# When
# Battered
# Women
# Kill

# When Battered Women Kill

*Angela Browne*

THE FREE PRESS
*A Division of Macmillan, Inc.*
NEW YORK

Collier Macmillan Publishers
LONDON

The Free Press
A Division of Macmillan, Inc.
866 Third Avenue, New York, N.Y. 10022

Collier Macmillan Canada, Inc.

First Free Press Paperback Edition 1989

Printed in the United States of America

printing number
1  2  3  4  5  6  7  8  9  10


**Library of Congress Cataloging in Publication Data**

Browne, Angela.
   When battered women kill.

   Bibliography: p.
   Includes indexes.
   1. Abused women—United States.    2. Conjugal
violence—United States.    3. Homicide—United States.
I. Title.
HV6626.B76    1987    364.1′523′088042    86-25789
ISBN 0-02-903881-2

# Contents

Contents

# Acknowledgments

Many people participated in the genesis of this book. Laura Wolff and Eileen DeWald, at The Free Press, guided the manuscript through the publication process and encouraged me during those times when it seemed it would never be done. Joanne Drouin, my secretary, assistant and friend, smoothed my work life and shouldered as many of the burdens as she could. Linda Gott and Heidi Gerhardt worked on references and source notes, and Kathy Cole prepared the indexing manuscript.

Other people have been involved in the "makings" of this book from the beginning. The book would not have been written without the contribution of my Quaker parents, Della and Loyde Osburn, who refused to let me become inured to brutality or suffering, and who have accepted with grace the fact that their daughter chose to study women who kill.

My thanks also go to:

Robert Elder and C. Robert Miller, my cherished "other family," who believed in me and encouraged me from my first involvement with this work;

Lenore Walker and Roberta Thyfault—the team with whom I began studying battered women and conducting homicide evaluations;

Dorian Welch, who was the legal counsel on my first homicide case, and who has remained a concerned friend and advisor ever since; Katharine Thayer, whose example of courage and intellectual honesty has been a guide;

Steve Ipsen and Tim Collins, for the long hours they spent in preparing the data and running the analyses (and for all the jokes and chocolate bars);

Phil Shaver, for his extensive editing of an earlier draft; and Carol Barrett, Carolyn Simmons, Ralph Woehle, Willow Simmons, Michael Patton, and Mitch Handelsman, for their guidance and participation in the research and writing up of study results.

I would also like to express my appreciation to:

The staff of the Family Research Laboratory at the University of New Hampshire, particularly to Murray Straus for his sweet spirit and unswerving belief in the value of this research, Larry Baron for his counsel and support, and Gerry Hotaling for his careful reading of the content;

Tessa-Storme Lyon and Ted Parkman, for their invaluable contributions to the process; Kirk Williams, for his optimism and blunt wisdom; and David Gillies, who kept the home fires burning and whose calm support helped smooth the year in which the book was written;

And to these friends, for enriching my life with their love, humor, and joy:

Bess Palmiciano, John Ahlgren
Jan Bamburger, Judy Meyers, Susan Turner
Gary Floyd, Cate Jones, Pat Foley
Lynn Miller, and David Gibson.

Most of all, I want to thank the women who shared the most painful details of their lives with me, and whose strength and endurance in the face of hardship inspired the writing: This is your book.

# Introduction

In the summer of 1979 I began working on a research project in Denver, Colorado that involved interviewing battered women from six states about violence they had experienced in a relationship with a spouse or lover.[1] The questionnaire used was 200 pages long, and took six to eight hours to administer. I would spend an entire day with one woman in a room equipped with a couch, a chair, and a tape recorder. We were on the second floor of an old building; all the windows stood open, and my most vivid memory is of the cadence of women's voices backed by the distant sound of sprinklers running on the lawn below us.

In what was usually a quiet and steady manner, woman after woman told of attacks by loved ones whose level of brutality paralleled that which I had previously associated only with assaults by strangers or with torture inflicted on prisoners in concentration camps. I came from a home where not even voices were raised. It was hard to believe what I was hearing, except that the accounts of different women from different backgrounds and circumstances were so similar.

Fall came and the furnace stuck on high. Again the windows stood open and, in bad weather, the snow blew in. Having a desk on the hall side became a high priority. But the project staff continued to interview women and I stayed on—amazed that a problem so serious could have been so long ignored; drawn by the challenges of trying to understand a phenomenon so vast and so well-hidden; and captivated by the strength and hope of the women before me.

The next summer, I was still there beginning work as a consultant on legal cases in which abused women were charged with the death or serious injury of their mates.[2] I remember some of what I was thinking the morning of my first interview with one of these women. What would it be like to spend the day with someone who had killed another person? How would she act? What would she say?

She turned out to be a lot like other women I knew—like

friends or family, like women in general—except that she had
lived through experiences that, even to her, seemed unimagin-
able. I began looking for books about women who killed their
partners, or even about partners who kill partners. I found only
two.[3] It seemed that the place to learn was from the women
themselves.

For the next three years I conducted interviews with accused
women, read corroborating documents, worked with their attorneys, and followed the outcomes of their trials. Some of the interviews took place in jails, the woman and I sitting in wooden
chairs at wooden tables marked with messages from other women
who had been there before us. One interview was conducted in
the house where the homicide occurred; bullet holes were visible
in the stairway and the man's coat still hung in the hall.

The evaluations now took 10 to 12 hours to complete, and
many more to code and write up. But the extensive questioning
was providing a wealth of information about the dynamics of
little-studied relationships, from the perspective of victims who
struck back in their own defense.

This book tells these women's stories, traces how their relationships progressed from affection to violence, and describes a pattern of events that led them to feel locked in with danger and so
desperate that they killed a man they loved. Examples are drawn
from the lives of 42 women from 15 states who were charged
with the murder or attempted murder of their mates. Many details
of these accounts were corroborated by hospital and police records and by the testimony of relatives and other witnesses;
although, in most cases, only reports by the women are recorded
here.

I have attempted to remain true to the ways in which the
women told their stories, in order to preserve a sense of how the
situations appeared to them. The decisions a woman makes in an
abusive relationship are based on her perceptions of patterns and
alternatives, so it is important to understand these perceptions as
thoroughly as possible. Thus, the scenarios have been edited only
as necessary to shorten the accounts and protect the women's
identities. All the names have been changed.

I struggled initially with how much to say—that is, how
graphic to be. My goal was to convey as nearly as possible the
essence of the women's experiences; therefore, the accounts have
remained fairly explicit. I am aware that this will upset some

readers and seem unnecessarily dramatic to others. Violence is popular in novels and movies, where we can tell ourselves it is just a story, that someone made it up. However, some things just aren't supposed to happen in our homes and families, and when these "stories" are presented to us as real, we are tempted to turn away. It is my hope that, instead of being put off by the violence, readers will make an attempt to imagine what it might be like to live with such brutality and to understand both victim and perpetrator. For those readers who have had similar experiences, the vignettes will sound hauntingly familiar.

If the accounts sometimes seem to be missing logical connections—"I asked him what he wanted for dinner. He hit me and knocked me to the floor"—it is because I am relating what the women told me about the incidents, based on their perceptions. If you find it confusing, that is how it seemed to the women as well. A part of what makes abusive interactions so powerful is their seemingly random, non-contingent nature. Battered women often spend years trying to understand what went wrong, hoping that if they can once comprehend it, they can then fix it. In the homicide group, however, the women's attempts to live with a violent and unpredictable mate eventually resulted in an act of violence on their part as well.

Obviously, the homicide cases are extreme examples of what can go wrong between partners. However, they have much to say to us about how men and women in our culture deal with intimacy and affiliation. We all resemble these individuals in some ways; with capacities for desire and fear and a need for possession, for inflicting harm on those we love, and for cutting ourselves off from an awareness of another's pain—be it emotional or physical—in the interest of our own self-protection or comfort. And these tendencies often show up most strongly in our relationships with the individuals with whom we live or are romantically involved. The value of understanding these extremes lies in the insight it can give us in evaluating our own lives and interactions, and locating where we are on this unclaimed continuum of abusive behavior toward those we love.

# *1*

# Setting
# the Stage

A woman calls the police emergency number begging for help. She says she just shot her husband. Officers arriving at the scene note that she is bruised and there is evidence of an altercation. While ambulance attendants work on the dying man, police locate the weapon and test the woman's hands for traces of gunpowder. Then they wrap her hands in plastic and lead her to a squad car, wending their way past neighbors gathered on the sidewalk. The woman is taken to jail, where she is interrogated. She attempts to reply to the officers' questions, although her responses are disoriented and confused and she will later remember little of what she said. At some point she is informed that her husband is dead. She is asked to strip to the waist, so pictures can be taken of her injuries, and is booked on suspicion of murder. Later, testimony reveals that she had been beaten and sexually assaulted by her mate on numerous occasions, and that he threatened to kill her shortly before the shooting took place. The woman has no prior criminal record; she has a family, and has held a steady job.

Neighbors are shocked by the killing; such things don't happen in their part of town. Relatives are grieved and defensive. They struggle with what to say when questioned; what to say in court, when the private lives of their family become front-page news. The man's family, who knew the most about his abusiveness, are in the worst position: Will they aid in this woman's defense, when she has just killed their son and brother? Could they have prevented it? Was his drinking to blame? Or was it her fault, for staying with him? They knew he sometimes hit her, but no one ever dreamed she would kill him.

What leads a woman who has occupied the role of victim, and who usually has no history of violent or illegal behavior, to use deadly force against her mate? What factors—in her perceptions, in the relationship, and in our society—precipitate the woman's committing a homicide? Why would a woman remain with a man who assaults her or threatens to take her life? And why are men the primary perpetrators of severe violence against their partners? What evokes this response in some men?

## THE INCIDENCE OF VIOLENCE IN FAMILIES

Early studies on criminal victimization focused primarily on violent incidents occurring outside the home. Most of these studies were conducted with incarcerated offenders—individuals labeled as comfortably "different" from the "rest" of us. Their problems were seen as stemming from unusual family backgrounds that were "unique" in being violent or disordered; or as attributable to a medical or psychological condition that provided a pathological explanation for their behavior.

Newspapers and other media emphasized the more sensational crimes and criminals. Assaults were depicted as occurring on city streets or in barroom brawls; rapes and murders were committed on the unsuspecting by deranged strangers; bad things happened to good people only when they were where they weren't supposed to be: out late at night, in a dangerous part of town, in a place of questionable reputation. An impression was formed that the risk of personal injury lay primarily in individuals outside one's circle of intimates. Violence in the family—if recognized at all—was rarely considered criminal unless a death occurred. The average family, it was assumed, afforded its members nurturance and protection. Individuals who left their homes and families were sometimes stigmatized, forcibly returned, or punished.

Yet current evidence identifies a reservoir of victimization that has existed almost unnoticed and, indeed, has been given permission to thrive within our culture. Research in the 1960s first began to document an unsuspected level of assaults within the nation as a whole. In 1968, in a nationally representative sample of 1,176 adults, one out of every 12 reported that they had been threatened or cut with a knife; one out of every 17 said they had been threatened or shot at with a gun; and one in 17 admitted having used a gun or a knife on another person in self-defense. (These incidents included only assaults that occurred as an adult, and excluded military action.) In addition, one-fifth approved of slapping a spouse on "appropriate" occasions; the percentage *increased* with higher levels of income and education, rising to 25 percent among the college educated. Contrary to popular impressions, experiences with violence were not confined to the poor or the working class. Violence was equally common among all income groups and education levels. The researchers concluded that "the privacy of the middle-class life-style preserves an illusion of greater domestic tranquility . . . ," but that, apparently, this was "only an illusion."[1]

The study of family violence, with an emphasis on child abuse, also began in the 1960s.[2] At that time, there were almost no reports of abused wives, and those that existed attributed the assaults to personality disorders in both the women and the men. Violence in families was thought to be infrequent and to result from psychopathology in the individuals involved, rather than being seen as a society-wide problem of much greater proportions.[3] It wasn't until the early 70s that sociologists started to study these assaults on a wider scale, and shocked the nation with their findings on the percentage of American families in which such attacks occurred.[4]

In recent years, there has been an upsurge of inquiry into violence between intimates. Some researchers explain violence in families from the perspectives of stress theory, resource deprivation, conflict and aggression theory, structural inequality, and theories that attribute the occurrence of violence to the patriarchy and general discrimination against women in our society.[5] Violence between romantic partners cannot be adequately understood, however, without consideration of the specific context in which it occurs: that of intimate relationships between men and women. Combining the more specialized topic of family violence with theories on relationships compels us to note the ways in which abuse by male partners and responses by female victims are extensions of our cultural *expectations* of romance and relating, and enables us to examine the similarities—as well as the differences—between relationships that include physical abuse and those limited to more "normal" interactions between couples.

In this country, a woman's chances of being assaulted at home by her partner are greater than that of a police officer being assaulted on the job. Books that document such abuse and describe the nature of the attacks have been written about the so-called "battered woman." Little is known, however, about the progression of such violence, or about those cases in which an abusive relationship culminates in death. Yet these issues surely deserve our attention.

Many spousal homicides are preceded by a history of abuse, and women jailed for the slaying of their mates frequently were beaten by them.[6] Many of these women sought help from the police or others prior to the lethal incident but either the urgency of their situation was not understood, or the alternatives offered were inadequate to allow them to escape. A more adequate understanding of the dynamics of relationships marked by violence could enable us to avert at least some of the homicides that now occur in desperation, and identify and intervene with those couples at risk for severe and continued assaults.

## VIOLENCE BETWEEN PARTNERS

How often does violence between partners occur? In a national survey of over 2,000 homes conducted in 1975 and published in 1980, Murray Straus, Richard Gelles, and Suzanne Steinmetz questioned married couples and found that more than one quarter (28 percent) reported at least one instance of physical assault in their relationships; 16 percent reported violent incidents in the year just prior to the study. Of these incidents, over one-third were serious assaults involving acts such as punching, kicking, hitting with an object, and assaults with a knife or gun. A follow-up survey conducted in 1985 found the exact same percentage reporting violent incidents in the twelve months prior to the study. These estimates are supported by the results of a Harris poll using similar questions, which found that 21 percent of women respondents had been physically attacked by a male partner at least once. This figure was much higher for those who had been recently separated or divorced; of these women, two-thirds reported violence in their former relationships.[7]

Other studies conducted in U.S. cities confirm these percentages. In a random sample in San Francisco, 21 percent of women who had been or were currently married reported at least one occasion of physical abuse by their mates.[8] Similarly, researchers attempting to find a group of nonbattered women to compare with a sample of physically abused wives in Pittsburgh found that 34 percent of their control group also reported being attacked by a partner.[9] Though the "majority" of respondents in these studies did not report violence, these figures mean that *over a million-and-a-half women in the United States are physically assaulted by a partner each year.*[10] Of course, many people just don't tell researchers about violence in their families, so these figures are underestimates of the true incidence of violence between partners. The true incidence of abuse between partners may be nearly double what people report in surveys.

## HOW SERIOUS IS FAMILY VIOLENCE?

Because we think of families as safe and even companionable, the phrase "family violence" seems almost a contradiction in terms. When the words are linked together, the emphasis shifts to the family, and the meaning of "violence" is modified by our particular images of home. "Domestic violence" has a tame sound—like a household pet, no longer wild. A "domestic problem" sounds minor and uninteresting; perhaps trouble with bill-paying or disagreements over the division of household chores. Somehow, we devalue incidents that occur in the home. News accounts still report serious assaults and even murders between partners as "the result of a domestic argument," masking the extremity of the acts and the history of threat and brutalization that frequently preceded such events.

Yet it would be a mistake to imagine that, although we now know more physical attacks are perpetrated by intimates than by strangers, attacks by family members are probably not as serious as those by outsiders. In comparing assaults involving intimates with assaults involving strangers, the 1980 National Crime Survey found that when the attacker was a stranger, just over one-half (54 percent) of the victims sustained injuries. However, when the attacker was related, *three-fourths* of the victims were injured. In addition, three-fifths of the attacks by relatives occurred at night, when most of the victims were "home safe." We lock our doors at night to keep the danger out. However, many people are actually locked in with the danger: Their place of greatest risk is their home.

## "MUTUAL COMBAT"

How mutual is the violence between romantic and/or married partners? When violent assaults occur in relationships, are men or women more likely to be the perpetrators? Are there differences between men and women when one looks at relatively minor physical assaults, versus more serious actions and injuries?

In the Straus, Gelles, and Steinmetz study of American families, nearly half (49 percent) of the couples who reported violence said that both partners had used some kind of force; in 27 percent of the cases, only the husband had been assaultive; and in 24 percent, only the wife had been assaultive. However, Straus and his colleagues noted that, because of men's greater average size and physical strength and their tendency toward greater aggressivity, the same acts frequently have quite a different effect in terms of pain, injury, and threat when performed by a woman and a man.[11] Men are also better able to avoid physical victimization than are women. As Mildred Pagelow (1984) observed:

> Men are, on the average, larger and muscularly stronger than women, so if they choose to strike back they can do greater physical harm than is done to them, they can nonviolently protect themselves from physical harm, or they can leave the premises without being forcibly restrained. (p. 274)

In the Straus study, assaultive actions were divided into categories of relatively "minor" (threw something at the other; pushed, grabbed or shoved; slapped) and "severe" (kicked, bit, punched, hit with an object, beat up, threatened with a knife or gun, used a knife or gun). Despite the seemingly equal appearance of assaultive behavior when looked at separately, when analyzing the results this way, Straus and his colleagues found that men had a higher rate of using the most dangerous and injurious forms of violence—such as physically beating up their partners or using a knife or a gun—and that when violent acts were committed by a husband, they were repeated more often than they were by wives. In addition, a large number of violent attacks against wives occurred when the women were pregnant, thus increasing the risk of injury and of miscarriage or stillbirth.

Although the Straus study has been cited often as evidence for the mutuality of violence, several other factors should be taken into account. First, the Straus sample was restricted to couples who were living together currently; recently separated or divorced couples were not included in the inquiry. Second, information on violent acts was gathered from only one member of a couple, without corroboration from the other partner or other sources, and without a means for ascertaining possible differences in the reports of the victims and the perpetrators of violence. Also, the study was not designed to ask about injuries sustained from the violence, nor about what proportion of the acts were in response to violence initiated by the other or in self-defense. Finally, questions about violence were set in a context of settling disputes in a conflict situation and, therefore, may not have elicited information about attacks that seemed to come "out of the blue." These are crucial factors for assessing the mutuality of combat, and some of them have been investigated in more depth by other researchers.

As noted earlier, separated and divorced couples appear to have extremely high rates of violence, especially violence perpetrated by husbands. Thus, a greater impression of "mutuality" may result when one studies intact couples than when divorced or separated couples are included. In the 1982 National Crime Survey, for instance, 91 percent of all violent crimes between spouses were victimizations of women by husbands or ex-husbands, while only 5 percent were victimizations of husbands by wives or ex-wives.

The identity of the person doing the reporting also seems to be important in assessing what weight to give responses. Studies of crime victims show a surprising tendency to forget even fairly serious attacks. Experience with women victims of a partner's violence confirms this. Battered women, especially those who have been victimized over a long period, tend to underestimate both the frequency and the severity of the violence they experience when their reports are compared to the reports of witnesses or to hospital and other records. Similarly, experts working with abusive men note that the men greatly *underreport* their violent actions; they minimize or deny assaultive behavior against their wives, and claim more involvement by the victim in justification of their violence than witness or police reports would support.[12] Thus, in a study combining estimations of violence by male perpetrators on female victims, one is faced with the possibility that the perpetrators will sound less violent and more victimized, while the victims will appear to have been less severely assaulted and more likely to victimize their partners, than is actually the case.

When one looks at the results of studies overall, men seem much more likely to assault their female partners, especially seriously, than women are to assault male partners.[13] For instance, in analyzing the records on almost 900 cases of family violence, R. Emerson Dobash and Russell Dobash (1978) found that when the sex of victim and offender was known, women were the victims in 94 percent and offenders in 3 percent of the cases. Almost the exact same proportions were found in records of the Minnesota Department of Corrections on 966 assaults; 95 percent were women victimized by a man they were currently or had been living with, and 5 percent were men victimized by women partners.

Undoubtedly, there are couples who engage in "mutual combat" with roughly equal levels of aggressivity. However, it seems likely that for a woman to physically assault a man involves some degree of confidence on her part that his reactions will stop short of a life-threatening response, i.e., that he will be able to control aggressive responses so they are not life-threatening, and that he will want to exercise that control where she is concerned. Studies of severely battered women suggest that they are not typically violent toward their mates, especially not in initiation and usually not in response. Their perception of danger is too great. It appears to be the "mildly battered" women who fight back. Even for those women, however, the husbands' level of violence is typically higher than that of their wives.[14] Women's use of violence is also more likely to be in self-defense than is men's violence toward their female partners.[15]

Another factor in assessing the mutuality of violence is whether or not injuries result. Partners may "trade punches," but they rarely "exchange" injuries.[16] Both national and city data show that, when assaults between partners occur, 94 percent to 95 percent of the time it is the woman who gets hurt. Research has found that, even when both partners are injured in an altercation, the woman's injuries are nearly three times as severe as the man's.[17] Injury patterns also differ: Multiple injuries, abrasions, and contusions are reported frequently by female victims of a partner's violence, but are not seen in their mates.[18]

One indication of the frequency of injurious assault by men on their partners is emergency room admissions records. Researchers on a National Institute of Mental Health project estimate that 21 percent of all women who use emergency surgical services are battered; almost half of all injuries presented by women to the emergency surgical service occur in the context of partner abuse; and half of all rapes to women over 30 are part of the battering syndrome.[19] Extrapolating such figures to the United States would mean that between 1.5 and two million women seek medical treatment each year because of an assault by a male partner.

Although threatening or attacking another person is illegal, very few of the incidents come to the attention of authorities when it happens within a family. Even if the assaults are reported, they are often not accorded the serious treatment given to attacks by strangers. Harris found that 43 percent of the women who had been abused told no one and only 4 percent of the reported assaults resulted in court action.[20] Even though these attacks tend to be more serious than attacks by strangers, the rate of prosecution and conviction drops sharply when there is a current or prior relationship between the victim and the assailant.[21] It is usually only when someone is seriously injured or killed that strict action is taken. Women reporting assaults or threats by partners are familiar with being referred for personal mental health counseling, or asked why they don't leave their homes, rather than being offered effective alternatives. Many of these women attempt to leave their partners, only to be caught and beaten for it; many try repeatedly without success to obtain protection. Left without adequate intervention, some of the altercations continue to escalate in severity until they result in death.

## HOMICIDE BETWEEN PARTNERS

Nearly one-fourth of the nation's homicide victims in 1984 were related to their assailants; 4,408 murders in that one year were committed by family members.[22] The rate of homicide among families in the United States is quite high when compared to that of many other countries; it is higher, for instance, than the rate for *all* homicides in countries such as England, Denmark, and Germany. Of homicides occurring within the family, by far the largest category is that of a spouse killing a spouse. Nearly half (48 percent) of intrafamilial homicides in 1984, or the deaths of over 2,000 people, were between partners. Of these, the majority of the victims were women: Two-thirds (1,310) were wives killed by husbands, and one-third (806) were husbands killed by wives.

Women don't usually kill other people; they perpetrate less than 15 percent of the homicides in the United States.[23] When women do kill, it is often in their own defense. A report by a government commission on violence estimated that homicides committed by women were seven times as likely to be in self-defense as homicides committed by men.[24] In his study of criminal homicide, Wolfgang (1967) noted that 60 percent of the husbands who were killed by their wives "precipitated" their own deaths (i.e., were the first to use physical force, strike blows, or threaten with a weapon), whereas victim precipitation was involved in only 9 percent (5 of 53) of the deaths of wives. A review of police records on spousal homicides in Canada also found that almost all of the wives who had killed their mates had previously been beaten by them.[25] In such cases, it's the abusive mate who becomes the final victim. A 1977 study at the Women's Correctional Center in Chicago revealed that 40 percent of the women serving time for murder or manslaughter had killed husbands or lovers who repeatedly attacked them.[26] Similarly, Jane Totman (1978), surveying women in a California state prison found that, of the 30 women who had killed their mates, 29 had been abused by them; 20 of the women indicated that the homicide had resulted from their attempt to protect themselves or their children from further harm.

In the majority of homicide cases between partners, there were many "cries for help" prior to the lethal incident. A review of homicide records in Detroit and Kansas City revealed that, in 85 percent to 90 percent of the cases, police had been called to the home at least once during the two years before the incident, and in half (54 percent) of the cases, they had been called five or more times.[27] In the Chicago study mentioned earlier, all the women who had killed abusive mates reported that they called for police help at least five times before taking the life of the man; many said the violence they endured became more, rather than less, severe after their attempts at gaining assistance.[28] Given their lesser physical strength and a history of physical jeopardy at the hands of the man, when abused women do strike back they typically use a weapon or an object as an equalizer.[29] However, Wolfgang (1958) found that beating, not the use of a weapon, was the usual method when a man killed a woman (p. 162). Women employed fewer acts of violence during the homicide incident as well; men were likely to employ five or more acts of severe violence in the killing of their partners.

Women charged in the death of a mate have the least extensive criminal records of any female offenders. However, they often face harsher penalties than men who kill their mates. FBI statistics indicate that fewer men are charged with first- or second-degree murder for killing a woman they have known than are women who kill a man they have known. And women convicted of these murders are frequently sentenced to longer prison terms than are men.[30] The following case illustrates the discrepancies in attitudes that may lead to this uneven sentencing:

> In 1978 an Indiana prosecutor, James Kizer, refused to prosecute for murder a man who beat and kicked his ex-wife to death in the presence of a witness and raped her as she lay dying. Filing a manslaughter charge instead, Kizer commented, "He didn't mean to kill her. He just meant to give her a good thumping."[31]

In contrast, each of the women in the present study had a documented history of physical abuse by the man she slayed. In many cases, the files contained police photographs of the woman's injuries at the time of her arrest and, in some instances, the woman was transported to a hospital for X-rays or treatment before being taken to jail. All of these women reported that the abuser had threatened them, and almost all had attempted to escape and had sought outside intervention against the violence. Yet of the 36 women whose husbands died, all but nine were charged with first-degree murder. None was charged with manslaughter. Their stories are unusual and little-known. But given the incidence of homicide between partners and the frequency with which a history of abuse is a factor, they cannot be called unique. Knowing the dynamics behind that final brief incident demonstrates how physical assault can gradually take over a relationship, and how women who find themselves trapped in a potentially deadly situation can become—suddenly—widows by their own hand.

## STUDYING WOMEN WHO KILL

Results of the homicide study are based on interviews with 42 women who were charged with a crime in the death or serious injury of their mates.[32] The women came from 15 states; seven of them were incarcerated awaiting trial at the time of the interview. Initial contact was made with the women when their attorneys requested an evaluation based on evidence that the woman had been physically abused by her partner prior to the homicide incident. Thirty-three of the women were charged with murder, three with conspiracy to commit murder, and six with attempted murder. (In reporting the findings, no distinction is made between cases involving attempted murder and the homicide cases, since the same dynamics applied to both types of events.) Of the women who went to trial after the interview, twenty (about half) received jail terms, 12 received probation or a suspended sentence, and nine were acquitted. In one case, the District Attorney's office determined that the killing was justified on the grounds of self-defense and dropped the charges. Jail sentences generally ranged from six months to 25 years; one woman was sentenced to 50 years.

The purpose of the study was to understand more about the relationships of abused women who kill their husbands, and to identify the dynamics that lead up to the commission of a homicide. Thus, the inquiry focused on the women's actions—e.g., the killing of a mate—in the context of their position as victims, and investigated the impact that violence and threat from a romantic partner, as well as other situational and societal variables, had on their perception of danger and of alternatives. In an effort to understand more about battered women who kill, and to identify the factors that characterize their relationships with their abusers, reports from women in the homicide group were later compared to those of 205 women who had been in abusive relationships but did not take lethal action against their partners.[33]

Women in the comparison group came from a six-state region, and from both urban and rural areas. They were recruited through public-service announcements, newspaper ads, and posted notices, as well as through referrals from physicians, emergency-room personnel, and battered-women's shelters. The women in the comparison group were self-identified and self-referred (i.e., called up and said they had been battered), and were considered eligible to participate in the study if they reported being physically abused at least twice by a man with whom they had had an ongoing intimate relationship or to whom they had been married.[34] Since nearly all the women in the homicide group were living with their mates at the time of the lethal incident or were only recently out of the relationship, women in the comparison group were limited to those either still with the abusive partner or out of the relationship less than one year.

## *Definition of Abuse*

When studying violent relationships, it is important to define what is meant by the labels being used. The terms "violence," "abuse," "battering," and "assault" are often used interchangeably, although the meanings may be quite different. Is a slap "abuse"? Is it battering? Could there be such a thing as a nonviolent assault? And what could possibly be meant by the phrase "minor violence"?

Actually, the word "violence" carries with it more of a connotation of physical force, whereas "abuse" can include meanings of misuse and may connote nonviolent as well as violent interactions. "Battering" and "beating" are more specific to physically forceful actions and actions that are repeated or that occur in a series. Thus, "battered women" are those who have been struck repeatedly, often experiencing several different kinds of physically violent actions in one incident, and usually, by the time they are identified, having experienced a series of such incidents, each consisting of a cluster of violent acts. Other issues that enter into the definition of violence in a particular context are whether there must be evidence of an intent to harm on the part of the perpetrator to call an act "violent," whether violence is judged by the act itself or only if injuries result from that act, and whether acts of coercion and restraint are considered violence or abuse.[35]

In the present study, "physical abuse" was defined as *any physically assaultive act by one person against another, with or without evident resultant physical injury*. These acts were those considered assaultive on the part of the women; the list of acts included in the study—pushing, shoving, slapping, hitting, punching, kicking, hitting with an object, throwing bodily, choking, smothering, burning, using a knife or gun, trying to drown— would also be considered assaultive in a U.S. court of law. To be included in the study, a participant had to have experienced at least two incidents of physical violence at the hands of a partner. Coercive physical acts like restraint or a physical threat of violent action (such as an upraised fist) were considered abusive but were not, in and of themselves, sufficient for inclusion in the study.

Information on other kinds of behavior was also collected in the course of the investigation. Factors such as excessive possessiveness or jealousy, surveillance, extreme verbal harrassment, and threats—as well as actions such as playing Russian roulette or forcing a woman to watch while a pet animal was killed—were often reported as a part of the cluster of events that occurred during abusive incidents. Frequently, such actions seemed to have an even greater impact on the women than some of the physical violence they experienced. However, because the study was not designed to measure psychological abuse alone, all women participants had experienced at least two physically violent incidents. Therefore, the term "assault," as used in this study, implies a physically violent attack. In both the homicide and the comparison groups, most women reported at least four occurrences of physical violence by their partner: the first occurrence of violence; a "typical" violent incident; one of the worst incidents, in the woman's estimation; and the last abusive incident before the interview.[36] For women in the homicide group, the final incident was frequently the one in which the tables turned and the homicide took place.

The impact on a woman of even a single incident of physical violence in a relationship should not be underestimated. Though women who are assaulted "only once" are rarely labeled as battered and still less often studied, any use of violence in a relationship can dramatically alter the balance of power, destroying a sense of openness and trust on the part of the woman and resulting in a permanent sense of inequality, threat, and loss.[37] Repeated assaults by a partner seem to have a cumulative effect on women victims, building on the shock of the first assault and taking them through a progression of emotions and attributions as they attempt to reinterpret their lives and their relationships with others in light of a pattern of continued attacks.

It is at this point that a comparison between women in abusive relationships who eventually kill their mates and those who don't becomes useful. Are there systematic differences between the women, or the relationships of abused women who kill and those who don't, that might explain such a drastic difference in outcome? And, given that violent interactions between intimates are usually carried out in the privacy of the home, are there differences that, if known by helpers outside the home, could be used to identify those couples particularly at risk, as well as serve as a yardstick for the women themselves? It is these questions that the present work begins to address.

## *Issues of Self-Report*

Of course, one question about studies based on victims' or perpetrators' self-reports is how seriously one should take an individual's description of such highly charged events. This is of special concern in the homicide cases, where one can no longer learn the deceased's version of the story and the survivor is facing criminal charges related to the incident. Would women in the homicide group overstate the violence—i.e., make the man "look bad"—in order to help their case? All these women were facing trial at the time they were interviewed. What effect might that have had on the accuracy of their reports?

Interestingly, it was usually easier to document the women's stories in the homicide cases than in the comparison group, since private records became available and some witnesses came forward to testify because they were no longer afraid of retaliation by the abuser. All available police and hospital records were carefully reviewed, and the testimony of family members and other witnesses taken into account, as were reports on the men from past acquaintances, employers, or service providers. This information was then compared to the history given by the women to check for reliability. When discrepancies were found, it was usually in the direction of understatement: As noted by other researchers, women tended to underreport abusive incidents and injuries. They were sometimes reluctant to report their mate's sexual abuse of a child or their own physical or sexual abuse in childhood, for fear of doing damage to other family members. And some women were reluctant to describe severe physical and sexual abuse by their mates out of a sense of shame, or for fear others would not believe them.

One of the cases in the homicide group—that of Karen and Hal Simon—was of particular interest in regard to self-report. A part of the documentation that became available after Hal Simon's death was his account, written in an alcohol-detoxification program, of his physical assaults on Karen. Hal's version of the incidents paralleled the narrative already given by Karen, except that, by Hal's account, the violence was more life-threatening and more severe. Medical records on Karen's injuries after specific incidents supported Hal's version of the story.

Previous inquiries have investigated spousal homicides and found a history of abuse as a factor. The present study began with an investigation of abusive relationships, and focused on those that culminated in homicide. Earlier studies of homicides between partners typically gathered their data from individuals who were already convicted of a crime in the incident. Most of these individuals were incarcerated at the time they were interviewed, or had served time for the offense.[38] Studying only those who have been judged guilty and sent to jail, however, may produce a bias in the results. For one thing, those who go to jail are disproportionately from economically disadvantaged and minority groups. In addition, those who are acquitted and individuals with mitigating circumstances who are not incarcerated are not interviewed in such investigations. In the present study, over one-quarter of the women who went to trial for homicide were granted probation or a deferred sentence, and just under one-quarter were acquitted. Thus, studying only those incarcerated for the death of a partner would have left out half of the present respondents and might give us a biased picture of homicides in which battered women are the perpetrators.

In the chapters that follow, one couple's history is used to demonstrate the progression of an abusive relationship from courtship through an escalation of assault and threat that eventually results in death. (Although based on an actual case, some facts have been changed to protect identities. Details of the violence remain unaltered, however.) Vignettes from nine other cases are used throughout to illustrate factors found to be common to the homicide group. These were selected for their representativeness of the sample as a whole and their importance in illustrating specific dynamics of the homicide relationships. The number of case histories is limited to 10 so that readers can follow these couples as additional details are given. The *combination* of events in abusive relationships is often as important as the events themselves. Establishing a context for violent events allows us to increase our understanding of the dynamics of abusive interactions, as well as patterns typical of the unfolding of violence in a relationship.

# 2

# Childhood Roots of Violence

## MEETING MOLLY

Molly Johnson was 35-years-old when I met her. Information on Molly indicated that she had been severely abused during the course of her marriage: medical records from a recent examination included notations of numerous scars from knife wounds and bite marks, marks on her forehead from blows with cleated boots, permanent damage to the joints of one hand, and a partial loss of hearing in one ear. When Molly arrived for our interview, I was prepared for someone whose appearance and demeanor reflected the severity of the abuse she had apparently suffered. Instead, I was faced with a very beautiful young woman. Bangs covered her forehead; she wore a high-necked blouse and a calf-length woven skirt. She kept her left hand hidden most of the time; later I saw that the fingers were bent out of shape and the back of the hand crossed with scars.

Molly was petite and fine-boned, with long dark hair and delicate features. Her voice was low-pitched, her manner poised and quiet. The initial impression was one of fragility. However, during the time I spent with her, Molly's iron self-control became apparent. The evaluation took nearly 10 hours. During those hours, Molly recalled for me the most painful incidents of her life, yet she never broke down. She occasionally altered her breathing, sat up straighter in her chair, or clasped and unclasped the arm of the chair with her right hand; her eyes were often bright with tears, and at times I could see her shaking. But the tears never fell.

At one point, while describing the final incident, Molly ceased talking and sat trembling, both hands pressed against her face. Still, her back was perfectly straight and she made no sound. Another time, when a memory was particularly painful, Molly crossed the room and sat partially turned away from me, gazing out the window as she continued her account in the same soft voice. Only after the interview did I learn that Molly was suffering from constant severe headaches and continued weight loss, and was unable to sleep more than three or four hours a night. Jail personnel reported seeing her lying silent and sleepless on her cot as they made their rounds. But Molly held all this inside.

At the end of the last day, Molly shyly showed me a journal she had been keeping since she'd been in jail—beautifully written, but so full of pain as to be almost unreadable. I encouraged her to continue writing; perhaps to study writing. I don't know if she has. The story Molly shared with me in those two days illustrates almost all the dynamics found to be crucial in the homicide relationships: frequency and severity of assaults, severity of the woman's injuries, the interaction of the man's substance abuse with the violence, sexual assault of the woman by the abuser, and the abusive partner's threats to kill the woman, himself, or a child. The progression of the relationship over time, and Molly's reactions to the continued threat and violence, is also illustrative of the patterns found in the homicide study.

### Women Who Kill

Who are the people who become involved in such extreme relationships? Could you identify them if you met them? What about the women in the homicide group? Is there something unique about them, their backgrounds, their childhoods, that leads to this outcome in their lives? And do they differ in significant ways from women in the comparison group, or is it only their relationships that differ?

Women in the homicide group were an average age of 36 (the age range was from 19 through 58) and had an average of two children. Over half (66 percent) were caucasian; 22 percent were black, and 12 percent were Spanish-American or Chicano. Nearly half (46 percent) came from working-class backgrounds, by the women's self-reports; one-quarter were from the middle class and one-quarter from the lower class; two women (5 percent) were raised in upper-class homes. Almost three-quarters (71 percent) of the women had finished high school, and 21 percent had attended college. Slightly less than half (48 percent) were employed most or all the time during their relationships with their abusers, while another 15 percent were employed sporadically.

Women in the homicide group had been involved with their partners an average of 8.7 years. Eighty percent were married to the abuser, and the average length of these marriages was seven years. The women tended to be with men from a lower social class than themselves.[1] Forty-three percent of their partners were from working-class backgrounds, another 43 percent from the lower class; 8 percent were from middle-class homes, and 5 percent from the upper class. Their average level of education was also higher than that of their mates.[2] Sixty-one percent of the men had completed high school, while 22 percent had gone on to college. Less than half (48 percent) were employed during most or all of their relationships with the women, while another 28 percent were employed sporadically. On this measure, the women and their mates were not significantly different.

When comparing these women to women in the comparison group, few differences can be found. Women in the homicide group were somewhat older at the time we interviewed them; the comparison group had an average age of 31, although they also had an average of two children.[3] Women in the homicide group did tend to come from a higher social class background than women in the comparison group.[4] Fifty-five percent of the women in the comparison group were from working-class backgrounds, 41 percent from the lower class, and 4 percent from middle-class homes. However, their level of education was not significantly different from women in the homicide group, nor were their employment patterns.

Women in the comparison group had been involved with their mates for approximately the same amount of time as women in the homicide group (an average of 8 years, versus 8.7 years—not a statistically significant difference). As with the homicide group, 80 percent of women in the comparison group were married to the abuser and the average length of those marriages was 7.7 years. Women in the comparison group tended to be from a similar social class as their mates. As with women in the homicide group, they were significantly more educated than their mates, although fewer of them were fully employed compared to their partners.[5]

There were no significant differences in the men's class of origin between the homicide and comparison groups: Thirty-nine percent in the comparison group were from working-class homes, 55 percent from the lower class, and 7 percent from middle-class backgrounds. The men's employment patterns were surprisingly similar, with only 55 percent of men in the comparison group employed during most of the relationship and another 20 percent sporadically employed. Men in the comparison group were significantly more educated than men in the homicide group, however; nearly three-quarters (74 percent) had completed high school, while 46 percent had had some college.[6] Details on the life histories of both the women and the men provide a clearer picture of the composition of the homicide group, as well as a beginning look at the impact of violence on these individuals.[7]

Molly grew up with her mother, father, and two brothers. She was the youngest child of the family. Molly remembers that her father was very jealous and controlling of her mother all during Molly's childhood, and didn't want her mother—who was extremely attractive—to go anywhere without him. He was harsh and critical with Molly, telling her how stupid she was and that she couldn't do anything right, but he never hit her. Molly thinks he was not physically abusive to her mother, either, but he did beat her brothers. Her eldest brother was too proud to cry, and her father would hit him harder and harder, trying to break him. Once Molly and her mother tried to pull her father off this brother, because the boy was being hurt so badly. The most critical thing Molly remembers about her childhood is the strictness of her father and how important it was to be good; to not displease her parents.

Jim's mother left his father when Jim was young. At first, Jim lived with his mother, but she often left him alone without adequate food or clothing and the neighbors wound up taking care of him. When he was 10 years old, Jim's father took him to live with him and Jim never contacted his mother again. His father was an alcoholic who had a difficult time keeping a job. He often beat the woman he lived with, and his methods of punishing Jim would probably have been considered battering by outside observers. Jim would never talk much about his childhood, except to say that his mother was "no good."

## EXPERIENCING VIOLENCE AS A CHILD

As with Molly and Jim Johnson, early experiences of being abused or witnessing abuse were often reported in the childhoods of both women and men in the homicide group. Nearly three-quarters of the women (71 percent) described some kind of physical violence in their childhood homes, including that of a father or other male partner abusing their mother, abuse of siblings, abuse of themselves by parents, and abuse from other relatives. (Even though these figures seem high, women in the homicide group were not significantly different from women in the comparison group in this respect: Sixty-five percent of women in the comparison group also reported violence in their home of origin.) Many of the women reported that their partners had come from abusive homes as well. In the homicide group, 18 percent of the women didn't know that information about the childhoods of their mates, but of those who did, 91 percent believed there was physical violence in the man's childhood home.

Much of the abuse reported for both the women and the men occurred in the context of "discipline" administered by a parent. (It is interesting to note, in this regard, the frequency with which abusive men rationalize the beating of their wives by saying, "I did it for her own good," or "I had to teach her a lesson. . . . ") Women in the homicide group remembered that, as children, they often accepted this violence as a legitimate form of correction. Mary Wheeler's case is an example:

Mary was raised with her mother, father, and a younger sister. Her father worked at a grocery store and her mother stayed home; Mary always thought of her father as the boss of the family. Mary's parents were quite strict and disciplined her harshly, but Mary thought this was the only way they knew. Her father beat her with a belt for talking back or disobeying; once, he caught her in the face with the belt buckle and permanently injured her eye. Another time, he hit her in the mouth with his fist for talking back, and cut her lip. Still, she feels he never really meant to hurt her and that he did the best he could.

———————

Irene Miller's childhood was characterized by many types of violence between different family members. Like Mary Wheeler, she accepted much of the violence as appropriate:

Irene's mother beat her with a strap from the time she was in school, but Irene says this was meant as punishment and that she "probably deserved it." She remembers that she "just stood there and took it," because she thought she should. These beatings would leave welts on her legs and back that lasted several days. Her mother would also get angry with her and her sisters and slap them, or throw them in the shower. As they got older, the mother was less physical with Irene, but called her a "cheap whore" and "no good" whenever they disagreed. Irene's stepfather beat her up once for coming in late, but usually he left the disciplining of the girls to their mother. He would "over-discipline" her brothers, however, causing them to have bruises and sometimes cuts. He was "physical" with his wife as well: On one occasion, he attacked her so severely she had to be hospitalized for several days.

———————

Other women were unsure of what was hidden behind their childhood memories:

Wanda Bowles grew up with her mother, father, and three siblings; she was the oldest child. She thinks her father might have beaten her mother, because she heard sounds at night and saw bruises. Her mother denies this, and says she bruises easily. When Wanda heard these sounds, she would take her brother and sister and hide in the closet until the house became quiet. Wanda's mother always said she was going to leave their father when the children were older, but she never did. Wanda doesn't think her father beat her—she can't remember the years before she was six at all—but she does remember that she was terribly afraid of him and doesn't know why. Wanda's younger brother was regularly attacked by her father, however, and frequently injured. When he grew up, he became fiercely protective of women and, in 1981, was accused of killing Wanda's husband for badly beating her daughter.

───────────

Even for women raised in upper-class homes, a hint of abuse shadowed their childhood histories:

Janet VanHorn was the only child of very traditional parents. Her mother was quite socially involved and traveled a lot, and Janet was cared for primarily by a maid. She adored her father and saw him as a romantic figure, but he was not affectionate and she never felt close to him. Social position and appearances were of utmost importance to her family, and Janet was raised to do the socially correct thing and to hide those things that might bring shame. As she got older, Janet realized that her father drank a great deal, and her mother implied that he sometimes hit her when he was drunk. Janet never witnessed the abuse, however, and didn't want to believe this of the father she loved. Janet's parents made all her decisions for her to the extreme; even picking the boy she was to marry when both children were young and insisting that she go through with the marriage when she turned 20. She was never physically abused, however, or even physically disciplined, and found herself unable to cope with the violence in her marriage when it occurred.

───────────

The partners of women in the homicide group seemed to come from homes that were even more violent and chaotic than those of their mates:

Randy Bowles was raised with his mother, father, and four siblings. His father was an alcoholic who would come home at two

o'clock in the morning and make the kids get up and rewash
the dishes if he was angry, or get up and eat something with
him if he was high. Randy's mother was "emotional and irrational" by Randy's account, always "flying off the handle" and
striking out. Wanda related that both of Randy's parents were
violent with each other, attacking one another both physically
and verbally. Both parents also battered the children, and the
male siblings fought violently with one another throughout
their childhoods and into adulthood.

Chuck Wheeler's parents were divorced when he was 10. His
mother was in a mental institution for a period of time, and
Chuck's father said he'd had her put away so that he could be
with another woman. Chuck lived with his father until he was
nearly 14. He told Mary that his father would get angry, throw
knives at him, and threaten him; finally, he ran away to rejoin
his mother, who was then living in Arizona. He returned to his
father briefly but fled again, and his father had him arrested as
a runaway. At 17, he joined the army to get out of a juvenile
detention center.

Mark Miller's mother died when he was nine or 10. In talking
about her later, he idealized her and said they had been quite
close. Mark's father was extremely strict and abusive; he battered Mark's mother, his stepmother, *and* Mark. He also probably molested Mark's sister, who left home at 16 to escape him.
In spite of this, Mark admired his father greatly and emulated
him, even in his choice of a profession. His father died suddenly when Mark was 26, and Mark was depressed for months.

———————

Another form of assault frequently reported by the women was
sexual abuse of the woman as a child, usually by a family member.
Over half of the women in the homicide group—57 percent—
reported being the victim of at least one completed or attempted
sexual assault during their childhoods. (Again, although this was
a significant part of their life histories, it did not differentiate
them from women in the comparison group, in which 54 percent
had experienced attempted or completed childhood molestation.) Most of these assaults were by a father, stepfather, mother's
boyfriend, brother, or other male relative, and included activities

such as being fondled, being forced to fondle the other person, forced oral sex, and attempted or completed intercourse. Threats and beatings often accompanied these incidents. Irene Miller's case provides a typical illustration of reports from the homicide group:

Irene Miller's stepfather attempted to molest her and her sisters throughout their childhoods, saying that such intimacies were "only what a father would do." Irene would tell her mother and her mother would confront him, but he'd cry and say Irene was lying, and her parents would work it out. One night, right after Irene started high school, her stepfather forced her to drink whiskey with him. She went to bed and to sleep and woke later to find him in bed with her, her nightgown pulled up above her waist. Irene screamed and ran from the room. She told her mother, who was going to leave him, but the stepfather cried and said he was sorry, and this time attempted suicide. He and her mother were reconciled, and Irene went to live with her grandmother.

## THE IMPACT OF VIOLENCE IN CHILDHOOD

What effect does exposure to violence in the family of origin have on becoming the perpetrator or the victim of violent acts in a relationship with an adult partner? Does such an effect differ for men and women? And are there differential effects of witnessing violence between other family members, versus experiencing direct violence (i.e., abuse by parents)?

There is still much debate about the impact of early exposure to violence on later involvement in abusive interactions. Drawn from social learning theory, the concept of an "intergenerational transmission of violence" explains how patterns of violent interaction can be "passed on" from one generation to the next. Children growing up in violent homes learn from observing, and then imitating, the behaviors of the people around them. In addition, they begin to develop their own ideas about how different emotions are expressed and what constitutes appropriate reactions for various situations. These concepts include ideas about what behaviors are appropriate for males and females, and the roles and responsibilities of different family members. Social learning theory suggests that when violence is present in the family setting, children will model those ways of dealing with relationships and apply similar methods of coping when they are faced with threatening situations later in life.[8]

In their 1980 national study of couples, Straus, Gelles, and Steinmetz asserted that, "Each generation learns to be violent by being a participant in a violent family—'Violence begets violence'" (p. 121). Findings from studies on the development of aggressive behavior support a theoretical connection between childhood exposure to aggressive acts and involvement with adult violence. For instance, exposure to aggression as a child is highly correlated with later anti-social or delinquent behavior in general, and with acts of violence in particular.[9]

## VIOLENCE IN THE CHILDHOODS OF BATTERED WOMEN

The intergenerational transmission theory was first applied to battered women in an effort to find something about women victims that explained their involvement in violent relationships as adults. Early theorists assumed that battered women were likely to come from homes in which they had been abused and, therefore, accepted violent treatment as the norm. Research on incest victims indicates a strong tendency for them to be re-victimized; Judith Herman (1981) suggested that a history of childhood sexual abuse may be associated with an "impairment of the normal adult mechanisms for self-protection" in dealing with later relationships (p. 30). Similarly, childhood physical abuse may have the effect of making a woman less skilled at self-protection, less sure of her own worth and personal boundaries, and more apt to accept victimization as a part of what it's like to be female. This might also be true if, as a child, the woman had watched her mother being physically abused by a male partner.

Findings on childhood victimization in the histories of abused women have not always supported the early theories, however. While some studies of battered women do find a positive relationship between childhood exposure to violence and later victimization experiences, other studies have not found this connection.[10] As noted earlier, the assumption has been that women who witnessed or experienced violence in childhood might feel more helpless if violence recurred in their lives, and thus cope less effectively than someone without prior experience with abuse. For the 71 percent of women in the homicide group who had been exposed to violence as children, this often seemed to be a factor. Many of these women reported slipping into deep depression when violence erupted in their own marriages or relationships, and experiencing reactions of helplessness, withdrawal, and shock. Women who watched their mothers being beaten when they were children remembered how determined they had been that nothing like that would ever happen to them. Some of these women had become involved with a man who later became their abuser in order to escape a violent home, and were thrown back into childhood patterns of interaction when the violence exploded in their adult world as well. As noted earlier, a high proportion of battered women in both the homicide and the comparison groups reported some type of abuse in their childhood homes.

Yet an explanation of "childhood violence" for the involvement of women in severely abusive adult relationships would be too simple. Early exposure to violence did not prevent the women from trying to escape their abusers (in studying 350 women and their spouses, Mildred Pagelow found that women who had been abused as children actually had a tendency to leave their violent partners more quickly than women who lacked prior experience with abuse), and simply having a framework from which to interpret the violence did not make the abuse seem any more acceptable or justified. In addition, focusing on just those women who had experienced violence in childhood would ignore nearly one-third of the women in the homicide group, who did not come from violent backgrounds.

Interestingly, women in the homicide group who had no previous experience with abuse reported much the same reactions to the violence in their relationships as those who had experienced or witnessed abuse as children—shock, helplessness, withdrawal, and depression. However, they gave a different reason for their responses: These women saw their *lack* of experience with prior abuse as a major factor in their inability to comprehend and deal with the violence when it occurred. As one battered woman told me, "I spent the first two years in shock, trying to understand what had happened. It was ages before I realized I had to make a plan." Maria Roy, in her study of battered women, observed similar reactions from those with no prior exposure to violence. She noted that "a large proportion of the women remembered a happy home life and . . . found their own husbands' acts of violence confusing and perplexing."[11]

Women who had no exposure to violence in the past often viewed the incidents as isolated occurrences, attributing them to particular circumstances or stresses in daily life, rather than suspecting that this might be a characteristic way of relating for their partner, and attempted to change their own behavior or the couple's interactions to avoid a resurgence of aggression. When such efforts failed, this type of attribution often led—again—to reactions of helplessness and depression.[12] Thus, the assumption that how well a woman copes with violent acts by an adult partner is primarily related to whether or not she was exposed to violence as a child is greatly oversimplified, and may mask the much more important issue of how a woman explains the violence to herself.

More male perpetrators than female victims come from violent homes. Since responses of the women seem mixed, and primarily in reaction to the violence coming in, one should look more closely at the individuals to whom they were responding. Alan Rosenbaum and Daniel O'Leary (1981), in a study of marital interactions, warned that there are serious problems with models that look to the wife/victim for reasons for her victimization and urged more inquiry into characteristics of the husband/assailant (p. 70). A recent summary of studies on husband-to-wife violence supports this. Gerald Hotaling and David Sugarman (1986), in reviewing the findings of empirical investigations from the last 15 years, note that the strongest precipitant of victimization in women is simply being female. Characteristics of the man with whom a woman is involved are actually better predictors of a woman's odds of being victimized by violence than are characteristics of the woman herself (pp. 24, 27).

## VIOLENCE IN THE CHILDHOODS OF ABUSERS

An association between the perpetration of violence against a female partner and exposure to violence as a child seems quite strong. In their national sample, Straus, Gelles, and Steinmetz

(1980) found that men who had witnessed violence between their parents were almost three times as likely to hit their wives as were men whose parents had not been violent. The sons of the most violent parents had a rate of wife abuse 1,000 times greater than sons of nonviolent parents. Similarly, Fagan, Stewart, and Hansen reported that exposure to violence in childhood was the strongest predictor of the prevalence of spouse abuse, as well as a predictor of the severity of injuries experienced by the wife. In fact, the majority of studies on abusive men find that a high percentage come from homes in which there was either abuse of a spouse, a child, or both.[13] Such findings are consistent with studies of homicides occurring between partners, which indicate that the majority of men involved in those relationships also witnessed abuse and/or were abused as children.[14]

## VICTIM OR WITNESS?

The impact that childhood exposure to violence can have on an individual's future interactional style is further highlighted by recent studies that attempt to separate the effects of witnessing violence between parental figures from those of experiencing violence in the form of child abuse. Although exposure to violence in the childhood home—whether as a victim or a witness or both—is highly associated with later involvement in violent relationships, the experience of witnessing abuse seems to be the most powerful factor for both men and women. Of 42 characteristics of female victims investigated by researchers,[15] only one— witnessing violence between parents or caregivers while growing up—is consistently related to future wife abuse. (Seventy-three percent of the studies found this effect, while 27 percent did not.) Similarly, men who witnessed parental violence are much more likely to later perpetrate abuse against a female partner than men who were the victims of child abuse but did not witness abuse between their parents or caregivers.[16] In the review by Hotaling and Sugarman, 94 percent of the empirical studies found a significant relationship for men between witnessing parental violence and later abusing a partner, whereas 69 percent found being the victim of child abuse to be associated with partner abuse and 31 percent did not.

In one study examining this difference, Rosenbaum and O'Leary analyzed child abuse and parent-to-parent violence separately in a sample of couples. Although they found no differences in exposure to childhood violence between abused and non-abused women, they found that men who abused their wives had a higher incidence of witnessing parental violence than did the comparison groups but were similar to nonviolent men in the incidence of child abuse. In another investigation, Debra Kalmuss looked at the differences in "experienced aggression" (being hit by one's parents) and "observed aggression" (viewing one's parents hitting one another), and found that the transmission of violence tended to be primarily role-specific: For male respondents, observed parental hitting doubled the odds of husband-to-wife aggression in their later relationships, and this was much more strongly related to the later perpetration of violence against a partner than was having been hit by one's parents. Kalmuss & Seltzer also looked at whether stress in an individual's current life or exposure to violence as a child were more predictive of partner abuse, and found that exposure to violence as a child exerted a strong effect on the presence of relationship violence, even when current life circumstances were not stressful—with witnessing parental violence still having the greatest impact.

## LESSONS LEARNED IN A VIOLENT HOME

How does early exposure to violent interactions affect the later perpetration of violence against intimates? Experiments using children and adults in a laboratory setting found that children remember and then imitate aggressive actions that are modeled for them. Boys imitated these behaviors more spontaneously than girls, even when not directly encouraged to do so.[17] Acts that were performed by an adult male were more likely to be imitated than those performed by women, especially by male children. This was particularly true if the male who was modeling the aggression was a person familiar to the child; children were as likely to imitate a man they knew well but didn't like as one with whom they had a close nurturing relationship.[18]

A premise of social learning theory is that those actions that are allowed in one's environment and that elicit a desired response (i.e., are rewarded) are maintained, while those that fail to elicit attention or reinforcement decrease in frequency.[19] Sonkin and Durphy, from their clinical experience with violent men, note that one reason men batter women is because it works: In the short term, the use of violence "puts a quick stop to an emotional argument or a situation that is getting out of control," and also acts as a relatively safe outlet for frustration, whether that frustration arises from inside or outside the home.[20] It ensures that they are listened to—especially when they are being threatening—and that their wishes and concerns are taken seriously. Thus, it may be that a man who perpetrates violence saw it "successfully" used by a male authority figure in childhood, and developed learned behaviors that led to the perpetuation of violence as a personal style of relating in adult life.[21]

Like women, men who grow up in violent homes also experience feelings of helplessness, fear, and loss of control, even when they themselves are not the victims; for example, when witnessing an attack against a mother or sibling that seems particularly unjustified or brutal, and knowing they lack the power to intervene successfully. As children, they may come to hate the abuser, and yet still learn that the most violent person in the household also seems to be the most powerful and the least vulnerable to attack or humiliation by others.[22] Although the lesson may be the same for boys and girls, men are usually heavier and physically stronger than women, and more able to replicate some form of physical dominance over others in adulthood.

This type of aggressive reaction is also more strongly rewarded, and certainly less curtailed, for men than for women in our society, which facilitates the adoption of force or intimidation as an interactional style.[23] Typically, girls are taught to reach their goals by winning the approval of others and adapting to existing circumstances, and to deal with threatening situations by suppressing angry or aggressive reactions in favor of persuasion and conciliation. Boys and men, however, are supported in much more dominant roles—are encouraged to be in control of their circumstances, rather than letting their circumstances control them; to change the things they do not like; to express anger or frustration more directly; and to mask or devalue expressions of adaptation and conciliation. In addition, they are taught to use their bodies in a physically more aggressive way than girls. Thus, when threatened with a perceived loss of control in an adult relationship, men raised in violent homes may follow the early models by resorting to violence themselves, in an attempt to maintain control and prevent the potential of further victimization and pain.

Men who witnessed abuse and/or were victimized in childhood seem to develop a sense, even when there's no danger, of always being threatened and at risk. Home life for most of the men in the homicide group was chaotic and marred by brutal attacks on themselves and on others. If these men later become the abusers in their own households, the tables are turned: They are not the victim any more, they are the assailant. Yet they *feel* as though they are constantly victimized, and react against it. This sense of threat, coupled with an inability to trust, seems to underlie many of the perceptions that trigger their anger.

Women in the homicide group reported that their mates had an expectation of betrayal and constantly attempted to head it off. As one abuser put it, "The best defense is a good offense." This fear of being hurt or betrayed by those closest to them led to restriction or surveillance of the women's activities, constant queries about the women's thoughts and motives, and physical attack—as a warning or as a punishment for imagined wrongs. Thus, violence for these men was not only a way of relating learned in childhood, but also an attempt to be "safe" from further vulnerability or humiliation.

Not only did these men have negative role models to follow, they also lacked positive ones.[24] Children raised in violent homes may never have the opportunity to witness more effective means of dealing with conflict or stress, or to learn how to initiate and maintain effective, nurturing interactions with those they love, particularly for those roles in which the violence occurred. Again, because of traditional sex-role socialization, the lack of a male role model for caring and empathic behavior between intimates can leave a boy from an abusive home with no patterns to follow except ones of violence and power. If violent actions are also valued by males in his peer group or in his neighborhood, the risk of perpetrating future violence is greatly exacerbated.[25]

## VIOLENT CHILDHOODS, VIOLENT MEN?

Given the predominance of violence in the childhoods of men who abuse their partners, what is the risk that a boy raised in a violent home will later become a violent adult? Current figures on the incidence of child abuse suggest that many more male children are exposed to violence than actually grow up to perpetrate violence against others.[26] Some men may react in exactly the opposite way—avoiding conflict with family members adamantly, or even avoiding the establishment of sustained intimate relationships, in reaction to conflicts in their childhoods that escalated into violence and abuse.

Individuals exposed to similar social situations do not all react in the same way; this has always been a dilemma in accounting for crime on an individual level.[27] Although social learning concepts such as modeling portray how violent behavior is learned and may be transferred from childhood experiences to adult interactions, they still do not explain why some men who witness violence as children do not grow up to batter their intimates, while others who did not come from abusive backgrounds later become violent. Factors that facilitate the development of favorable modes of relating to others, in spite of exposure to abuse as a child, need to be identified. Perhaps if we identify factors that mediate the negative lessons learned in an abusive home, we can then intervene effectively with children who are particularly at risk of perpetrating violence in their adult relationships.

# 3

# Courtship and Early Marriage: From Affection to Assault

Molly looked a lot like her mother, with the same features and dark, curly hair, and that seemed to worry her father. Although she was quite shy, she was voted "most popular" her junior year in high school. However, the attention she received made her father angry. He wouldn't let her attend most school functions and didn't allow her to date until she graduated. Molly remembers that she was depressed much of the time during high school because of her father's restrictiveness and the tensions at home.

Shortly after graduation, Molly began to date an older man who was gentle and polite; they were married when Molly was 19. Within a year of their marriage, Molly's husband was sent to Viet Nam, and when he returned he seemed changed. He never abused her, but he would disappear for weeks at a time and never say where he'd been, and when at home he was silent and withdrawn. They were divorced four years later.

## THE COURTSHIP OF MOLLY AND JIM

Molly met Jim Johnson in the fall of 1978, when she was twenty-nine. Jim was thirty-five, tall and muscular, and strikingly good-looking. Friends indicated he had had a long string of relationships with women and never wanted to settle down, but with Molly it was different. Jim's interest in Molly began at their first meeting and never abated. He was dependable and attentive, rearranging his schedule to be with her and dropping other activities and even former friends with whom she felt uncomfortable.

In the following months, Jim was with her every moment Molly would allow. He occasionally spent time away from her and went drinking with old friends, but when he came back he was as gentle and considerate as ever and he never drank heavily around her. Most of the things they did they did alone together. Jim said Molly was too fragile for his male world, and that he found relief from the daily pressures of life just being with her. And he did seem at peace; his friends said he was the happiest they had ever seen him, and Molly was glad to be a part of that. From what she knew of his past, she felt like he'd had a hard life.

Thinking back on that time, Molly remembers that she just felt fortunate Jim had noticed her. He didn't seem to mind her shyness; wasn't always pushing her to talk more or to party with him, like other men she had dated. And he was always attentive and there—something that was important to her, after the long absences of her first husband. In May 1979, Molly married Jim in a quiet ceremony by a justice of the peace with two of Molly's employers in attendance.

There wasn't any abuse during the first few months Molly and Jim were married. Jim was working steadily and was good to Molly. At his urging, Molly quit work and stayed home; she enjoyed setting up a household again. But then Jim quit his job during a fight with his boss and couldn't get another one. He wouldn't hear of Molly going back to work, telling her he had married her and would support her. They stayed in the apartment another month, and then Jim put everything in storage and he and Molly moved into his van. They were living at the coast and would move the camper from rest stop to rest stop. Jim usually left in the truck during the day to look for work;

Molly waited for him to come home, then fixed supper on the camp stove and they'd move to another location for the night.

Molly tried hard to be supportive; Jim was a proud man and she knew it was a difficult time for him. He was very quiet and moody, but most of the time they got along alright. The only serious arguments they had were when Molly attempted to persuade him to let her look for work, even if just on a temporary basis. The first time Jim yelled at Molly was over this issue, and Molly never brought it up again. Jim refused to let her go with him into town, and persuaded her not to tell her family and friends where she was until they got themselves settled. Molly knew Jim was embarrassed about the change in his circumstances and complied. It seemed to her that it rained all fall; she read a lot, and tried not to let herself get depressed.

As the weeks went by, Jim began coming back later at night, often drunk. When drinking, Jim was different than Molly had ever seen him—yelling at her, calling her names, accusing her of not loving him or of wanting to leave him. And sometimes, he raped her. Molly didn't think you could call it rape, when it was your own husband, but he was very rough during lovemaking—pinching and biting and treating her with anger. At these times, he was like another person; he didn't seem to know her or realize what he was doing. Molly began to have constant bruises and bite marks. But Jim was always cold sober by morning—quiet and depressed and terribly sorry. He would apologize and stroke her face, and drink less and spend more time with her for the next several days. Molly prayed he'd find work soon. She kept telling herself things would be alright once he got a job and they moved out of that van.

## The First Beating

Jim found employment just before Christmas, and they moved from the van to an old house in town. He was gone most of the time now, getting things in order and working overtime to pay back bills. But Molly was ecstatic; so glad to have a home again and to be moving things into shelves and closets. After unpacking, she began fixing the house for Christmas. Jim didn't want her to spend much money, but she put up a tree and made some decorations. She also made a couple of presents for Jim.

When Jim came home from work on Christmas Eve, he seemed alright. But suddenly he became very irritated, angry that she hadn't reminded him to get her a Christmas gift. The more Molly tried to reassure him, the more angry Jim became. He tore the tree down, then began to hit Molly in the head with his fists. Molly attempted to pull away, but Jim grabbed her by the hair and slammed her head back against the wall with all his force. Molly came to with Jim throwing water on her. When he saw that she was conscious, he hit her in the stomach, carried her to the bedroom and had sex with her, and then fell asleep. Molly slipped into the bathroom and cried. Jim had never beaten her like that and she could not understand it. She thought maybe it was because his brother had been killed the month before in Viet Nam.

The next day, Molly had black eyes, a swollen nose, and bruises on her face and stomach. Jim said he was sorry, but added that if she had reminded him to buy her something for Christmas, it wouldn't have happened. He made her put makeup on her face so he wouldn't have to look at the bruises, and while she was doing that, he fixed the tree. But Molly hid the presents, for fear of making him angry again. For the next few weeks, Molly just felt numb, realizing that Jim had hit her. She'd go up to the attic and sit staring out the window for hours. They had an income and a house. This is when things were supposed to be getting better.

=====

## FIRST IMPRESSIONS

Molly's initial impressions of Jim were similar to those reported by the majority of women in the homicide group about their mates. Women noted that these men were, in the first weeks and months they knew them, the most romantic and attentive lovers they'd ever had. Such characteristics as early and intense interest; a constant concern with the woman's whereabouts and activities; a desire to be with them all the time; wanting to do everything together, often alone; and major changes in the men's life-styles were mentioned over and over again. The women remembered that the men showed a particularly intense concern with what they were thinking and feeling, watching them closely and responding strongly to any perceived shifts; and this the women also saw as evidence of sensitivity and love.

The women often perceived these men as unusually communicative and open as well; the men's need for an early commitment and their expressed fears of being hurt seemed endearingly honest and vulnerable. In the early stages of a relationship, with all the attendant insecurities and unknowns, neediness can be a charming quality in a partner. A man who wants you so would never turn around and leave you; a man who cares so deeply and is so aware of your moods seems unlikely to later treat you badly.

One woman, raised in an abusive family, remembered that her partner was "a wonderful man" when she first met him, "very observant and gentlemanly." She wasn't used to men like that and drank in his attentions. She did know he "liked women" and that he was used to "stepping out"; she caught him in an affair once and nearly left him. But he was so sorry and so charming; his intensity over her convinced her she was really the one he cared for. He pressed her to move in with him, and then to marry him, and she felt they had worked through their problems. In those early days, he laughed easily and drank lightly; it was three years before she realized he was an alcoholic. His temper started to change in the second year: You could say one thing and he would laugh at it, and then later become angry over the same thing. She learned that much of the time he was lying to her about his past and his activities; he quit his job two months before she found out he wasn't going to work. The third year they were married he began "dating"; the physical abuse started soon after.

Even with some indications of prior trouble, women often believed the men had changed, and they made their commitment to the men as they were when they met them.

When Wanda met Randy Bowles, he was on antabuse and not drinking; he seemed kind and quiet. He talked to her about his dreams and plans, was enrolled in college classes and excited about making a fresh start, and never forced his attentions on her. Wanda says it was like out of a storybook; he was so good to her. Then Randy became ill and stopped taking antabuse. Wanda moved in to take care of him, and things went so well that she stayed on. They were married a month before Randy started to drink again. He still treated Wanda with consideration, but gradually dropped out of school and then quit his job. Staying home, he began to drink more and more heavily, and the verbal abuse began. . . .

## EARLY WARNINGS

Violence is a part of many types of intimate relationships between men and women, not just the relationships of women in the homicide group. In surveys of American college students, for instance, 21 percent to 30 percent report at least one occurrence of physical assault with a dating partner.[1] Typically—in 72 percent to 77 percent of the cases—violence occurs only after a couple has become seriously involved, is engaged, or is living together; rather than in the early, more casual stages of dating.[2] Victims have difficulty interpreting assaultive behavior from someone they thought they knew so well. Violent episodes are attributed to specific circumstances (or even to love, as discussed later), and the relationships continue despite the outburst. Although many respondents report that their relationships worsened or terminated after the violence, in 26 percent to 37 percent of the cases, individuals say the relationships "improved" or became more committed after an assault.[3] (It is interesting to note that, in at least one study, men were twice as likely as women to say that their relationships improved after the use of violence, whereas women were more likely to say the relationships deteriorated.)[4] The longer the couple is involved and the more serious their commitment, the more likely they are to remain together after a physical attack.[5]

It is sometimes difficult to separate the warning signs of future violence from more typical romantic interactions. Couples newly in love do think primarily of one another, want to spend time together and, in the process, often isolate themselves from other acquaintances. Verbal expressions are intense and emotions easily triggered. Since our romantic tradition is based on gender stereotypes and premises of possessions, characteristics of a partner that suggest a potential for future violence are often hidden within behaviors culturally sanctioned as appropriate for men who are in love. A clustering of these behaviors, however, particularly in the areas of intrusion and possessive control, should be carefully evaluated for the history that might underlie their outward expressions.

### *Intrusion*

Many of the behaviors that women in the homicide group initially thought so romantic, over time became the triggers that led to

their assault. The men's constant desire to know their whereabouts, for example—which at first made the women feel missed
and cared for—stiffened into a requirement that they account for
every hour and led to violent reprisals when their partners were
not satisfied with their explanations. Women reported being followed to work or to friends' houses, constant phone calls to make
sure they were where they said they would be, and sudden
appearances to check up on them. The early interest in their activities became confounded with suspicion and distrust, and arriving
home a few minutes late could mean a beating.

## *Isolation*

This need for constant knowledge of the woman's whereabouts,
combined with a preference for not letting the woman interact
with people other than themselves, led in most cases to severe
restrictions on the women's activities, especially once a commitment had been established. Men in the homicide group cut their
partners off from friends and family, refused to let them work outside the home, and treated activities the women wanted to pursue
without them as a personal affront. There had usually been some
indication of this tendency to isolate the woman from outside
contacts in the early days of the relationships: Women remembered that their partners had often not wanted them around their
friends and had shown little interest in, or even expressed jealousy of, the women's friends. In the first stages of the relationships, however, this unwillingness to be a part of a larger network
had gone unnoticed in the intensity of being together. Such isolation left the women at great risk once the abuse began, reducing
their resources and the chance that others would be aware of their
plight or intervene.

## *Possession*

The dynamics of touch and intimacy also changed for these
women, from the gentle but persistent persuasion reported as
characteristic of the early experiences with the abusers to forceful possession without regard for the women's wishes or well-
being. For many women in the homicide group, physical intimacy
changed from a joy to the most threatening part of the relationship. They found they were unable to predict when lovemaking
would be affectionate and when assaultive; consequently, they

felt at risk any time intimate contact was initiated. Now women remembered that, even in the good days, there had been something determined about the way the man guided them through a room at a party or indicated by touch that they were his. In the early days of courtship, this had seemed more protective than controlling.

That the women should be confused about the meanings of touch is not surprising. Possession is an accepted part of romantic interactions between men and women, and many of these behaviors would be hard to distinguish from more normal ways of relating until they began to degenerate over time. In our present culture, even the violent forcing of physical intimacy is frequently seen as an indication of true love: In the popular genre of Harlequin romance novels, for instance, dashing "heros" tear women's clothing and leave bruises on the bodies, thus alerting the reader that they really love them and will probably marry them by the end of the tale. Ironically, such unions are presented as a stroke of immense good fortune for the women involved: Marriage to an assaultive man *is* the "happy ending" to the story.

## Jealousy

Another factor woven throughout our tradition of romantic love is the expression of jealousy. From the "chivalry" of dueling to folklore and ballads about crimes of passion, jealousy has been used not only as a yardstick by which to gauge affection, but as a justification for violence. In the homicide group, the men's tendencies toward extremes of jealousy were often masked by an initial emphasis on the positive dimensions of being alone, or were only implicit in their constant inquiries about the women's activities and thoughts. Yet all the women reported that this became a serious problem in their relationships with their abusers. Many violent incidents were triggered by a partner's jealous rage and, in almost all cases, the men's jealous suspicions far exceeded all bounds of possibility by the end of the relationships.

## Prone to Anger

Reports of women in both the homicide and comparison groups suggest other warning signs, less confounded with our concepts of romantic love, although still supported by cultural stereotypes for male behavior. Even before their partners became physically assaultive, the women noticed that many of these men seemed easily angered. Their mood could change from laughter to fury without warning, and what might set them off was hard to predict. More importantly, this anger was often completely out of proportion to the circumstance that occasioned it, and it was this pattern that later left women victims of violent attacks for something so minor as forgetting to turn off the oven or leaving the checkbook in the car.

Early outbursts of violence were frequently directed at objects or against pets, rather than against persons. Women reported watching their men rip pictures off walls or smash furniture, when the reasons for their distress were not exactly clear. An aggressive approach to life was frequently displayed in driving behavior as well. Women recounted occasions of recklessness in which the men seemed to deliberately put both their lives in danger, and reported them deliberately running into things such as stop signs or parked cars, or using the car as a weapon or threat. These behaviors demonstrate a man's willingness to do damage, and provide an indication that a potential mate may someday direct his destructiveness against his partner as well.

## Unknown Pasts

Many of the women knew almost nothing about the pasts of their men when they first became involved with them, or even at the point at which they made major commitments. Most had spent relatively little time with their partner's friends early in the relationship and few had mutual acquaintances who knew the man well. Thus, their impressions were based almost exclusively on their own interactions and on the sides of the man they were allowed to see. The women were often so blinded by the men's intense interest and desire to know about *their* pasts that they didn't notice how little they knew about the men's.

Such knowledge might have helped them. The majority of men in the homicide group had a history of violent interactions, if not with prior female partners, then with peers or family members. Women told of finding out later about assaults by their mates on former wives or girlfriends, relatives, or even employers. Yet the women often did not learn of these incidents until sometime after they had made a commitment to the man and had already had an investment in the relationship. Some of the men had a reputation among their male friends as fighters, and had earned nicknames of Duke or Knock Out. Many also had a history of arrest, both as juveniles and adults. Yet, in some cases, the women were so isolated from the men's pasts that they were even unaware of criminal records until that information was uncovered in preparation for the women's trials.

While other warning signs may be hard to separate from more typical romantic interactions, a prior history of violence is a factor that should not be ignored. Even if prior assaults were not directed at female partners, it is very hard to keep repeated violence compartmentalized in one area of one's life.[6] Aggressive responses in one area of interaction often spill over into another, and women whose mates have a prior history or current mode of responding violently to their environment should consider themselves at risk for similar assaults. The case of Randy Bowles—whom Wanda first saw as a "kind and quiet" man—illustrates both the importance of the things the women *didn't* know, and the generalization of violent behavior to many targets:

Randy had a long record of arrests. When Wanda first met him, he was on parole for shooting a girlfriend's husband in the stomach. Wanda knew only that he had been in an alcohol detoxification program, and didn't find out until later that he had also been in jail. Sometimes when drunk, Randy would tell Wanda about the fights he had been in and talk about people he had hurt as though he were proud of it. He said he had shot the other woman's husband because he was jealous, but that if he had it to do over again, he would shoot the woman instead. He warned Wanda not to cross him, or he would do the same to her. . . .

As Randy's drinking grew worse, he became increasingly abusive to Wanda, her nine-year-old daughter, Christie, and others. Once, he hit her sister's husband with a baseball bat and had to be forcibly restrained. He also attacked a neighbor with a bat and broke his glasses and his nose: twice, he threatened the man's son with an axe. Randy and his brother got into violent fights that resulted in both being injured, and Randy was frequently involved in fights in bars. If he lost, he came home and attacked Wanda and Christie. Wanda took a picture of Randy after a fight once, hoping to persuade him to stop drinking, but he just laughed and tore it up.

═══════════

## WHEN VIOLENCE STARTS

As with findings on dating violence, although the signs were there, for most of the women in the homicide group, the onset of violence did not occur until after they had made major commitments to the men. This is consistent with what is known about battered women in general. Studies of abused women have found that the majority—73 percent to 85 percent—do not experience physical assault until after they have married the abuser.[7] Often the violence occurs within the first year the couple lives together; many of the first incidents are around the time of the wedding or shortly thereafter.[8] Violence that occurs before marriage typically is triggered by the man's jealousy, or is the result of a woman's attempt to end the relationship. Lee Bowker (1983) noted:

> Many of the suitors assumed that their future wives were personal property and became violent whenever the women showed any independence, particularly where that involved contact with other males.[9]

Assaults before marriage tend to be isolated incidents that happen only once or twice, however. Especially when the issue is jealousy, women report thinking that these attacks would not be repeated after marriage, when the men felt more secure.

Again similar to other findings, women in the homicide group often described the first incident of violence as seeming to come "out of the blue." They saw them as bewildering but isolated events, inconsistent with the rest of the man's behavior, or as the result of a specific issue between the partners that would be resolved with commitment and understanding. Particularly when the first signs of abusive behavior were related to sexuality and jealousy, women usually did not label them as abuse or realize that they might represent the beginning of a pattern of assault. Yet, in almost every case, the onset of physical violence was preceded by other abusive behavior, extensions of earlier warning signs present in the first stages of courtship.

Abuse started early in Janet's relationship with Rick VanHorn. She had known Rick only a couple of weeks when, although his manner remained smooth, he began to force sex on her if she didn't immediately respond to his attentions. Janet was dating other people, and Rick became terribly jealous when they were apart. After separations, he would check her body during love-making for signs that she had had sex with another man. Yet he was courteous and attentive in other ways. Janet was too ashamed and confused to tell anyone what was happening or to seek advice. She wouldn't have talked about her sex life, anyway. She also thought this might be just the way passionate men *were* with the women they loved. Rick was pressuring her to get married, and Janet believed he would relax once she made a commitment and he knew she was really his.

It never occurred to Janet that Rick's taking her by force in their sexual relationship might expand to other forms of physical domination. She minimized the force by responding, and ceasing to see other men. She was already afraid to cross Rick, although she didn't really stop to analyze this fear.

For Janet, the first physical beating occurred after the marriage that was supposed to solve all their problems:

Janet and Rick had been married about a week. They were alone in her father's house after dinner, standing by the mirror in the dining room. Janet turned Rick to face the mirror and said something about what a nice-looking couple they made. The muscle in Rick's jaw pulled. Without comment, he turned and silently began hitting her in the head with his fists, gradually working down. Janet was trapped in the corner and couldn't get out. She fell to the floor, and he kicked her until she lost consciousness.

Janet woke up in bed. She was unable to get up for several days and Rick stayed home and cared for her. He was gentle and concerned; he fed her, brought her ice packs, ordered her flowers. Rick told her father that Janet had been in a car accident, although she didn't think her father believed him. Janet was totally confused. Hurt and at his mercy, she was afraid to ask why this had happened. She said nothing and tried to control her fears. When she was able to be up again, Rick took her away for a delayed honeymoon. Months later, when she asked Rick about the incident, he would say only that it was good for a wife to be beaten.

———————

For other women, the early warning signs were less obvious. Duke Ortega didn't like to talk about his past. Apparently, he had a history of arrests; Maggie knew that he had been in correctional institutions as a boy, but she didn't know what for. When Maggie met Duke, he used drugs for recreation, but drank only about once a week. Maggie lived with Duke for two years and, although his drinking increased and he could be rough with her when intoxicated, the first incident of actual violence did not occur until the day Duke and Maggie were married:

They had had an argument that morning. Duke was tense about the wedding and left and went to a bar. But he arrived for the ceremony on time and the wedding proceeded smoothly. After the ceremony, Maggie and Duke and the wedding party returned to the house to celebrate. Duke had invited some friends over, and they arrived late in the evening and were drinking heavily. Maggie asked Duke to come talk to her in the bedroom and told him she wanted the people to leave. She just wanted the two of them to be together. Duke didn't say anything; he just looked at her, hit her in the mouth with his first, and then rejoined the party. Maggie remained in the bedroom and finally fell asleep. The following day, Duke acted as if nothing had happened; Maggie was too depressed to bring it up.

The next incident of violence occurred only a week later. Duke came home late at night and Maggie was already asleep. She awoke to find him choking her, his face distorted, "like another person." Maggie struggled to get away and to get her breath. She managed to escape out the back door and hide behind a wall, but she had no clothes and had to ask to be let back in. When Duke passed out on the bed, Maggie packed some things and stayed somewhere else for the night. But Duke came looking for her the next day. He seemed surprised at the marks on her neck and claimed not to remember doing it at all. He admitted he had been drinking too much, and thought maybe it was the pressure of getting married. He was sorry and begged her to come home. Maggie knew you should give folks a second chance. She had been with Duke two years and this had never happened before. She decided to try again.

Frequently, the onset of physical violence was preceded by a pattern of verbal name-calling and denigration:

Chuck Wheeler had a quick temper and Mary never knew what he was going to do next. He often became angry, but in the early part of their relationship he took his fury out on furniture and walls, confining his abuse of Mary to calling her names and making fun of her in public. The first physical incident occurred when they had been married about a year. They were bowling with friends, and Chuck started laughing at Mary about what a poor bowler she was. He was sitting in the row behind her, and would reach over and hit her on the head with the clipboard, saying, "Dummy! Dummy!". At first it seemed like he was only playing, but then he became increasingly intense, bending down and punching her arm forcefully with his fist. The more he struck her, the more angry he became. Mary was really frightened. She didn't understand what he was upset about or why it had escalated so. Finally, one of his friends made him stop and Chuck left the bowling alley without her.

Chuck didn't return until the next day. He said he was sorry and that he knew he'd made a fool of himself; he didn't know why he'd done that. He was upset by the swelling of Mary's arm, and said it wouldn't happen again. Mary didn't ask him where he'd been the night before; she did not want any more trouble.

She just decided to try to be a better wife and mother and not to do things she couldn't do well. The marks on her arm lasted for several months. After this, the physical abuse occurred several times a year.

═══════════

In most cases, although the violence may have been preceded by verbal abuse or other signs of difficulty, the actual assault was triggered by a seemingly minor occurrence or seemed to have no trigger at all:

Sharon and Roy Bikson had been married about two months. It was summer, and Sharon stacked the dishes in the sink after the evening meal: she decided to take a bath and then do the dishes later. Roy told her she should do them now, but she replied that they would be fine there, or why didn't he do them? Sharon started to leave the room when Roy—suddenly furious—grabbed her. He spun her around and began to slap her face repeatedly. Sharon jerked free, but Roy caught her and pushed her down, hitting her in the chest with his fists and slapping her. She attempted to say something to him, but there wasn't time to get her breath. Roy finally stopped when he noticed that Sharon's face was swollen. Sharon started to throw up and he brought her a washcloth and some water. She cried later and told him, "I've never hurt anyone in my life. I've never done anything to deserve that. . . . " Roy said he knew it, but that she had brought it on herself: She was too rebellious. Washing the dishes was woman's work, not something a man should do.

═══════════

## RATIONALES FOR VIOLENCE

Many things can become "reasons" for a violent assault. As noted earlier, studies of battered women find jealousy and attempts to terminate a romantic relationship with a male partner as the most common reasons given for assaults that occur prior to marriage. Studies of dating couples also pinpoint jealousy as a major rationale for violence, as well as anger over sexual denial and disagreements over drinking behavior.[10] Male respondents who assault partners in serious premarital relationships often insist they were "goaded" into the violence, claiming their assaults were the result of jealousy and perceived rejection; whereas women are more likely to attribute the occurrence of violence to power struggles and see the assaults as related to the use of alcohol or drugs.[11]

In the homicide group, explanations for violence ranged from the man's jealousy and possessiveness, to major life events such as getting married or the loss of a job, to more basic issues regarding control and the functions attached to men's and women's roles. At the beginning of a relationship, these explanations may be hard to refute. Especially if violence has never occurred before, the cause of an assault may be linked to a specific circumstance by both the women and the men. A concrete reason for an unexpected attack is comforting; women often attempted to adapt their behavior in light of the reasons given, in an effort to prevent further trouble.

But a focus on the rationales for violence too often distracts us from the real problem, although these justifications typically become the emphasis of the couple's later discussions. The period just before or just after marriage is stressful for many people; longterm relationships almost always involve times of irritation with the partner; most couples have some differences of opinion on gender roles or the division of household chores. It is the choice, or the *willingness,* to use violence in response to daily events that is the issue here. Aggression in these cases often seems to be more of a response to the man's internal state than a reaction to external circumstances or the realities of a situation with the woman. To the extent that these internal responses are triggered by, but are not proportionate to, events in the outside world, a woman's attempts to avoid future violence are bound to be unsuccessful.

## WOMEN'S RESPONSES TO EARLY ASSAULTS

Women reacted to initial assaults with shock and disbelief; sometimes attempting to discuss the incidents with their partners, often withdrawing into silence and confusion and attempting to avoid any further confrontations while they thought it out on their own. As one woman, who had not had any exposure to physical abuse prior to her marriage, described the sequence of shock and denial: "You wonder if it's something wrong with you that is causing him to behave this way; what the fact that your partner is violent with you says about you. You tell yourself things might be better if he wasn't so unhappy at his job, if you lived in another house, if you weren't working, or if you were. You begin to question if it really is as bad as you are making it out; if you're exaggerating; if you're going crazy. You wonder if anyone would believe you if you told them. But you keep it all inside, so you never do find out how others might judge the situation if they knew. Sometimes you wonder if it ever happened. In an odd way, you attempt to protect your sanity by denying your own reality."

Most women in the homicide group did not attempt to seek help after the first incidents of violence—or refused outside intervention if it was offered—as a result of their shock, confusion, and shame. Again, this is typical of women's reactions to assault by their intimate partners.[12] A few women attempted to leave the men after the onset of violence (e.g. the case of Maggie Ortega). However, most of these women were talked into returning by the men's assurances that the violence would not occur again, and by their own sense that they should give the relationship another chance. In some cases, even when women made serious escape attempts, the very sources they turned to for help persuaded them to return.

Bella Harris went back to her mother's after the first few beatings, but Isaac always came after her. He would beat her again for leaving, right in her mother's house, and force her to go home. Her mother said there was nothing she could do to stop those assaults, since she "didn't have a man around" to control him. She would go in the next room and busy herself with cooking, and pretend she didn't hear. Bella fled to another relative's, but Isaac found her there and forced her home at gunpoint. After that, her mother told her, "All this running away don't do no good. You're like a little kid, always running from your home. Isaac's going to beat you when he finds you, anyway. You might as well stay with him. You're grown up now. Don't be coming here, running from your husband. . . . "

Another woman told of leaving after the initial assault and staying at a friend's home where the man was unable to find her. However, her husband kept calling her family and threatening them. Her parents were frightened, and finally her sister persuaded her to go home "for the good of the whole family." Women also talked to clergy who told them the abuse was a cross they must bear and advised them to be better wives; of marriage counselors who searched for what the women had done to provoke their husbands and assured them that the violence would not have occurred without some contribution on their part; and of attorneys who told them the assaults sounded too minor to really be worth a court case, and advised them to see their ministers or a marriage counselor instead. Such responses play into the women's tendencies to minimize the seriousness of the violence and to blame themselves for their partners' behavior, and decrease the likelihood that the first assault will be the last.[13]

# *4*

# Typical Violence

When the night mask takes center stage
When the overwhelming rage
Takes you over the edge
   of humankindness

The sink holes that were once your eyes
   pierce their way into my being
   and deaden my soul.

I go to the Island of Catatonia
Where the voices of despair cry
   This can't be happening
     again.
Where the waters of forgetfulness
   lap the shores of unconsciousness.

Until I remember the trick
   of jumping out of my body
So that I can slip through the crack in the wall
   where my soul becomes whole once again.
I wait.
The fury will subside.
I ride the current.
The mask will dissolve and melt back into
   your face.

I return to untie the knots in my stomach
   to ice the burning of my bruises
   To face the aftermask.

The calm after the storm—
A relief.
But my eyes scan the wall
    mapping the spot where the crack appeared.

For I know in the dark corner of my heart
That I will have to make the journey yet
    another time.

Anonymous*

During that first year together, Molly and Jim moved three times; with each move, Molly's life became more isolated. Jim took over all the grocery shopping and errands and, at the second house, wouldn't let Molly go outside unless he was there. He also sold her car. At the third house, he made Molly keep the blinds drawn whenever he was away and forbade her to talk to the neighbors. He never allowed her to write to her family, even once they were settled. He quit explaining why. Molly felt like she was living in a dream: Her family didn't know where she was, she was confined to the house, she was out of touch with her friends.

Molly kept waiting for Jim to get better, or at least to understand what was wrong. She knew things were not going well at work and thought maybe that was the reason he seemed so depressed. She considered slipping a letter out to her family, but didn't know what to write to them, so she never did.

The second violent incident occurred on Valentine's Day, 1980, although Molly does not remember much about it. The third occurred several months later, in a bar. (Jim still took Molly out with him some evenings. Most of the time now he seemed calm and content with her, as long as she was with him or he knew she was home alone.) On this occasion, Jim told Molly to put money in the jukebox. She was standing by the machine when the bartender walked over to put in some quarters and said something to her about a selection. Jim got up so fast he knocked over his chair. He picked the bartender up off the floor and accused him of having an affair with his wife, threatening to kill him. Someone phoned the police, and Jim and Molly left. In the van, Jim knotted one hand in Molly's hair

---

*The poems in this book were written by a woman who has experienced battering in an adult relationship.

and pounded her head against the dashboard. A police cruiser finally pulled them over and Jim was jailed for drunkenness.

While Molly drove herself home, she considered leaving Jim. She had the van now, and some time while Jim was in jail. But they lived in a small town and Molly felt sure she would have to go far to get away from Jim. He already talked as though something terrible would happen if she left. On top of that, she thought she was pregnant. Where could she go with no money and no car? Besides, she loved Jim and hoped he would change; she saw alcohol as his main problem.

Molly's nose was swelling so that she could hardly see and her head buzzed. When she got home, she made ice packs for her face and went to bed. Maybe when Jim came back, she could talk to him about his drinking. Maybe now he would see what was happening. And Jim wanted a baby, a son. When he knew she was pregnant, he'd be careful with her.

•   •   •   •   •

By the next year, the physical abuse was occurring once a month. Jim would pull back and hit Molly with his fist for no reason, then tell her to get up and sometimes knock her down again. If he was really upset, this would go on until she couldn't get up again. At first, Jim said he was sorry for these incidents, and occasionally brought Molly gifts, although he still blamed the violence on something she had done or forgotten to do. In June, he hit Molly in the head and she fell and later miscarried. Her dreams of improvement were shattered. Molly could not remember the Jim she used to know.

Molly stayed because Jim said he would kill her family if she left, and she believed him. In addition to his violence toward her, she was beginning to find out more about his violence toward others—men he worked with, men in bars. Jim warned that her parents' home would be the first place he would go if he came home and found her gone; he said he would see them die first and then kill her. Though he said this only when he was drunk, it was then that he was most violent. Molly got so she never left the house if she thought he might come home. She began having constant headaches and dizziness, and was living on Empirin III. She knew she ought to do something, but it was enough just to get through the day. She tried to remember all she knew about being hopeful. She tried to take it one day at a time.

By 1982, Jim was drinking more heavily. He had left his last employer the previous fall, and was doing odd jobs to make money. Abuse often began when he arrived home in the evening; he would accuse Molly of having affairs and then begin hitting her. He insisted on having sex nearly every night, and this frequently involved violence as well. Molly always had bruises, teeth marks, and abrasions. Jim also required sex after beatings, and this was especially painful when Molly was injured. She began to welcome unconsciousness as a refuge; it was so much easier than experiencing what was going on. There were no more good times. Molly simply lived in fear of Jim's rage and tried to avoid things that might set him off. But Jim became more and more unpredictable, and when he came home angry, there was nothing she could do.

Molly gave birth to a son in August. Rather than being pleased, Jim found the baby annoying and would sometimes go to his room and break his toys or spank him in irritation. He seemed aware of how much Molly wanted to leave him, and added the baby to his list of warnings against her departure. Yet he often talked to Molly about leaving her, and sometimes threatened her with the revolver he kept in the pickup—holding it to her head and saying that he didn't love her, that she wasn't good enough for him.

After Kevin's birth, Jim began dating. He would come home at night and tell Molly about the women he had been with— young and beautiful, no stretch marks, no kids. He admitted that he abused her sexually, but said it was because of her age; she wasn't a virgin anymore and she deserved it. Molly started making plans to escape but, with the baby, and without a car, money, or friends, she wasn't quite sure how. She persuaded Jim to let her take in ironing, and began hiding some of her earnings under the sink.

## PATTERNS OF VIOLENCE

Types of physical abuse reported by women in the homicide group ranged from being slapped, punched with a fist, kicked, or hurled bodily to being choked, smothered, or bitten. Women reported attacks in which they were beaten with an object, threatened or injured with a weapon, scalded with hot liquid, or held under water. Sexually assaultive acts also were frequently mentioned. The typical battering episode involved a combination of assaultive acts, verbal abuse, and threats.

Usually there was a pattern to the violence, both within the incidents and over time. Women learned to identify this pattern and often to see changes in the man just before an attack. By the time these changes became apparent, however, it was usually too late to escape. The women attempted to withdraw into silence, leave the room, or reason with their partner but, by this point, everything they did seemed to be wrong. Once an attack began, there appeared to be little one could do to calm the assaulter.[1]

For Maggie Ortega, the violence most often came without warning, usually when Duke was drunk. Maggie never knew when Duke would become aggressive or she would wake up to being punched in the face and yelled at. You couldn't reason with Duke at times like that. His voice got loud and his face changed expressions—tightening and pulling back. It was like dealing with a stranger, and it ran its course until he was through. Maggie would try to get away, although Duke was much larger than she was, or would call the police if she could get to the phone. After violent incidents, Duke was almost always sorry, except near the end of the relationship, when he seemed to cease caring.

Many times, the women reported, verbal disagreements would escalate into a physical attack.

Irene and Mark Miller's arguments usually started over the kids or money. The more heated the conversation became, the more upset Mark became. He'd get a look in his eyes and start to breathe differently; then, Irene would know there was going to be trouble and she would try to leave the room. That's when the hitting would start. Even if she just sat there, Mark exploded eventually. He'd always go for the throat and choke her, then throw her across the room or down on the bed. He would also hit her with his fist or the back of his hand, bang her head on the floor, kick her in the stomach, bite her, take a hand or foot and bend it back or twist it at the wrist or the ankle. Once Mark got started, he could not be stopped. He would suddenly stop himself and ask, "What happened? What did you do?" as if he had nothing to do with it. He'd be concerned over Irene's injuries, get her an ice pack, or help her stop the bleeding, telling her, "I love you. . . . You're my whole life! You're the only woman I've ever loved. . . . " He would change from a violent to a very gentle person. Afterward, Mark would send Irene flowers and cards with money in them, and things were alright for two or three weeks, until something else upset him.

---

Possibly in keeping with early childhood lessons, physical abuse also frequently involved a sort of "teaching model," with the man in the role of parent or trainer. Sharon Bikson described the violence in her relationship with Roy:

He felt I was a child. He'd say, "I'm going to teach you a lesson; raise you right." He'd make himself angry, lecturing me. I was always caught off guard by his attacks. They seemed to be mainly dependent on his mood, rather than on things going on around him. He would slap me, hit with his fists, twist my arms behind my back, call me names, and say awful things about—and to—my mother. And then he'd tell me it was for my own good. If I tried to say anything, he'd call that "talking back" and I'd get hit. But if I kept quiet, he'd say I was ignoring him. No matter *what* I did, it just got worse and worse, once it got started. He'd say, "You're going to dance to *my* music . . . be the kind of wife I want you to be. . . . " I was always afraid he was going to kill me. He'd curse and shout, his eyes seemed to dilate, he would spit or foam at the mouth. He didn't seem to know his own strength at those times, or care what happened or how badly I was hurt.

---

It didn't take much for Roy to reach this level of anger.

Sharon drove the new car to work, and Roy became upset about that. How did she know he might not want to drive it later? In talking about it, he became more and more enraged, fuming: "You just piss me off. I hate you for buying the washing machine. I hate you for turning on the light in the bathroom while I'm sleeping. . . . " He threw her to the floor, then pulled her up and began banging her head against the wall. . . . The most severe violence began after Sharon filed for divorce and attempted to live apart from Roy.

---

In some cases, the women never knew the reasons for the assaults, except when they were related to their attempts to leave.

Hal Simon battered Karen only when he was drunk. Something would just bother him and, like a reflex action, he would begin punching on the right side of her head with his fist, gritting his teeth, breathing hard. He would quit when he got tired, and wander off and do something else. Later, he would be sorry and apologize; but as the relationship progressed, he no longer seemed contrite, and threatened to kill her if she tried to leave or told anyone. Karen attempted to escape several times, but Hal found her and beat her badly for disobeying.

Their final year together, Hal didn't hit Karen in the head as much, but used the gun more, or hit her where the marks would not show. Each time, Karen was afraid he would finally kill her, or beat her to the point that she didn't know who she was or what she was doing. After assaults, she would always check to see if she could remember her name, her dog's name, her street address. She began drinking heavily to handle the tension and fear.

---

Many severe incidents in the homicide group were precipitated by the man's inability to tolerate the woman's being away from him or away from home.

Bella had gone to the movies with her sister. Isaac believed her place was at home, and had beaten her so badly in the past for going out that she usually never left the house. But this evening, he said he wanted her to go. Then he changed his mind while she was gone. He began telling the children that he was going to kill her when she returned, and they were all going to stay up and watch. The youngest girl began to cry, and Isaac made her go to the top of the stairs so she wouldn't give it away.

When Bella got back, Isaac began shouting, "Damn you, damn you. Who said you could go to the movies?" Bella tried to reason with him, saying, "You did, honey. You told me to go." But Isaac chased her toward the living room, yelling, "I'm going to kill you, you bitch. I'm going to kill you this night!" Bella ran from side to side in the room, but couldn't get to the door because Isaac had it blocked off. Isaac forced her into a corner, holding her up with a hand in her hair, and began hitting her repeatedly in the head with his fist. Bella could hear the children screaming and kept crying to them to get help. She was sure Isaac would kill her if no one intervened. Then he began to bang her head against the wall. Bella was too dizzy to resist anymore, and just hung on. The attack ended a few minutes later when a relative stopped by and restrained him.

---

## EXPRESSIONS OF REGRET

At the beginning of the homicide relationships, most of the men expressed contrition after attacking their partners. This was especially true for the onset of violence: Nearly all—87 percent—expressed some regret after the first assault. A higher percentage of men in the homicide group than in the comparison group showed contrition following the first incident (87 percent versus 72 percent).[2] But after that, the percentage of men in the homicide group expressing remorse dropped sharply, while the percentage in the comparison group stayed about the same.

The abusers' distress following assaultive incidents often made the situation even more confusing for the women. Particularly at the beginning of a relationship, it was tempting to think that the violence would not occur again. After physical attacks, most of the women were in shock, hurt, and depressed, and in need of reassurance and love. Though their fears remained, they reached out for the thread of something to hope for.

After the times he hurt Maggie, Duke Ortega would say that he was sorry, that it wouldn't happen again; he'd hold her in his

arms and sometimes cry. Duke—and Maggie—blamed the abusiveness on his drinking. Duke often said he didn't even remember the attacks that had caused her injuries. They talked a lot
about his drinking less, and Maggie tried to believe everything
would be alright.

---

Yet, when the abuse continued in such relationships, expressions of remorse became harder to understand.

Isaac was often terribly sorry after abusing Bella. He'd sit at the
kitchen table and weep, saying, "I've got to stop my evil ways!
I don't know why I *do* you this way. Come here, baby. Did I
hurt you bad?" Bella would get so confused: Isaac was this sorry
after he hurt her, and yet it kept happening again and again. He
would leave the house in the morning and they would be laughing and talking, but he would come home furious at night.

---

Especially in the early stages the women made repeated
attempts to understand the explosions and to look for ways to
work through the problem with their mates. The case of Susan and
Don Jefferson provides an example:

Susan couldn't understand the batterings, why they kept happening. At first, she felt sure they could work it out; in between
the batterings, Don was so nice and good to her and she didn't
want to give up on them. She kept asking herself, "What am I
doing wrong? The house is nice. . . . I keep it up nicely. . . . I
prepare food for him. I have a good job; I'm not just sitting
around. . . . I'm not having any affairs." She never could understand what set him off.

After violent incidents, she would try to reason with him,
often leaving the house first to protect herself from further
abuse, then returning in a few hours to try to talk it out or
understand what was happening. Don was always quiet and passive after the incidents, shaking his head and saying he didn't
really know what was wrong. He would tell her he was sorry; it

wouldn't happen again. So, they'd patch it up and start over "fresh," and Susan would try to forget. . . .

---

Over time, however, the women increasingly lost hope in their abusers' desire or ability to change, even if contrition continued. Many of their partners gradually ceased to show remorse—the percentage of men in the homicide group expressing regret declined to 73 percent after the second or a typical violent incident, and to about 58 percent after the worst incident—even though, in most cases, the attacks became progressively more severe.[3]

---

Toward the end of his life, Duke no longer seemed sorry about hurting Maggie. He became increasingly violent, and trying to talk about it could set off another angry attack. Maggie was more like a punching bag or a sexual outlet than a person to him; the only time he noticed her was when she got in his way. Violent assaults just "occurred" in the course of his day. Maggie didn't think he thought about them at all.

---

Whether most abusive men show contrition after incidents, even in the early stages of a relationship, is still a matter of debate.[4] Women in the homicide group often reported that the man had said he was sorry (or had done something to indicate remorse, such as buying the woman flowers or being especially affectionate), but had also said the incident was her fault. In some cases, the men never expressed remorse for their assaults (e.g., the case of Sharon and Roy Bikson), but considered them justified by the woman's actions or attitude. For many of the women, the mere *cessation* of violence—the calm after the storm—was a positive occurrence.

---

Randy Bowles didn't apologize for his violence. Usually after violent episodes, he just became quiet. Sometimes, as though to tell Wanda he was sorry, he wanted to make love. Typically, however, he would be nice the next day, or wait beyond the next day to take a drink. Since he was usually angry when drunk, these brief periods of quiet and peace were Wanda's only good memories of their last few years together.

―――

Many times, even the men's attempts to make up were tinged with danger. Anything that seemed to be a lack of response or appreciation on the part of the women could trigger a renewed assault.

Mark Miller always wanted to make love to Irene after an attack, no matter how upset she was or how injured she might have been. It seemed to be part of his attempt to convince her that he was sorry and that he really loved her. If Irene refused, he would get upset, so she usually gave in to avoid more trouble. The few times Irene resisted, Mark became enraged and started beating her over again.

―――

## THREATS TO KILL OTHERS

In spite of their expressions of regret these men threatened further violence against the women, other people, or themselves. Men in the homicide group made significantly more threats to kill than did men in the comparison group: Eighty-three percent had threatened to kill someone, as compared to 59 percent of men in the nonhomicide group.[5] Given their experience with the men's capacity for violence, the women took what they said quite seriously. Some of the threats were implied in conversation or by action.

As Roy Bikson's assaults became increasingly severe, Sharon Bikson would tell him, "The way things are going, someone is going to get killed here!" She hoped that would help, that he would realize how rough he was getting. But he would just laugh and say, "You're damn right they are. But it's not going to be *me*."

―――――――――

Many threats of other men in the homicide group were much more explicit.

―――――――――

Isaac Harris often threatened to shoot Bella. He kept a loaded shotgun by his bed and she was afraid that someday he would use it on her. He would start talking about it, sort of fantasizing out loud, and keep bringing it up all day; just follow her around the house saying, "I ought to get my gun and shoot you. Get that gun and blow half of you away!" Several times, Bella woke up in the morning to find Isaac standing beside the bed, looking down at her with a strange expression on his face, like he was trying to decide what to do, his hand resting on the gun propped against the wall. Every other week or so, Isaac would begin to talk about killing her. Bella thought someday he would.

―――――――――

The women reported that threats by the men were particularly related to the woman's leaving the relationship, telling someone else about the abuse, or being with another man. In warning the women not to leave, the men also made threats toward those people the women might go to for shelter, such as relatives or friends, as well as threatening separation from or the loss of their children. The threats frequently involved detailed verbal fantasies as well; descriptions to the woman of what would be done to her, how it would feel, how her body would look afterward, and even how her relatives would react to news of her death. These episodes made a deep impression on the women, even when physical violence was not employed. Guns were also used to intimidate when physical assault did not occur.

One night, Mary, Chuck, and their two children were sitting at the table eating dinner. Mary was talking about a friend she had seen that day when, suddenly, Chuck jumped up and began shouting, "I've had enough of you. I've had enough of your shit!" He grabbed a rifle from behind the door and began firing down at her from the end of the table, his face distorted. Mary could feel the impact of the bullets and was terrified. She waited for blood to come, for the sensation of pain. Then Chuck started to laugh wildly, telling her he only had blanks in the gun and not to be such a fool. The children were sobbing, but he made them all finish their meals, even though one of them became sick. After this incident, Mary was always afraid Chuck would kill her with the gun. She never forgot the sight of him standing over her, or the look on his face when he pulled the trigger. She knew he could do it again *for real*.[6]

———

In other studies of homicide between partners, threats have been found to be an important forewarning of the events to come; lethal acts were rarely unheralded.[7] And often, the partner making the threats became the final victim.[8] In the homicide group, the men's threats to kill—both veiled and direct—became one of the most important dynamics of the couples' ongoing interactions; they intensified the women's perception of danger, limiting their perception of alternatives for escape, and providing a means of control by the partners, even when physical force was not used.

## SUICIDE THREATS

In addition to threatening to kill others, 61 percent of the men in the homicide group threatened to kill themselves. Many of these threats were made when the men were depressed or if the woman talked about ending the relationship. However, it was sometimes difficult to tell what was intended by the message. The case of Janet and Rick VanHorn provides another illustration of the use of a gun for intimidation, in combination with an apparent suicide threat by the man:

Rick was fascinated with guns. He owned four or five and amused himself by shooting squirrels in the backyard at night. He would lie on the couch in the den and force Janet to hold his .357 Magnum to his head while he positioned her hand on it, then tell her that someday he was going to do that and make her pull the trigger. Janet would cry and beg him not to talk that way. He always seemed faintly amused by her reaction.

———————

Men in the homicide group were not significantly different from men in the comparison group, in which 51 percent had threatened to commit suicide. There were, however, significant differences in suicide threats made by the women. Almost half of the women in the homicide group—48 percent—said they had talked about killing themselves, compared to 31 percent of women in the comparison group.[9] Many of them had also made suicide attempts, but were found by the abusers or their children and received emergency care.

Some researchers now contend that battering relationships account for one in four of all female suicide attempts seen at emergency services in metropolitan hospitals.[10] If the number of suicide deaths that are related to a battering situation could be known, it seems probable that our estimates of how many people die as a result of abusive relationships would increase.

## ESCALATION OF THE VIOLENCE

The frequency with which abusive incidents occurred increased over time, with 40 percent of women in the homicide group reporting that violent incidents occurred more than once a week by the end of the relationship. Only 13 percent of women in the comparison group reported abusive incidents occurring that often.[11] (Over 63 percent of women in the homicide group reported abusive incidents occurring more than once a month, compared to 45 percent in the comparison group.) Over time, the abuse also tended to become more severe: Eighty percent of those in the homicide group reported that the physical abuse worsened during the course of their relationships, compared to 58 percent in the comparison group, and 90 percent (vs. 73 percent) reported that the psychological abuse became more severe.[12] As these relationships progressed, all the women in the homicide group became convinced that their partners either could or would kill them, based on the severity and frequency of the violence, verbal threats to kill, and an apparent dimunition of concern by the abusers for the harm they were inflicting.

## PHYSICAL INJURIES

Injuries to women in the homicide group ranged from bruises, cuts, black eyes, concussions, broken bones, and miscarriages caused by beatings, to permanent injuries such as damage to joints, partial loss of hearing or vision, and scars from burns, bites, or knife wounds. Interestingly, although the number of abusive acts reported by women in the homicide group was not significantly higher than the number of acts perpetrated against comparison-group women, these acts were apparently done with much more force. When asked about four specific incidents, women in the homicide group were much more severely injured in both the second (a typical) and the worst (or one of the most frightening) incidents and, overall, sustained more, and more severe, injuries than did women in the comparison group.[13]

Again, this illustrates the necessity of gathering information on both assaultive actions and their outcome if the context in which violence occurs is to be fully understood. The *force* with which an act is carried out, the number of *repetitions* of the act, and the *clustering* of different acts together play a major role in determining the amount of damage that is done. Both the repetition of violent acts and a clustering of types of acts within a single incident increase the potential for injury, as victims are overwhelmed by the rapidity of events and are unable to recover in time to protect themselves from the next blow.[14]

The clustering of acts during an assault also frequently produces a distinctive pattern of injuries in battered women, characterized by multiple injury sites; a concentration of injuries to the central part of the body (head, face, neck, throat, chest, and abdomen), rather than the extremities; and multiple types of injuries from one event, particularly abrasions and contusions.[15] When such a pattern of injuries is seen in a woman—particularly in combination with evidence of old wounds and with vague complaints of physical aches and pains—physical abuse should be suspected, regardless of the explanation given for the current complaint.[16]

## VIOLENCE TOWARD CHILDREN

In both the homicide and the comparison groups, women were not the only victims of the men's violence in the home. According to the women's reports, 71 percent of the men in the homicide group had physically and/or sexually abused the children by the end of the relationship. (Just over half—51 percent—of men in the comparison group had also abused their children.)[17] Again, some of this abuse could later be documented through other witnesses or service provider and school records. Irene Miller's case provides an example of a partner who physically abused the children from a previous marriage:

Mark was especially abusive when Irene's children were younger. He hit, kicked, and slapped her son and told him he was being punished for being "stupid." He also pushed and slapped her daughter, threw her across the room, called her names, and made suggestive sexual comments about her. When Mark's car pulled into the driveway at night, both children would run and jump up on the couch (they called this "being good"), and the boy would shake. Even after Mark was dead, Irene says she still felt a sense of dread whenever a car turned into the driveway.

Sometimes, abuse of the children involved sexual assault as well. The women were often reluctant to report this type of abuse, out of concern for those still living. However, in some of the homicide cases, there were reports of the man's molestation—particularly of daughters in the household—whether they were his own children or the woman's children by a previous marriage. Many times, the children were too afraid to tell their mothers about the abuse prior to the abusers' death. In one case, the daughter began running away and, shortly before the homicide took place, was committed to a hospital for a suicide attempt related to her father's sexual abuse of her.

There were no significant differences between the homicide and comparison groups in the number of women who reported

abusing their children during their relationship with their partners (15 percent of women in the homicide group and 23 percent
of women in the comparison group). There is evidence from
other studies, however, that battered women are up to eight times
more likely to abuse their children when they are with an abusive
partner than when they are not in an abusive relationship.[18]

Even in homes in which the children were not physically or
sexually abused, evidence on the transmission of violence
reminds us of the potential impact of witnessing abuse between
one's parents. As small children, we all have fears and fantasies—
perhaps of monsters in closets or strange dangers lurking under
the bed. For children in violent homes, however, their nightmares
are real. Hearing one's mother cry out in pain, or her body fall
against the next wall; seeing actual attacks, or even the evidence
of them later is abusive. To stay with a violent man because he
has never hit the children is to underestimate the effect that witnessing abuse can have on them when it occurs or how it may
distort their most important relationships in the future.

## SUBSTANCE ABUSE

To what extent were alcohol or other drugs implicated in the
men's violence toward their female partners? Again, there were
significant differences between the two groups of men on this
measure.[19] Forty percent of abusive men in the comparison group
(a high figure) became intoxicated every day or almost every day;
yet, in the homicide group, 79 percent of the men became intoxicated this often by the end of the relationship. Over one-third
(36 percent) of men in the comparison group became intoxicated
once a month or less, whereas only 10 percent of men in the
homicide group were reported in this category.[20] There were also
significant differences in the frequency of drug use between the
two groups. Nearly 30 percent of men in the homicide group
used street drugs every day or almost every day, while only 8 percent of men in the comparison group used them that often. The
use of prescription drugs was also significantly higher for men in
the homicide group.[21]

Women in the homicide group reported that violent assaults
frequently occurred when the men had been drinking. The fol-

lowing episode with Wanda and Randy Bowles typifies alcohol-related incidents by the women:

It was late summer, and Wanda and Randy were attending a barbeque at the home of some of Randy's relatives. Randy was drunk and began making fun of another guest at the party. Wanda reached out with her foot and pushed on his chair, trying to make him stop. However, Randy had the chair titled back, and when she pushed it, he fell over. Wanda knew right away she was in trouble. Randy got up and started to come toward her, and Wanda ran toward the front of the house.

Randy caught up with her as she reached the driveway. Inexplicably, he didn't seem angry about the chair; he began yelling at her about other men at the party—saying she was his and nobody else's, and he would tell her what to do. He grabbed her around the neck, choking her, screaming at her about trying to leave him. Wanda was on tiptoes and couldn't get her breath to explain. Several men ran up to them, pulled Randy away, and took him inside.

Wanda was in the car, trying to get it started, when Randy came out of the house. He yanked open the door and wanted to drive, attempting to reach past Wanda and get the keys. Wanda was trying to tell him he was too drunk to drive when Randy jerked her out of the car. He bent her backward and, banging her head on the hood, began to choke her again, yelling, "I want to drive. You're supposed to trust me. I'll drive the car, goddam it!" The men came and intervened again, but Wanda decided the only way to end the incident was to let Randy do what he wanted. She went around to the passenger side and let him take over.

Randy drove half the way home, but then pulled over and told Wanda to drive. He was yelling about his relatives and how they were always interfering, punching her on the arm, saying, "Listen. Listen to me." Wanda couldn't drive with him hitting her; she finally pulled over near the curb and waited until Randy passed out. Then she drove the rest of the way home and got a blanket from the house to put over him; Randy slept in the car until morning. Wanda had a bruised arm, a sprained finger, and abrasions on her neck and face from this incident.

Like other research on violent behavior, research on marital violence often shows an association between alcohol and aggression. This association is particularly clear for men who abuse their female partners.[22] In contrast to the clear pattern of results for abusers, however, most studies of abused wives that employ a comparison group do not find a significant relationship between alcohol consumption and becoming a victim of a husband's violence.[23]

Although a strong association has been found between substance abuse and the occurrence of violence in marital relationships, it should be viewed as a disinhibiting, but not a causal, factor.[24] While under the influence of alcohol, individuals may behave in ways they would refrain from when sober, and may also take longer to realize the consequences of their actions than if they were not intoxicated. The use of alcohol and other drugs may serve a multitude of purposes for individuals involved in abusive interactions. For instance, Gelles speculates that the perpetrators of violence may drink to excuse their conduct.[25] This may be particularly effective when the excuse of intoxication is also accepted by others, as it was by women in the homicide group.[26] In their work, Sonkin and Durphy also suggest that violent men may use substances in part to dull the guilt and sadness they feel for abusing loved ones.[27] However, this connection is hard to establish, since other evidence of contrition appears to decrease over time.

Research does indicate that abusive men with severe alcohol or drug problems are apt to abuse their partners both when drunk and when sober, are violent more frequently, and inflict more serious injuries on their partners than abusive men who do not have a history of alcohol or drug problems. In addition, substance abusers are more apt to sexually attack their partners, and are more likely to be violent outside the home.[28] The precise nature of the relationship between substance abuse and these men's violent behavior has not yet been disentangled. For women in the homicide group, the link between alcohol consumption and violence often provided a way for them to understand their mates' assaultive behavior, especially at the beginning of their relationships, and gave them hope that, if the man would only stop drinking, the violence would also cease.

For most of these women, however, violent assaults became

more frequent and more severe as their relationships continued, while the men's expressions of remorse or concern over their actions seemed to diminish. Women in the homicide group were subjected to repeated attacks, most consisting of a combination of violent actions, and often sustained multiple injuries as a result of these episodes. Such assaults were frequently accompanied by name calling and threats, and many of the women reported that the atmosphere of intimidation, continued even when physical violence was not occurring, in the form of verbal warnings or threats with a knife or a gun. Severe physical attacks seemed to be triggered by relatively minor events, and sometimes the reasons for the attacks were completely unknown to the women, as when they were awakened in the night by the onset of an assault. Many of the men in the homicide group were assaulting their own and/ or the women's children in addition to the women, and were threatening, or behaving violently toward, others. The frequency with which the men became intoxicated or used other substances also typically increased over time, and this added to the women's perceptions that the men were totally out of control.

# 5

# The Psychology of Intimate Relating: Differences in Women and Men

What is it about the women in these relationships that makes them try and try again? Are they passive, helpless creatures, or are there strengths there that we typically do not see? Our tendency is to devalue physically abused women for being, or staying, in such a spot. Yet perseverence in the face of hardship; attempts to understand, soothe, and smooth over; assigning a higher priority to the care of others than to one's own well-being are qualities that have been taught and valued for decades as a vital part of a woman's role. Unselfishness and self-sacrifice—asking little and giving much—are held as virtues, especially in relation to one's family. Thus, it should not be surprising that the first coping strategies women utilize when violence occurs in their relationships most typically are attempts at peacemaking and resolution. In addition to seeming the safest response in the face of an aggressive mate, they are the most deeply ingrained culturally, and the most logical for a situation that involves emotional investment and usually love by the time the violence begins.

## "WOMAN'S WAY": STRENGTH OR WEAKNESS?

The traits of affiliation and sensitivity developed through women's roles of nurturing and sustained intimate relating are fre-

75

quently seen as weaknesses in a culture built on male yardsticks of autonomy and success. Perceived as weak by men and even by women, these qualities are both valued and denigrated: valued for their manageability and the comfort and stability they bring to the lives of others, yet belittled as indicating a lack of strength, independence, and maturity.[1] Theories of personality and development have been based largely on men and male ideals.[2] Thus, traditional models of psychological development place a heavy emphasis on the importance of individuation, task mastery, and autonomy, all a part of the prescription for being a successful male.

"Women's" traits, even women's strengths of compassion and care, have been described as somehow deviant from this traditional model; weaker, less effective, and less developed.[3] In particular, the importance attached by women to connection—what Kaplan and Surrey have called the "relational self" in women, or the quality of relationships with others being at the core of one's self-concept—is seen as less mature and less well-adjusted than the more autonomous perspective attributed to men.[4] The result has been a dichotomy, with women assigned the "lesser" tasks of caring for and nurturing relationships with others, and men assigned the "more important" role of mastering themselves and their environment, leaving the impediment of too many needs and emotions behind. In the male model, intimacy and relatedness often appear as threats to the more highly valued goals of autonomy and independence.

## AFFILIATION VERSUS INDIVIDUATION

One explanation for the differences in approaches to relationships by women and men is suggested by Nancy Chodrow, in her discussion of early childhood experiences with a parent.[5] Chodrow points out that, for both boys and girls, the primary caretaker in the early years of life is usually the mother. Thus, girls' impressions are formed by a basic connection to someone very like themselves, while boys' connections are with someone opposite to their gender. As children of both sexes mature, girls can continue to model their behavior on the female parent and have less need to divorce themselves from close association, whereas boys are encouraged—both by society and by their parents—to separate themselves from their mother's example as well as her person, and to begin building their own identity on the male role.[6] (All such theories are generalizations and represent trends, or patterns, in our society. There are always some individuals who differ from these patterns; although, if the trends are truly normative, all members of a society are affected by them.)

This difference in childhood experiences contains several implications for adult modes of intimacy. For women, there is an implicit continuity from being mothered by a woman to maturing into a woman herself. There is also a basis for the development of a special capacity for empathy, as the girl-child is raised and nurtured by someone like herself and, therefore, is more easily able to feel another's pain as though it were her own.[7] For a boy, the path toward development lies not in a continuation of attachment but in *separation* from the early caretaker, and in a definition of himself as different, "masculine," and independent. Often, this translates into different standards of self-control and self-expression, as well as a male ideal of not needing others and the development of a more conflicted response to closeness or dependency.[8] In writing about the impact of these childhood experiences on adult intimacy, Carol Gilligan speculates:

> Since masculinity is defined through separation while
> femininity is defined through attachment, male gender
> identity is threatened by intimacy while female gender
> identity is threatened by separation. Thus males tend to have
> difficulty with relationships, while females tend to have
> problems with individuation.[9]

―――――

Dare me not to touch you closely
or the pain we both shall bear
I bury my heart inside a stone
To avoid the weight of the words
　—"I care."

I see your eyes soft seeking mine
I feel the tingle of your touch
　But stand your distance!
　　don't hug me now!
　For I might like it
　　much too much.

And if I let my walls break down
Who then would I be?
How could I then define myself?
As part of you or
all of me?

Anonymous

## The Relational Self

While men's identities are apt to revolve around achievements and activities in the outside world, women's identities are more generally defined in relation to their intimates—partners, children, other family, and friends.[10] Because of this relational structure, women often fear being isolated or finding themselves without a mate, and look to close affiliation for safety and fulfillment; men, on the other hand, are more likely to see danger in intimacy and look to outside areas of achievement for self-worth and security.[11] Women also tend to assume responsibility for the maintenance of relationships, and internalize the blame when relationships fail, even if other reasons for the failure seem obvious.[12] Thus, while men may stress their independence and autonomy and fight to protect it, women tend to emphasize relatedness and continuity, often at the expense of taking a more definitive stand or drawing clear boundaries between what they will and will not accept.

This difference in an emphasis on continuity versus assertion is seen very early in childhood, in the play styles of girls and boys. In studies of children's games, for instance, boys tended to emphasize competition and responded with enthusiasm to the conflicts that arose, whereas girls' games were based primarily on cooperation and they were likely to end a game if conflict broke out, rather than risk losing a friend.[13] In some cases, the network of connections in which an adult woman is invested becomes so important to her sense of self-worth that, as Miller suggests, "the threat of disruption . . . is perceived not as just a loss of a relationship but as something closer to a total loss of self."[14]

## The Responsibility for Taking Care

In their societal roles, women have learned not only to base their identity in their relationships, but also to judge themselves in

terms of their ability to care for others. (Men, in contrast, sometimes judge themselves by their ability *not* to care.) This "ability" is again primarily ascertained by others' happiness and well-
being. Thus, when things go wrong, women often ask: "Am I giving enough? Am I being selfish? Am I being loving enough? The
phrase "to care for" comes to mean both the *emotion* of caring
and *actions related to* care-giving—feeling love, and therefore
"being there" for and doing for the other person. These compo-
nents become fused, and one without the other seems
insufficient.

When comparing concepts of morality, for example, Carol Gilligan found that men and boys emphasized rights and autonomy,
whereas women's concept of morality centered around care-giving and an understanding of responsibilities in relationships. Men
begin with their responsibility to themselves—a responsibility
they take for granted—and then consider the extent to which
they have a responsibility to others as well. Women more typically begin with their responsibility to others, and only later, if at
all, consider the ways in which they have a responsibility to
themselves.

## CULTURAL CONDITIONING AND VIOLENT
## RELATIONSHIPS

As with the standards established by our romantic tradition for
courtship and physical intimacy, cultural conditioning into men's
and women's roles plays a crucial part in the dynamics of assaultive relationships. "Female intuition," or attentiveness to the
cues of others' feelings, wishes, and concerns—developed
through close and sustained contact with intimates, and developed as well to safeguard women's existence in a society primarily determined by males[15]—becomes heightened in women who
live with violent men. When angry responses can be so out of proportion to the precipitant, victims become especially attuned to
the perpetrator's moods, scanning the environment for things that
might upset them, and attempting to predict and moderate their
reactions. A battered woman gradually comes to spend most of
her time monitoring the abuser's whereabouts and state of mind,
and anticipating his wants or frustrations. Abused women in
threatening situations are likely to know their partners better than

they know themselves.[16] Denied the freedom of expression or
movement that would allow experimentation with the full range
of their own characteristics and abilities, they see themselves primarily in the context of a troubled environment and in relation
to a troubled man.

## *Identity and Abuse*

Yet, deriving even a portion of one's identity from a relationship
with an abusive man is a risky proposition. In addition to hazards
that are usually part of a dependent relationship —e.g., others'
insensitivity, inattentiveness, and the normal fluctuations a couple experiences in closeness and affection over time—in a violent relationship, the person who knows the woman best and who
is in the most intimate contact with her seems to value her so
little as to batter her. It is very hard for a victim—any victim—
not to internalize the implications of this kind of treatment and
deeply question her own worthiness. In addition, a battered woman's difficulty in maintaining a self-image apart from the one
reflected by the man and his treatment of her is often exacerbated
by isolation from outside activities and people who would provide more objective information. The man's moods, definitions,
attributions, and opinions dominate the environment. Even if the
woman knows his abuse or accusations are unreasonable and
based within some problem of his own, repeated incidents, combined with a victim's confusion and distress and the vulnerability
fostered by injury and depression, make the abuser's definitions
especially hard to resist.

## *To Turn Away*

The importance of meeting other's needs—taught to women in
our society—makes it hard to leave a relationship marred by violence. A powerful dynamic is set up when the other person's
needs seem not to have been met, i.e., they still seem unhappy or
dissatisfied. Women are socialized in our culture to hold themselves responsible for the affective—or emotional—states of
their partners.[17] Thus, especially in the early stages of an abusive
relationship, women will often try harder and harder to meet
their mates' needs, looking to themselves for solutions to the others' distress: "If I gave more, was more understanding, was more

loving and less demanding, . . . was more quiet, or more respon-
sive, . . . more active, or less of a go-getter. . . . '' Such attempts
at solutions are rarely successful, however, when only one person
is actively involved in the resolution process.

Based on the morality of giving care, it also seems *wrong* to
walk out on someone who is in pain, especially when you are inti-
mately acquainted with that pain. Women in the homicide group
said they felt like they would be ''deserting'' the man in leaving
him, or even in thinking about leaving him, although the relationship was becoming destructive to them. Especially early in
the relationships, they tended to take into account how the man
would feel and the damage their leaving might do to his life; to
empathize with his troubledness, and try again. This sensitivity to
others' feelings leads to weighing others' needs and wishes quite
heavily in judgments and decisions. Thus the batterers' expressed
and apparent need for the women, as well as their pleadings or
warnings not to leave, figured prominently in the women's decisions about whether to stay or go.

## FEAR OF FEELING: VIOLENCE AND INTIMACY

Not only are women more sensitized to feelings, both in themselves and in others, than are men, but, because of their socialization as the ''weaker sex,'' they are also better able to acknowledge emotions of weakness or vulnerability. Conversely, men—
encouraged to avoid or at least deny sensations of vulnerability
and weakness—sometimes learn to fear situations that might produce such feelings, or to turn to other reactions to cover them
up. Jean Baker Miller suggests that men have been ''conditioned
to fear and hate weakness'' and that they ''try to get rid of it immediately and sometimes frantically.''[18] Thus, when they have these
emotions, they may look for alternate explanations and put the
blame on others—e.g., their woman partner—for ''making''
them feel uncomfortable, or simply for making them feel too
much. Women in the homicide group reported the irony of being
attacked *because* the man cared. Just the perception that another
person mattered so, seemed so vital to his daily existence and
happiness, became something to defend against: The man's need
for the woman seemed to him a power in her hands, and he would
lash out to balance the equation.

## The Dangers of Proximity

An extreme example of men's anxiety about feelings of weakness and vulnerability appears in the reactions of abusers to closeness and need. Much of this may stem from their childhood experiences. In a violent home, vulnerability and dependency become associated with the risk of harm and being at the mercy of a more powerful and often damaging person. The sense of helplessness a child feels when confronted with an angry and assaultive adult, or when witnessing one family member being attacked by a much stronger family member, may leave a desperate need to have complete control in intimate interactions as an adult. Just the normal variations of intimacy and affiliation in a day-to-day relationship could be expected to produce exaggerated levels of arousal and anxiety and, thus, exaggerated responses.[19]

As mentioned in Chapter Three, lessons learned in a violent (or even highly conflicted) home often differ for boys and girls. In an abusive home, children come to associate intimacy with emotional and possibly physical pain and injury. Particularly in a home in which the aggressor(s) is/are male, boys learn that the way to be safe is to dominate and control: girls, on the other hand, may perceive safety in trying to please and in acquiescing.

For boys raised in an abusive environment, later feelings of vulnerability may be unbearable. The arousal engendered by emotions of love and desire becomes more anxiety-provoking than pleasant. Many abusive men seem caught between two poles: a pressing desire to fill the void in their lives by establishing an intense connection with another who is completely "theirs," and an equally pressing need to protect themselves from the vulnerability and potential pain they have learned to associate with such closeness.

Given the depth of their fears, no amount of reassurance by an adult partner will suffice. Abusive men tend to respond to intimate relationships with a deficit of positive behaviors and an overabundance of negative acts. As is often found with abused children, their needs for attention and reassurance are extreme and their expectations of intimacy unrealistic. This leads to angry and frustrated feelings when such expectations are not met. The insecurity and inability of these men to trust is displayed in their intrusive personal style and easily triggered responses of anger, extreme jealousy, and violent outbursts in response to threats of loss or loss of control.[20] Excessive dependency on their mates is revealed by their attempts to make their partners dependent on them, and by their exaggerated control over their partners' behavior.[21]

## Labeling and Mislabeling

Many men who are violent toward their partners appear to be restricted in their labels for emotions. Almost everything they feel becomes labeled as desire or anger and, often, those get confused.[22] In an extreme of the cultural pattern for men, a wider range of emotions—sadness, insecurity, hurt, and fear—is rarely identified.[23] Most strong emotions, particularly unpleasant ones, become translated into anger and then externalized as somebody's "fault." The "offender" is labeled and punished, and the abusive man becomes the victim and, therefore, is "justified" in his aggression. This externalization of responsibility for emotions can go to great lengths. Women talk of being blamed even for the men's sense of remorse after an assaultive incident ("You set me up to be violent, so I would feel guilty. You made me hurt you so I would feel bad."); sometimes these attributions trigger a resurgence of the violence against them. Expressions of anger serve at least the short-term function of short-circuiting feelings of vulnerability, and have the advantage of being more socially acceptable for men than expressions of insecurity or fear.[24] Yet, in the long term, they create increasing distance between the abusers and the ones on whom they so desperately depend.

## Distance and Intimacy

Because of their perception of threat in closeness, abusive men need to maintain total control over the type and extent of intimacy in their relationships, although their own definition of how close they want to be keeps changing. In studying men who assault their wives, Donald Dutton and James Browning note the frequency with which the need for control or dominance, and issues of intimacy or distance, appear as factors precipitating assault.[25] When the arousal of closeness becomes too threatening, this stimulates a need in these men to create some form of distance. This may be done by leaving the home, by denigrating the partner, or by striking out. Yet once the distance is created and/

or the woman has withdrawn from her mate's violence, the aver-
sive arousal connected with the threat of closeness diminishes,
and the old need for attention and proximity returns. At this
point, the man may again lash out ("Pay attention to me!" "Why
are you so quiet?" "Are you trying to make me feel guilty?"), or
may attempt a loving, and often sexual, reconciliation.

Movements by the woman that decrease her proximity to the
abuser (i.e., having her attention on other matters, engaging in
outside activities or wishing to be with friends, withdrawal, or
actual attempts to leave) are perceived as rejection and threats to
the man's control; thus, they seem to jeopardize both the structure and the system of dependency he has established. Yet,
attempts by the woman to move closer—to be more intimate, to
discuss the relationship, to uncover the man's feelings for her—
threaten his sense of control over his own emotions, as well as
over his initiation of intimacy and the amount of it he will allow.
Unable to find a happy medium, such men continue to experience
discomfort, and to blame the discomfort on the woman who triggers these emotions in them and whose "power" they fear. They
sometimes seem to batter the woman in order to reduce her to a
nonentity—someone they no longer desire, unattractive to themselves as well as to others, someone unable to elicit confusing
longings and feelings and dreams. They are unable to go about
their daily lives without feeling extreme discomfort. Their need,
and therefore, their jeopardy, is too great. They must obliterate,
or cut off, the things they desire, in order to separate at all. Their
need to be understood and appreciated demands that they receive
affection and respect, yet emotional survival seems to demand
that they stand alone.

Extreme fears generated by caring for and needing another person become self-perpetuating. Because the triggers are frequently
so deeply rooted in the past, and the emotional cues often relatively unrelated to their current partner, the feelings of threat and
anger become increasingly disconnected from reality. This is
seen, for example, in the extreme jealousy frequently demonstrated by abusive men. Given their inability to trust and their
need for exclusive possession, the possibility of "their" woman
with another man is the worst scenario they can imagine. Often,
they spend much of their time away from the woman in obsessive
thoughts and fantasies about her possible infidelities; if they find
her desirable, so must everyone else. By the time they bring their

fears and suspicions home, imagined "signs" become "proof" of what they've already convinced themselves is true. The women's denials in these situations only further confirm their "guilt" in the abusers' minds. Afraid of closeness because of the risk of loss, and afraid of distance because that loss may have already occurred in their absence, the abusers put themselves and their partners in a hopeless situation.

## WHEN EMPATHY FAILS

If these patterns sound familiar—except for the violence, and the extreme jealousy—it is because they are relatively normative. The need for control at any cost, whether by denying or relabeling one's feelings, creating distance between one's self and a loved one, or taking a stand and refusing to negotiate, is seen frequently in romantic relationships. The distinguishing factor in the homicide group is the *extremity* of the men's reactions to their fears of intimacy and loss, and the use of violence as a mechanism of restriction and self-definition. Empathy—a quality typically not nurtured in men, nor considered necessary for the performance of male roles in our society, would have provided some measure of protection against the damage done in these defensive efforts to protect one's self. Yet, in the homicide cases, the capacity to feel with another seemed virtually missing in the abusers, and this failure of empathic understanding facilitated their increasing infliction of harm.

It must be remembered that, in the majority of cases, abused women do not know they are becoming involved with a violent man until after a major commitment has been made in the relationship. At the onset of violence, they usually perceive the aggression as an atypical occurrence—out of character with what they have observed of their partners' other interactions, and attributable to specific circumstances or stresses. Their sense of commitment and concern, and their love for their mates—as well as women's cultural conditioning toward continuity and the responsibility for taking care—often leads them to search for explanations for the violence and to seek solutions, rather than leaving at once.

Yet, attempts to understand what has "gone wrong" in a violent relationship can keep a woman at risk in an abusive situation for far too long, especially if it is a part of the man's pattern to express remorse after assaultive incidents or to talk over possible improvements. In a woman victim, the capacity for empathy, although desirable for the prevention of violence, may become a hook in itself: Those things she understands, she may then accept—what Gilligan terms "an understanding that gives rise to compassion and care."[26] Contrary to the persistent stereotypes of women being "emotional" rather than "rational," women's repeated attempts to analyze the abusive situation, to identify a meaningful sequence of events, and to reason with their partner about the occurrence of violence, represent a cognitive approach toward problem-solving. Women's reliance on communication as a mode of conflict resolution was displayed time and again in the homicide cases as the women attempted, often in the face of great danger, to communicate their concerns to the abuser. Looking for an adequate and a positive solution, these women sought a happy ending to the situation they were in, as opposed to severing their relationships, walking out on their homes, and starting over.

We often talk about battered women's slide toward hopelessness as a factor in their staying with an abusive man.[27] But hope can be as great a hook: hope for change, hope for improvement, often in the face of overwhelming odds. As one woman expressed it, "I go to bed pretty beaten down at night, but my soul gets back up in the morning." The fact that battered women maintain a home and often care for children as well as caring for the abuser, while they are being physically attacked and threatened, testifies to the depth of their resiliency and strength. As Gilligan notes, "the image of women arriving at mid-life childlike and dependent on others is belied by the activity of their care in nurturing and sustaining family relationships."[28] Women's strengths of perseverance, caring, and responsibility, applied in a no-win situation, do eventually lead to depletion and despair. Yet it is vitally important that the strengths be recognized, for they are generalizable—to leaving, to beginning a new life, to survival, and to the establishment and maintenance of more constructive relationships in the future.

Women in the homicide group, like many other women, carried a strong belief in caring as a powerful and healing force. They had grown up in a society that teaches its women: "Be thoughtful, be considerate; don't think of yourself, think of others." Along with others in this society, these women share the conviction that "if you're good, if you're caring and loving; if you try hard, and are unselfish; good things will come to you."

We are a nation that believes in happy endings. The thing that makes sad endings so compelling is that we desire the happy ones so much. These women shared with many others a commitment to "making it good, making it work out." Yet the problem here was in the application. Women's strengths, applied in situations where there is little hope for change—at least without outside expert intervention—are spent in vain, and eventually are seen as pathological.

There is the danger that women will construe their caring as a weakness, and identify others' refusal to care as strength; that— in an effort to be invulnerable and unhampered by their awareness of, and reactions to, the emotions and needs of others— women will emulate a model of autonomy that leaves out empathy and the responsibility for care and sensitivity. Yet the importance of connection, empathy, and care are seen in the effects of their obverse, when applied in self-protection. Gilligan sees the "origins of aggression in the failure of connection,"[29] and suggests that what is needed is not the abandonment of women's special emphases, but for a woman to achieve "the right to include herself among the people whom she considers it moral not to hurt."[30] Women need to construct a foundation within themselves for their self-image, built on a recognition of their ability to love and persevere as evidences of their strength; and from this basis then be free to choose where to invest those strengths in places where they can be constructive. In the homicide group, the depth of the men's disturbance, combined with the tendency for aggressive acts to escalate both in frequency and severity, eventually outweighed all possible good that could have been accomplished by the women's remaining with them.

# 6

# The Outer Limits of Violence

## MOLLY AND JIM: 1983

Molly had been depressed. Jim was no longer working and they were falling deeper and deeper into debt. He also refused to let Molly work now, because he said he did not trust her. The money under the sink had been spent for food and Jim had sold most of the things Molly owned before they got married. All the living room furniture was gone, as well as Molly's dishes and the special things she had kept from her family. Molly almost never talked anymore, except to her son. Jim said he knew she was thinking about leaving, but warned that she would not get far; he said he'd see to it that she never managed to leave with the baby. He would take the rifle down from the wall when she was quiet for too long, and Molly would try to perk up and seem more cheerful.

The baby became the focus of Molly's life. When Jim was away, she would talk and even sing to Kevin, to make them both feel things were alright. She promised herself they would get away when Kevin was a little older. But Kevin was so tiny now. She didn't want to take any chances with the safety of her son.

In the spring, Jim took the money he had made from selling their things and went to another state to buy a truck he had heard about. He was sober and kind to Molly just before he left. He said he knew things had been rough lately, but that getting the truck would turn the corner. He could start his own towing-

and-repair business and set up a garage in the shed; he knew where he could borrow some tools until he got started; he thought he would be happy doing that. They could pay off their debts and then maybe get some more furniture for the house. Molly felt hopeful for the first time in a long while. All she needed was a year of peace, or maybe two, until Kevin was older and she felt she could leave with him and get a job. It was sunny and beautiful, and Molly threw herself into spring cleaning, opening the house up to the outdoors, marveling at the sense of peace and relief she felt with Jim gone.

Jim came home the day before Molly expected him and caught her in the backyard talking to a neighbor woman. He seemed to take it quietly; he asked her to come inside, and he was sober. But as soon as Molly stepped into the kitchen, Jim flew into a rage. He told her to put the baby down. Then he began hitting her with his fists, throwing her against cabinets and appliances, knocking her to the floor, pulling her up, and hitting her again. He pulled one small cabinet completely off the wall, breaking the glasses, and threw everything in the kitchen that was movable. Molly had never seen him this angry. Over and over he kept saying, "I can't trust you. I just can't *trust* you."

Finally, Jim dragged Molly into the living room and demanded that she take off all her clothes. He put them in the fireplace, and then got her clothes from the closet and added those to the pile, saying she wouldn't be needing them if she was going to be a whore. He yelled and yelled at her about being outside, saying he would teach her not to do that; screaming, biting, pinching, pulling hair, kicking her in the legs and back. Molly held her breath and prayed it would be over soon. This time, she was not sure she could make it through. This time, she thought she might die.

After about an hour, Jim seemed to wear out. He walked into the kitchen, and Molly pulled herself to the bathroom and tried to stop shaking. She could hear the baby crying, and knew he needed to be changed and fed. But Jim burst in and accused her of trying to hide something there, saying this proved she had been unfaithful. He told her if she wanted to be a whore, he would show her what that was like. He pushed her forward over the sink and raped her anally, being as rough as he could, pounding her head against the mirror as he did so. Molly started throwing up, but he continued. When Jim finally let go of her, she fell to the floor. Molly had dark hair down to her waist, which Jim had always loved; now he grabbed the scissors from the bathroom cabinet and began shearing it off, scraping her scalp with the blades, ripping out handfuls in his anger. When he finished, he pulled Molly to her feet and forced her to look at herself, shaking her violently and saying, "How do you like how you look *now?* No one will look at you now, will they? No one will *ever* want you now!"

There was no more physical abuse that night, but Jim continued to rage at Molly until early morning, forcing her to sit on the floor of the bathroom, even though she was shaking and bleeding. He was pacing and screaming, and seemed tireless. It was even more frightening, knowing he was sober. Although she had taught herself not to respond, Molly could feel the tears rolling down her face and couldn't stop them. She had never been in so much pain. Eventually, Jim left her sitting there, warning her not to move, and went to bed, but woke up later and yelled for her. When she got to the bed, Jim picked her up and laid her down beside him, and then put his arms around her before going back to sleep.

The next day, Jim told Molly she was never to go outside the house again, for any reason. Molly was bleeding, throwing up, badly bruised, and unable to walk, but Jim seemed unconcerned with any of her injuries. He brought the baby to her so she could take care of him, and told her to put iodine on her cuts. He warned her that she would "lose" Kevin if she ever did anything else to disobey him. Molly didn't know what that meant, but she was determined to be more careful.

After this, Jim stayed around the house more and came back frequently to check on Molly if he was away. Molly felt ill for months. She moved slowly and just tried to take care of Kevin.

## FALL

Jim wrecked the truck, injured himself, and was hospitalized for several weeks. After he returned home, he drank heavily and was abusive every day. He would hit Molly with his crutches, throw his food at the wall, and chew snuff and spit it in her face. He felt the accident had ruined his business and he blamed Molly for driving him to it. He kept her awake until early morning while he raged, and threw bottles of beer at her or poured hot coffee over her if she fell asleep. In the morning, while Molly got up with the baby, he would sleep in. As Jim's injuries healed, sexual abuse occurred almost nightly. Molly's bite marks and cuts became permanent scars. When he had been drinking, sex would go on for hours because he couldn't climax. Jim would blame Molly for that, grinding his teeth, banging her head against the headboard and choking her. He also threatened her or traced on her with a fillet knife during sex. When he woke up in the morning, it seemed as if he did not remember the incidents at all.

Because of the accident, Jim said he could not pull his boots off and insisted that Molly do it. Sometimes, when she bent down for them, he would kick her across the room. Molly tried to protect herself during such attacks, but she didn't cry or scream. She would just concentrate on her breathing and wait for it to be over. Jim got angry and said she wasn't feeling enough pain; sometimes, he hit her harder, but Molly remained silent. She would think, "He might have my body, but I'll try not to let him have my mind." Still, she stayed—exhausted, ill, not knowing where to go. She kept telling herself, "If I could just get some more sleep; if I could make myself eat again, get my strength back. . . . " Jim was so wild now, she did not think she could get away with the baby without someone getting killed.

## 1984

By their last year together, Jim had several girlfriends. He would tell Molly, "I want you to know . . . I've got a date this evening." When he came home early in the morning, Molly was supposed to be waiting up for him. Jim would make her sit and listen while he told her details of his evening—how young the women were, how beautiful. Especially if he had been drinking, he would become angry with Molly for not being like that and start hitting her. Lectures or retaliation could last until dawn. Jim slept very little now, except when he passed out.

One night in April, Jim came home from a date about 3:00 a.m. He didn't say much when he walked in, but seemed angry. He went to the refrigerator to get something to eat, but then came back and knocked Molly against the wall and threw a chair at her. Still without speaking, he jerked her to her feet and slammed her backward into a partition. Molly's back broke through the plasterboard, and she came to on the floor with Jim pouring water over her. He told her to get up and fix his supper, but then changed his mind and made her sit in a chair while he lectured her instead. He was angry that she wasn't young and beautiful like the women he was dating, that she was not a virgin anymore, that she had had a child. As he talked, he kicked Molly in the legs; then he threw a knife at her, which missed. Jim picked up the knife and slowly cut x's across Molly's hand, talking all the while about how ugly she had become. Then he told her to bandage it up and make supper.

Molly started to move around the kitchen, but Jim thought she was not hurrying enough. He threw her back in the chair and hit her in the head with his fist. Molly tried to get up and run, but she was too dizzy. Holding her head, Jim began hitting her face with his hand, over and over, stopping to pour water on her from a pan whenever she seemed to be passing out. Finally he let her fall, and when she landed face forward, he stomped on her back with his foot. Something snapped, and Jim heard it and quit. It was daylight, but he stayed in the kitchen until Molly managed to prepare food for him. Afterward, he wanted sex. He seemed to realize Molly was injured, because he picked her up and put her on top of him. The next day he told her it would not have happened if she had been 16 and a virgin.

Jim took Molly to the hospital and said she had been in a car accident. Molly had black eyes, cuts, fractured ribs, and a concussion. Jim let the emergency staff care for her, but then took her home. A month later, he moved in with a girlfriend.

---

## THE WORST INCIDENTS OF VIOLENCE

The violence in these incidents seems mindless, inexplicable: How could a man do this to his wife? What was he thinking and feeling? *Was* he thinking and feeling? And how did the woman bear it? How could she be the recipient of such inhumane treatment for so long? Why didn't she do something about it? What would we do in her situation?

I know these accounts are unsettling to read. After years of working with violence, I still find them troubling to write. It is almost impossible to believe this level of victimization could occur between partners at home; that a man could move from romance and affection to seemingly endless brutality; that a woman could live in such a violent situation and still keep her mind.

Yet Jim's attacks on Molly are typical of the assaults experienced by women in the homicide group as their relationships progressed. Incidents described as the "worst" by these women usually consisted of a series of severely violent actions, and fre-

quently involved loss of consciousness and the infliction of permanent injuries. Some women defined the "worst" incidents as
those involving the abuse or endangerment of a child, sometimes
done by the abuser in retaliation. For several women in the homicide group, the abuse of a child eventually became the last straw
in their relationships, even though they had taken abuse themselves for many years.

Wanda Bowles was late getting home from work and Randy
became more and more angry after she arrived, speculating on
what she had been doing to cause the delay. His suspicion that
Wanda had been unfaithful led him back to an old anger that
Christie, Wanda's 10-year-old daughter by a prior marriage, was
not his own. He was furious with Wanda for having had anything to do with another man, even though it was before he
knew her.

Christie was in her bedroom, and Randy decided that she was
hiding. He called her out and made her sit on the sofa while he
lectured her about being a "bastard" and how no good her
mother was. The lecture went on for about 30 minutes, with
Randy pacing away and then coming back to stand over her with
his fists clenched. His eyes had "that wild look" they got when
he was on the edge of becoming violent. He kept turning to ask
Wanda, "Are you listening to this? Are you listening to this?"

Suddenly Randy stopped in front of Wanda, then walked over
to Christie and hit her hard in the face with his fist. He immediately turned back to Wanda for her reaction. She was afraid to
say anything, knowing he would hit Christie again if she did.
Randy kept yelling at Wanda and pacing around the room.
Christie was sitting still and trying to be quiet. Wanda could
see her shaking, hands over her face, blood and tears running
through her fingers, but she felt powerless to help her. Randy
was so angry with Wanda, he did not seem to notice that Christie was bleeding.

Finally, Christie asked if she could wash her face. Randy
seemed to become aware of the blood for the first time and
became quiet. He let her go to her room while Wanda fixed
dinner; then he made her come back out and watch TV with
him. When they went to bed that night, Randy put his arms
around Wanda before going to sleep—the closest he ever came
to saying he was sorry. They never mentioned it again, but

Wanda never forgot it or got over it. She kept seeing Randy's fist going toward Christie's face in slow motion. She could not get over having to stand there and watch Christie bleed, and not be able to help her. From that point on, Wanda was determined that somehow she had to end Randy's power over their lives.

## SEXUAL ASSAULT

As illustrated by the case of Molly and Jim, the most violent incidents often included sexual abuse. Thus, a discussion of the "worst" incident by the woman's definition often became a report of sexual assault by a partner. The subject is not one even many experts on "battering" want to write about in any detail.[1] Because of our tardiness in identifying forced sex in marriage as abuse, and because or our naivete about the seriousness and variety of acts involved in this kind of abuse, it has remained a hidden and little-understood area. Yet I believe we have made a mistake in so completely separating "sexual" from "physical abuse" in our investigations and thinking. In summarizing findings from her study of battered women, Irene Frieze notes that "marital rape is typically associated with battering and may be one of the most serious *forms* of battering [italics mine]."[2]

Certainly, there is not much question that sexual abuse is "physical"; and the seriousness of many of the reported incidents (in addition to the fact that a mutual act is being carried out against one person's will) qualifies it as assaultive. As Diana Russell observes in her book, *Rape in Marriage:*

The continuum of violence and the continuum of sex merge in the act of wife rape. Wife rape should be considered in discussions of both the issue of violence in marriage and the issue of sexual relations. To date, it has been ignored in both contexts.[3]

In the present study, battered women in both groups reported a high incidence of rape by their mates. Over half—59 percent—of women in the comparison group reported that they had been forced to have sexual intercourse on at least one occasion. However, in the homicide group, over three-quarters—76 percent—reported being raped by their mates.[4] In the homicide group, if it happened at all, it usually happened more than once or twice: 14 percent said they were raped between one and three times, 22 percent said it happened more than three times, and nearly 40 percent said they were raped "often." (This last figure compares to 13 percent of the comparison group who said that rape occurred often.)

In understanding sexual assault in these cases, it is important to ask about more than just forced sexual intercourse. The majority of women in the homicide group—62 percent—reported that their mates had forced or urged them to perform other sexual acts against their will; sometimes, acts they considered particularly abusive or unnatural. This compares to 37 percent of women in the comparison group reporting being threatened with or forced to endure such acts.[5] Of the women in the comparison group reporting forced or threatened sexual acts, 69 percent said that it happened only once and 31 percent said it occurred occasionally. No one in that group said it occurred frequently. In contrast, 39 percent in the homicide group said it had happened once, 42 percent said it happened occasionally, and nearly one fifth—19 percent—said it was a frequent occurrence.

Sexually abusive acts reported by women in the homicide group included the insertion of objects into the woman's vagina, forced anal or oral sex, bondage, forced sex with others, and sex with animals. One woman reported being raped with her husband's service revolver, a broom handle, and a wire brush. As with other types of violence, sexual abuse by partners typically involved a variety of assaultive behaviors:[6]

In many of the homicide relationships, the men required sex after beatings, and this seemed like rape to the women. At times, it was also extremely painful because of injuries sustained in the earlier assault. In one fairly typical case, the man wanted sex every day during the last two or three years they were together, whether or not there had been violence, and this was almost always abusive. He would choke, pinch, or bite the woman; he also forced a variety of objects into her vagina, and compelled her to perform oral sex on him, holding her by the head and pulling out chunks of her hair with his hands. It seemed to her that he hurt her in order to become sexually excited.

In another case, the woman reported that her partner forced some kind of sexual activity on her three or four times a week during the final year of their relationship. He would rape her with food objects and penile attachments or begin to masturbate on her face and stomach when she was sleeping. Often, she woke during the night to find him forcing anal intercourse. He was very rough with this; she bled after most incidents. Her arms and shoulders were always bruised from being held down. He seemed to intend to hurt her. She would stuff the corner of a pillow in her mouth to keep from screaming: He beat her if she cried out, and she knew it terrified the children. She began getting severe stomach cramps at night, and eventually developed ulcers. Several times, he also tried to force sexual activity between her and the family dog. She resisted desperately, and he would try to hold her down and still control the dog. Finally, he gave up, but she was always badly bruised from these attempts and sometimes received a beating afterward for resisting.

———————

As indicated by these accounts, sexual assaults in the homicide relationships tended to be quite severe. This is supported by other research findings, which indicate (again, contrary to our usual assumption that violence perpetrated by a stranger is more serious than violence occurring at home) that the *closer* the relationship between rapist and victim, the more violent the sexual assaults tend to be.[7] Most of the women in the homicide group reported that they were afraid to resist sexually abusive acts or their mates' sexual demands, particularly if these followed other types of physical assault, for fear of being hurt even more seriously.[8] This fear was based on reality: When they did resist, it almost always resulted in an increase in the use of physical force.

Sexual assault in these cases appeared to be related more to the abusers' need to demonstrate their absolute dominance and control over the women than to sexual enjoyment or sensuality. In fact, as the men became more violent in their sexual activities, they also seemed to experience progressively less pleasure and often had difficulty achieving an erection or reaching orgasm. It is possible that a part of these men's increasing brutality during sex was an attempt to achieve the intense levels of excitement they had experienced earlier in the relationships, when there was still the thrill of infatuation and conquest. With their insistence that "their woman" meet all their expectations and desires—an unrealistic presumption in any relationship—they may have been unwilling to accept the more everyday level of sexual relating that comes with familiarity.

Over time, sexually assaultive acts in the homicide relationships became increasingly brutal and bizarre. Many incidents involved a combination of violent acts and threats; sometimes they lasted for hours and resulted in the woman being severely injured.

During the last year of one relationship, the man came home from work already upset. He grabbed and twisted the woman's wire-rim glasses and began gouging her eyes with them. Blood was running down her face, but he decided they should watch TV. He put a comforter on the floor and demanded that she undress; he wanted sex. Instead of using his penis, he used a squash; he said he thought she would enjoy it. Afterward, he made her take a bath with him and forced intercourse in the tub, banging her head against the tile wall. Then he had her sit on the couch in the living room while he went to the kitchen for another beer (his fourth or fifth since he'd been home). He tried to get her to drink it with him, and when she refused, he forced the bottle into her mouth, breaking off a tooth. He pushed her down and "fucked" her with the bottle, pushing it violently into her vagina and anus. Then he drank the beer.

The abuser went back to the kitchen—she thought to get another beer—but turned out all the lights as he returned. He made her lie down on the blanket while he fantasized about mutilation, threatening, "I'll destroy you. I'm going to cut your nipples off. Maybe I will cut your clit out, too." He often fantasized about violence, and she hardly listened. She was thinking mostly about her eyes; they were both swollen shut and the pain in her right eye was intense. She wondered if she was blind. Then she felt the coldness of a blade across her chest. This was the first she had been aware that he had a knife, and she was afraid to breathe. Still talking about what he was going to do to her, he began pulling the blade back and forth across her nipples and her face. Somehow, being unable to see made it all the more terrifying. Finally, he put the knife down and forced intercourse in many different positions, some of them quite painful. Then he made her perform oral sex on him until he climaxed.

This incident covered a span of about six hours, finally ending in the early morning. The woman had a chipped front tooth and permanent scarring on her face and chest, and lost most of the vision in her right eye. She resigned from her job and quit going out socially. The doctor she visited in secret asked no questions about how she sustained such strange injuries. Because of her husband's position in the community, as well as out of her own sense of shame, the incident was never reported.

In addition to brutalization, sexual abuse was also used by men in the homicide group as a mechanism to humiliate and control. In one case, the abuser gave the woman a list of conditions she was to agree to, in exchange for him stopping his violence:

- The children were to keep their rooms clean without being told;
- The children could not argue with one another;
- He was to have absolute freedom to come and go, and could have a girlfriend if he wanted one;
- She would perform oral sex on him any time he wanted it;
- She would have anal sex with him.

Two days later, he decided to implement the agreement. They were giving a party for their daughter's graduation when he called her into their room and locked the door. He sat on the edge of the bed and made her kneel in front of him, forcing her to perform oral sex and being as rough as he could, ramming his penis far down her throat, even though she was gagging and crying. He kept saying, "You agreed to it. You *said* you would do this. So this is what you're going to do." Finally, he ejaculated in her mouth and let her go. She went in the bathroom and vomited while he dressed and left the room. Guests were arriving, so she went downstairs and hosted the party. She could not understand why he had tried to hurt and humiliate her, when she was doing what he wanted. In this relationship, although the "physical" abuse supposedly ceased at the time of their agreement, sexual violence immediately took its place, and continued to escalate until his death.

———

Many women said when the abuser was intoxicated, sex could go on for hours; this in itself was like a battering. Again, women reported being pinched and bitten, as well as having their heads banged against the headboard or being choked or smothered as the man became increasingly frustrated with his inability to climax. Often, these episodes ended when the man passed out.

## THE PREVALENCE OF MARITAL RAPE

Marital rape is sometimes reported in relationships in which no other type of physical abuse occurs.[9] However, it seems to be most frequently reported as a form of physical domination in otherwise violent relationships.[10] In a random sample of 930 women in San Francisco, Diana Russell asked questions to determine how many had been sexually abused by strangers, husbands, or other family members, and found that 1 out of every 7 women who had ever been married reported rape by a husband or ex-husband. In fact, more women reported sexual assaults by husbands and ex-husbands than by acquaintances or strangers.[11] Finkelhor and Yllo reported similar findings in a representative sample of 326 women in Boston. Again, more than twice as many women reported being raped by husbands as by strangers.[12]

Women whose husbands are physically assaultive in other ways are particularly likely to experience marital rape. In Irene Frieze's study of battered women in Pittsburgh, over one-third of the "battered" group said they had been raped by their mates. Forty-three percent of these women also reported that sex was unpleasant because of being forced.[13] Similarly, Mildred Pagelow finds that 37 percent of her sample of 325 battered women reported sexual assaults by their partners.[14] And in Shields and Hanneke's study of the wives of violent men, 45 percent of the women whose husbands were violent within the family setting reported that they had experienced marital rape.[15]

Most researchers who have studied rape within marriage agree that these figures probably represent severe underestimates of the problem. Information about sexual assault within marriage is especially difficult to obtain. Many women do not define even forceful sexual advances as assaultive when these acts are perpetrated by their husbands. For example, Pagelow notes that, of women in her 1980 study who reported they had *not* been raped, many still said that they had submitted to sexual demands in order to prevent beatings, or out of fear of their partner. Some of these women even reported physical assaults during sexual activity so severe that they were injured or lost consciousness, yet did not define these as *sexual* assaults.[16]

Even when specific questions avoid the label "rape," the extreme sense of shame and degradation experienced by many victims may prevent their disclosing the occurrence of sexual aggression by a mate, even when assured anonymity.[17] In the current study, the ability to obtain such information from women in the homicide and comparison groups may have been partly due to the long period of time (eight to ten hours) interviewers spent alone with each respondent, so that a high level of trust and comfort in talking about sensitive topics could be developed. However, even with these optimal conditions, women were more reluctant to talk about their partners' sexual assaults than about any other type of abuse.[18]

## THE IMPACT OF SEXUAL ABUSE

Sexual abuse, in a negative sense, is an "optimal" kind of violence. It is possible to inflict an intense level of physical pain over a prolonged period of time without killing the victim; and to cause a wide range of injuries, from superficial bruises and tearing to serious internal injuries and scarring. The psychological impact of sexual assault can also be extreme, especially when the attack is violent and threatening, and the psychological aftereffects may last for years.[19] In addition, sexually assaultive actions by a male partner are among the most risk-free forms of violence a man can engage in. A women is the least likely to reveal this type of abuse to others. Although she may seek help for, or talk about, a cracked rib or broken jaw, her feeling of humiliation usually inhibits her willingness to discuss sexual abuse. Even if a sexual assault does become known, societal sanctions against a partner are almost nonexistent. Marital rape is exempt from prosecution in most states: By 1980, only three states had eliminated the marital rape exemption from their laws, and five states had modified it. However, by 1982, 13 other states had *extended* their exemptions to include cohabiting couples as well as the legally married.[20] Thus, a maximal amount of damage can be done, both physically and psychologically, with a minimal risk of disclosure, or of penalty if the assault is revealed.

The woman is not the only person damaged by these acts. The repeated perpetration of a brutal activity against another human being becomes dehumanizing for the assaulter as well as the victim. (Especially when this violence was directed against the person closest to them, their most intimate contact and partner, it must have had a tremendous impact on the personalities of these men.) And, although supposedly a "hidden" act, sexual abuse of a woman by her partner can have a devastating effect on children living in the home. One battered woman told me about hearing a single cry of anguish from her teenage son as her husband pulled her toward their bedroom, threatening rape, after a physically abusive incident that had lasted hours and involved the children as witnesses.

What is a teenage boy learning from incidents like this? Will he grow up to dominate a woman partner in similar ways? Will he shy away from close relationships altogether, for fear he might be like his father; for fear of what he *might* do? Or will he be able to establish a satisfactory relationship with a woman, only to have the act of lovemaking be so overlaid with feelings of pain and anger that part of his heart will break each time he is intimate with his mate?

Most of what we now know about the effects of sexual assault on victims has been based on isolated instances of rape by nonfamily members. Our knowledge about sexual abuse by one's partner is still very limited. And, although we are now beginning to recognize the impact that witnessing *other* types of physical assault between parental figures has on children, we have yet to investigate the impact of knowing one's mother is being sexually abused by her mate. We do know that sexual assaults by a partner, sexual assaults occurring over a long period, and assaults involving verbal threats have a particularly traumatic effect on women victims.[21] For example, in Russell's study, women who had been raped by their husbands perceived these assaults as having more damaging, long-term effects on their lives than sexual assaults by strangers. Russell concludes:

> We have strong evidence that rape in marriage can be extremely traumatic, particularly when accompanied by violence . . . [Our] findings clearly indicate that violent rape is the form of wife abuse most upsetting to these women.[22]

In the homicide group, sexual assaults tended to occur relatively often, to be quite violent, and to involve a combination of sexual and other physically abusive acts and threats. The effect of these assaults on the women was profound, as indicated by the weight accorded to them in the women's descriptions of their relationships, and the emotionality and difficulty with which they recounted sexually abusive incidents. The impact that repeated sexual assault had on the women's perception of alternatives and on their sense of endangerment cannot be overestimated. As one woman put it, "It was as though he wanted to annihilate me. More than the slapping, or the kicks . . . as though he wanted to tear me apart from the inside out and simply leave nothing there."

## PRINCIPLES OF AGGRESSION

Although it is hard to imagine, knowing the final chapters of their stories, intimacy between men and women in the homicide group frequently began as tender and sensitive lovemaking. Women remembered the men's intensity and desire, and often their gentleness. They may have interpreted the man's focus on sexual intimacy as love for them and missed an obsessive component; again, this would be hard to distinguish from the desire for intimacy that typifies the early stages of most relationships. Yet, for the majority of women in the homicide group, this special connection degenerated from isolated instances of abusive behavior to brutal and dehumanizing attacks, accompanied by verbal threats and deliberate degradation.

How does violent behavior build to such extremes? Accounts of severe batterings seem to lack motivation and rationale: The man comes home already mad and begins a beating that may last for hours; the woman wakes up in the night to find her mate choking her and never knows why. Women in the present study often did not know the reasons for their abuser's behavior, and this contributed to their inability to define and cope with the situation. Most existing reports are on the men's actions. We still do not know much about the motivations for those actions. Since the women did not understand the violence, and the men were not available to interview, my own account must remain largely silent on this as well.

Yet it seems that the men in this study did not understand their own violence. Many of them expressed remorse and contrition after early assaults, and seemed distressed and bewildered. A possible measure of their distress is their general self-destructiveness. The majority of these men—61 percent—had talked of committing suicide. Injuring and nearly killing one's partner is, in itself, a self-destructive act. And violent men who habitually get into fights with others of equal strength (i.e., men in bars) deliberately put themselves in situations where they are likely to experience serious bodily harm. In the eventual homicide incidents, many of the men *dared* their partners to kill them, or ran against the gun as the women were firing. In their general self-destructiveness and the escalation of their brutality against their wives, it was as though they were driven by something even they did not understand.

Hal Simon, writing in his journal about his relationship with his wife, Karen, recounted his awareness of the lethality of his aggression and his attempts to control it. He noted:

> It was important for me to keep my temper under control so I wouldn't cause her to die from my fists. I had to keep saying to myself, "Karen is my wife. I love her, and I don't want her to die."

But then Hal goes on to recall the assault that occurred just after this resolution, and his reactions to it:

> But on this night, I had been drinking since early morning. We had just returned from visiting friends. Karen was in the bed-

room, and I heard this talking and thought she was fussing about my drinking again, and all that control just flew out the window. I got the 38 Colt, and went straight in there and demanded to know what the hell she was talking about, with the gun pointed right at her face. Then I backed off and kicked the hell out of her with my foot. I thought to put the fear of God into her. She fell off the chair toward the wall, blood coming from everywhere. My first thought was to just let her lie there, which I did; standing over her with the gun, daring her to get up so I could finish what I started. Finally, I calmed down and she still hadn't moved. Blood was over her and on the floor; she was passed out and I was the cause of it. I checked her pulse and couldn't find it and started trying to bring her back. If only she would be alright, I would quit drinking for good.

When she did talk again, all she wanted was to leave me, but I loved her too much to let her do that. The next day, I disabled the car so she would not go and leave on her own, and cancelled the phone. I couldn't take her to the doctor, which I knew she needed so desperately. I had to look at her face like that, all grotesque and swollen beyond recognition. I stayed with her as much as I could. Later, I told everyone she had fell off a ladder. I didn't want to lose my job because I was a wifebeater.

## *The Escalation of Aggression*

In trying to understand the causes of violent behavior, Turner, Fenn, and Cole observe that aggression is "not the only response, or even the most likely response" to life events. They contend that "social learning processes determine which members of society develop, through direct or vicarious experiences, aggression as the habitual mode of coping."[23] However it is arrived at, once aggression becomes a primary way of responding to everyday life situations, a damaging pattern can begin. Aggression tends to worsen over time. In laboratory experiments, researchers have found that perpetrating acts of aggression increases, rather than decreases, the likelihood of an individual's aggressing again.[24] The perpetrator gradually becomes desensitized, so that initial reactions of "distress and self-reproof" (or contrition, as measured in this study) become "extinguished with repeated performance of aggressive acts."[25] Being aggressive toward another person also seems to create a need to justify the violence by degrading the victim. This denigration may then lead to *further* violence or reprisal, as victims now seem to "deserve" the treatment they are receiving, and such a cycle may serve to perpetuate an attack.[26]

Repeated instances of aggression also tend to become more and more severe, and this escalation is surprisingly hard to deter. In laboratory experiments, researchers have tried interrupting subjects who were administering electric shocks, to see if this would lessen their aggression, or have provided buzzers so the participants could call in the experimenter for advice if they became uncomfortable with their own behavior. They have also attempted to prevent the escalation of aggression by making the aggressors aware of what they were doing or by directing their attention to external aspects of the situation. Only the presence of a "hot line" buzzer had any effect; and, although it did lessen the severity of the punishments administered, it did not prevent the escalation of aggression over time. No matter *what* the experimenters did, the attacks became more intense with successive trials.[27]

Although it is often difficult to generalize from laboratory experiments to situations in real life, one obvious parallel occurs in family violence cases in which a police officer comes to the scene, talks with the abuser, and suggests that he take a walk around the block to "cool down." Judging from what we know about the nature of aggression, this interruption should not be expected to deter an escalation of the aggressor's violence after the police have departed.[28] In fact, abused women often report that their abusers are more angry, and the violence more severe, following these types of interventions.

This escalation of aggressive acts is not necessarily tied to the performance of the victim. Even when "victims" in laboratory experiments gave more and more right answers over time, the levels of "punishment" administered to them by other subjects continued to intensify.[29] Thus, while there is a strong tendency in cases of wife abuse to ask what the woman did to upset her abusive mate, or to attribute increases in violence to increased frustration with a partner, the escalation of aggression seems more contingent on the abuser's having begun aggressive acts in the first place than on characteristics or behaviors of the recipient.[30]

Aggressive tendencies do seem to be stimulated or reinforced when a victim displays pain or submits to an aggressor.[31] This would suggest that, in meeting the abusers' demands for compliance and submission, women or children in abusive families may actually be reinforcing the very pattern by which they are being victimized. Yet it is hard to see a way out of this dilemma. Penalties for talking or fighting back with an abusive man are severe: Almost all the women in the homicide group said that resistance only worsened an attack. And many battered women (like Molly Johnson) reported that their abusers sometimes hit them harder when they did not express their pain, until they inflicted enough damage to achieve the desired effect.[32] Victims also acclimate, or adjust, to punishment over time and cease to respond as dramatically, which then contributes to an intensification of the aggression against them, as the abuser attempts to reach the same level of impact achieved with earlier attacks.[33]

All in all, this leads to a no-win situation for a woman victim. In the homicide group, once an attack was begun, there was very little the woman could do to control the situation. All they could do was endure. And once a pattern of aggression was established, the assaults tended to increase in frequency and severity, while reactions of contrition on the part of the abusers—or even an awareness of the extent of the harm they were inflicting— decreased. In spite of his professed love for his wife and his awareness that recent assaults had brought her very close to death, Hal Simon beat Karen again, several times, before the incident in which she killed him.

The women's despair and terror as this spiral of violence intensified, coupled with the effects of repeated assaults and injuries on them physically and cognitively, led to a sense of entrapment and desperation. Although still present, earlier emphases on the responsibility of caretaking and the maintenance of relationships paled in significance, as more basic questions of survival and escape became the focus of their lives.

# 7

# Fear and the Perception of Alternatives

**P**robably the most frequently asked question about women who are being abused by their partners is, "Why don't they just leave?" Especially when the abuse is severe, it is hard to understand why a woman would stay around for the next attack. Actually, many women do leave; they are among our friends and neighbors, and possibly our families. The majority of them, however, are never identified as abused women. Typically, they do not realize how many other women have shared the same experiences; being afraid that other people would not understand or would think less of them if they knew, they do not discuss the abuse they suffered in the past. They may still blame themselves for having become involved with an abusive man in the first place, or for the failure of their interactions with him, and so carry their memories and the lingering confusion alone. In the comparison group, over half (53 percent) of the women had left their battering relationships by the time they were interviewed; many had never talked about them before. Even in the homicide group, women left or attempted to leave their violent partners. Some had been separated or divorced for up to two years prior to the lethal incident.

The question, "Why don't battered women leave?" is based on the assumption that leaving will end the violence. While this may be true for some women who leave after the first or second incident (these women are rarely identified as battered, and still less often studied), even the smoothness of those separations depends on the abuser's sense of desperation or abandonment and his willingness or tendency to do harm when faced with an outcome he does not want or cannot control. The longer the relationship continues, and the more investment in it by both partners, the more difficult it becomes for a woman to leave an abusive mate safely. Some estimates suggest that at least 50 percent of women who leave their abusers are followed and harassed or further attacked by them.[1] To separate from an individual who has threatened to harm you if you go increases—at least in the short run—the very risk from which you are trying to escape.

Additionally, getting away is not as simple as it sounds. After a crime such as a rape or robbery committed by a stranger, victims often change apartments or even houses to avoid another offense by the attacker. But it is difficult for an abused woman to just "disappear" from her partner or husband. Even if it were possible to sever an intimate relationship so cleanly, couples often hold property in common, have children in common, know one another's daily routines, families, and places of employment, and have mutual friends. It is extremely difficult for an abused woman to go into long-term hiding. Another way to look at this issue is to ask, "Why should the *woman* leave?" Why should the victim and, possibly, her children, hit the road like fugitives, leaving the assailant the home and belongings, when he is the one who broke the law?

As mentioned in Chapter Five, women initially remain with these men out of love and commitment. They may hope for a favorable change and make attempts toward understanding and resolution, especially in the early days of a relationship when the violence is less frequent and less severe. Often, they are ashamed to let others know what is occurring in their relationships, and lose time attributing the problems to themselves and attempting to make adaptions that will eliminate further assaults. They also worry about the impact a separation might have on the children, and may stay for their sake, if the man is not abusive to them. Yet, as the severity and frequency of abuse increases, three additional factors have a major impact on the women's decision to stay with violent partners: (1) practical problems in effecting a separation, (2) the fear of retaliation if they do leave, and (3) the shock reactions of victims to abuse.

## PRACTICAL PROBLEMS IN LEAVING

The point at which many outsiders suggest a woman should decide to leave a violent relationship—immediately after an abusive incident—is precisely when she is least able to plan such a move. Frightened, in shock, and often physically injured, all she wants to do is survive. Shelters that house abused women are now established in many cities (although in rural areas, these facilities are often lacking or are located many miles from the women's home).[2] Yet they are often full. Even when a shelter has room for a woman, the maximum stay is usually less than six weeks, so the woman still must find alternative housing, provide for her children if she has any with her, obtain whatever legal help may be necessary, and plan for her continued safety from further abuse. During this time, the woman will also be trying to decide whether to file for a divorce, and where to find money to pay for fees and services—decisions most people find difficult to make, even under the best of circumstances.

If the woman leaves her children behind, the man may refuse to let her have them and may charge her with desertion. If she takes the children with her, however, she disrupts their daily lives and runs the risk that any retaliatory violence may involve them as well. If she initiates divorce proceedings against the children's father, he will usually be granted some kind of visitation rights, and the woman may be enjoined against moving out of state, even after the divorce is final. In many cases, the abuser fights the woman for custody of the children, and sometimes wins.[3] In litigation concerning custody, a man's violence against his wife is not the issue before the court, especially if there is no evidence that he has physically abused the children. In addition, if he seems established and has a job, while the woman appears in transition and unstable, he may be considered better able to care for the children, regardless of his wife's accusations of violence.

A move into hiding is particularly difficult to manage. If the woman is working, she must try to keep the transition from interfering with her job, since that job will now be crucial to her survival. Yet, if she has reason to fear retaliation by her partner, she must weigh the necessity of going to work against the danger that he will follow her there and cause her further harm. If she has school-age children, she must choose between keeping them out of school and her concern for their education, or be faced with the danger that their father may remove them from the school grounds if she lets them attend. She must also find a place to live where the man cannot find and harm her: she must weigh the benefits of leaving town for her own safety against the disruptive impact it would have on her work situation and her children's lives, as well as the complications such a move could produce in following through on litigation. If the woman does move, she might not be able to go to her family, because the man would be apt to find her there and could endanger her family as well as herself. Obviously, if an abused woman is forced to relocate to a new city or state, away from her source of income and from family and friends—especially if she is moving children with her—the alternatives become more and more difficult to accomplish.

In one instance, the woman had lived with the man for a year before the first incident of threatened violence. After two more physically assaultive incidents during the next two years, the last one endangering the couple's infant son, she decided to leave her mate and file for divorce. Although she loved him, she knew his verbal abuse was uncalled for and was unwilling to risk further physical assaults. She wrote a letter explaining why she was leaving and, taking their child, went into hiding with relatives. She called a few nights later to let him know she and the baby were safe. She also consulted an attorney to file protection orders and help her obtain a divorce.

At the same time, the husband went to court to obtain custody of his son. He claimed that his wife had been depressed and emotionally unstable in recent months, and cited her "unexplained disappearance" from their home as evidence of her unpredictable mental state. He expressed strong concern for the safety of his child, and requested that she be found and the child removed from her care. Based on his allegations, when the woman appeared in court to obtain an order of protection, her son was taken from her and custody was awarded to the state until a temporary hearing could be arranged. The state placed the child with the abuser's family, since their place of residence was considered the most stable. The woman was allowed to have her baby one weekend every other week until temporary orders were established.

Even this visitation right was soon canceled, after further charges were made against her by the husband and his family. At this point, she was allowed only brief supervised visits each week; this supervision was provided by her husband's relatives, and her husband was frequently present. Formally, the husband was now charging her with neglect, although the charges were unfounded and she had performed all the child-care duties while they were together. Privately, he was pleading with her to come back and warning that she would never have her son again if she did not. Each court date was postponed by the husband's attorneys, as she was urged by family members to "come home." At the time of this writing, the case is still pending. The woman has been separated from her small child for nearly a year, and forced to remain in almost constant contact with her husband. Welfare is now recommending that custody of the child be awarded to the husband's relatives, with whom the baby has been staying. As one state worker told me, the fact that their stories are so contradictory makes both parents seem unreliable.

This woman's story provides one answer to the question, "Why don't battered women leave?" The woman acted independently and rationally: She left the situation when she began to realize that it would not improve; she refused to tolerate vicitimization; she sought legal remedies. She escaped her abuser before the violence became serious. She may also have lost her child.

## FEAR OF REPRISAL

In the homicide group, many of the women stayed because they had tried to escape and been beaten for it, or because they believed their partner would retaliate against an attempt to leave him with further violence. Almost all of the women in both the homicide and the comparison groups—98 percent and 90 percent, respectively—thought the abuser could or would kill them; and many, especially in the homicide group, were convinced that they could not escape this danger by leaving. Susan Jefferson's case is an example. After Don's death, Susan said:

We were separating, but I don't think that would have solved anything. Don always said he would come back around—that I belonged to him. Just that day he had gotten an apartment, but it was only right down the street. I knew he would come after me if he saw someone he didn't know come to the house. I was scared. It seemed like the more I tried to get away, the worse things got. He was never going to quit.

———

The women's fears of retaliation were supported by their past experiences with the men's violence, as well as by threats of further violence if they attempted to leave. As noted earlier, 83 percent of men in the homicide group had made threats to kill, and the women took these threats quite seriously. In the case of Karen and Hal Simon, Hal wrote in his journal:

Every time, Karen would have ugly bruises on her face and neck. She would cry and beg me for a divorce, and I would tell her, 'I am sorry. I won't do it again. But as for the divorce, absolutely not. If I can't have you for my wife, you will die. No one else will have you if you ever try to leave me.'

———

Abused women's primary fear—that their abusers will find them and retaliate against their leaving—is justified. Some women who have left an abusive partner have been followed and harassed for months or even years; some have been killed.[4] The evidence suggests that, in many cases, the man's violence continues to escalate after a separation.[5] In a 1980 report to the Wisconsin Council on Criminal Justice, investigators noted: "Simply leaving the relationship does not provide adequate protection for some women. . . . " Thirty percent of the assaulted women in that study were separated from their partners when the attack occurred. Many had called the police for help, and still the assaults continued. As one woman, charged with the death of her husband, reported:

I knew if I ran he would find me. He tracked down his first wife with only her social-security number. Can you imagine what it would be like to go through life knowing that a man who intends to kill you may be just around the corner?

Violent men do search desperately for their partners once the woman leaves.[6] Often, they spend their days and nights calling her family and mutual acquaintances; phoning her place of employment or showing up there; driving around the streets looking for her; haunting school grounds, playgrounds, and grocery stores. If they believe the woman has left town, they frequently attempt to follow her, traveling to all locations they think she might be found. She is theirs. She *cannot* leave and refuse to talk to them. They may nearly kill their mates, but they do not want to lose them. Some of the women in the homicide group had been separated or divorced for up to two years before the final incident, yet were still experiencing life-threatening harassment and abuse from men unwilling to relinquish their connection.

For many battered women, leaving their mates and living in constant fear of reprisal or death seems more intolerable than remaining, despite their fears of further harm. Women in hiding relate how they are afraid to go into their apartment when they get home; to go to work in the morning or to leave at night; to approach their car in a parking lot; to visit friends. They know if their estranged partner finds them, he may simply retaliate and not wait to talk. And if he does begin a conversation and they do not agree to go home, they know it may trigger an attack. Every sound in the night, every step in the hall, every pair of headlights pulling up behind them might be him. Accomplishing daily tasks against this wall of fear becomes exhausting. Added to the other difficulties these women are facing, and the life-changing decisions that must be made, it is often too much and the women return home. Shelter personnel who work with battered women struggle against their frustration when women return to their abusers; yet in many cases, the women are simply overwhelmed.

## ESCAPE ATTEMPTS

The point of, or even the discussion of, separation is one of the most dangerous times for partners in a violent relationship. Abusive men threatened with the loss of their mates may be severely depressed, angry, agitated, homicidal, or suicidal.[7] Even attempts to discuss a separation can set off a violent attack.

Susan couldn't take it anymore. She had been living with Don for six months, and the violence kept getting worse. Something happened nearly every week; Don would say he was sorry, but it never got any better. She decided that the only solution was to leave. When Don came home, Susan sat down to talk with him about it. She told him that she couldn't stand the fights, couldn't understand what was happening, couldn't take the things he said to her. She wanted him to understand. She wanted their parting to be amicable.

Don began acting very strangely—running around and pulling furniture in front of the door; acting as though he was angry, but laughing and joking at the same time. Susan had never seen him behave like this and was suddenly very frightened. It seemed crazy to her. Don kept saying, "You're not going anywhere! You're my prisoner here. I'm going to put bars on the doors and windows, and keep you here. . . . You're my prisoner." He would laugh like he was kidding with her, then suddenly act furious and throw her across the room or onto the floor. He would smash things in the room with his fists or his foot, and throw things against the wall. He made her sit in a corner like a child, saying, "Sit here. Face the wall. Hold still now. You just sit there and listen to me. Look at me now. . . . Don't look at me like that. . . ." He had a stick, and he'd hit her with it if she tried to move or speak to him. Susan was wearing a cotton shirt and he reached down and tore it off, slapping her across the back and face with it. He'd laugh; then suddenly grab and choke her, shaking her by the neck, panting with anger and exertion. Susan kept thinking, "I may never leave this house alive."

Finally, Don said, "OK. You go ahead and leave." Susan thought about not having anything on above the waist, but decided that was unimportant. She made it as far as the door when Don grabbed her and pulled her back inside, laughing, then saying angrily, "No . . . you're not going anywhere like that. You're my prisoner here. I'll never let you go now. I'm going to keep you here forever." He resumed hitting her with the stick and his hands and made her sit on the floor again. Finally, he said again that she could go and Susan ran outside and to the corner, but Don was right behind her. He started yelling at her on the street about "deserting" him. Then he suddenly became quiet and passive, took her hand, and walked her home. Susan remembers the feeling of the sun on her back and her hand in his. She knew any further move on her part would only anger him. They cleaned up the house together and threw out the broken things. Then Don made her take a nap with him, although he left the heavy furniture stacked in front of the door.

─────────

Irene Miller's experience also illustrates how dangerous it can be for an abused woman to talk with her mate about separation. The threat of abandonment is so devastating to some men that they would rather kill the woman than see her go.[8] Irene's case is typical of many women in the homicide group, in that repeated attempts at separation and escape always failed.

Irene gradually came to from a beating the night before, frightened, exhausted, and throwing up. Mark came into the bedroom to check on her, and Irene told him she thought they should get a divorce; she couldn't stand any more beatings, just please let her go. She reminded him of how much worse the violence was getting. This time, she wasn't sure if she'd been sleeping or unconscious. She confessed she was afraid he would kill her someday, and tried to persuade him that being apart would be the best thing for both of them.

Mark's mood changed suddenly. He denied that he beat her and held her down on the bed, shouting, "You'll *never* leave me. I'll fucking kill you if you ever try to do that!" He grabbed her ankle and was bending her foot back, like he was going to break it, then came for her face. Irene turned on her stomach to protect herself and Mark grabbed a heavy vase from the dresser and hit her on the back of the head, splitting the skin open. Then he began hitting her repeatedly with the vase, yelling, "I'll kill you. I'll fucking kill you." Irene screamed to her son to get help, and Mark left the room to pursue him.

Irene was still struggling to get up when Mark came back. He tilted her head up toward him, she thought to see how badly she was hurt, but instead jammed his forefinger into her eye.

Irene cried out and reached up reflexively, and Mark bit her hand so deeply that it required stitches. A neighbor pounded on the door, yelling at Mark to let him in, but Mark ignored him. He began to choke Irene, but then seemed to notice the blood running down her head for the first time. He seemed worried about that and quit being violent, saying to her, "Honey, what happened? What did you do here?" He was still trying to curtail the bleeding when the police arrived. Mark fought with them, and it took three men to subdue him. He was taken to jail, and an ambulance transported Irene to the hospital, where she had stitches and surgery on her eye.

After she was released from the hospital, Irene left Mark. She pressed assault charges against him and she and the children stayed with various relatives. But when Mark got out of jail he began calling everyone they knew, begging to talk to her, begging them to help him find her. She obtained a restraining order and filed for divorce, but after Mark was awarded weekly visitation rights to the children, she found it impossible to keep their whereabouts a secret.

Irene got an apartment, and she and the kids moved in. Mark would come to visit the children while she was at work and then refuse to leave. The children were too afraid not to let him in and, if Irene locked the door, he broke in. Irene tried to have the restraining order enforced, but the police said it had already been violated when she let him visit the children at home. Arresting Mark always meant a fight; Irene thought they just didn't want to get involved.

In desperation, she took the children and left the state. It took Mark several months, but he quit his job and found them. Irene and the children moved again. Again he found them. After this, Irene just gave up. She thought, "What's the use? I can't get away from him. All I'm doing is moving my kids around the country like gypsies." Both children were nearly a year behind in school, and both were doing poorly. She took them back to the schools they were used to, and as soon as she settled in, Mark moved in too. They were "reconciled" in March 1982. Mark died in January the following year.

———————

Many times, women attempted escape when they could sense that an attack was imminent, or during a break in an assaultive episode.

It was Saturday morning, and Karen and Hal Simon were sitting at the kitchen table. Hal was already drinking when Karen said they were spending too much money on beer. Hal always warned Karen not to tell him what to do. He reached over and, holding her wrist, put his cigarette out in the palm of her hand. Karen ran to the sink to run cold water over it and, to calm him down, said she was sorry. But Hal followed and slammed her into the counter, yelling at her about never leaving him alone. He hit her several times and then said he was going to get the gun. Karen knew what that meant and just stood there; they had been through this before. She never knew if someday he would really use it, but she knew she didn't have time to get away. She had terrible nightmares about him shooting her in the back as she ran across the yard, so she never tried.

Hal came back with the rifle. He pressed it against her temple and clicked the hammer, then began ramming it into her stomach, yelling, "I'll kill you, goddamn it! I'll kill you this time!" Finally, he laid the gun down and went outside. Karen could see him pacing around and knew he was still angry. He'd talk to himself about all the things she had done wrong and really attack her later.

When Hal left to get more beer, Karen fled, taking her small dog with her. Hal had nearly killed the dog several times when he was angry. She couldn't bear to leave it at home, knowing what would happen to it. Hal never allowed her to have keys to the car, so Karen walked all the way to the nearest town and asked for directions to the police department, hoping they would help her. She told them she had to get away from Hal before he killed her. The police advised her to swear out a warrant for his arrest, but Karen was so afraid of what Hal would do that she hesitated. Finally, she called a friend for advice, but the friend called Hal and he showed up at the police station a short while later. Hal was furious. He said she was not going to swear out a warrant against anyone; she was his wife, and he was taking her home. He took her elbow and walked her out the door, and nobody intervened.

All the way home, Hal was saying, "You goddamn bitch! You think you're going to leave me? When I get home we'll show you about leaving!" He snatched her over close to him, holding her clothes so she couldn't jump out. Karen was so terrified she couldn't focus on anything. She just sheltered the dog in her arms and prayed. When they got to the house, Hal came around and jerked her door open. He yanked her out of the seat and onto the ground, then began kicking her in the ribs. Each blow knocked Karen farther across the driveway. She knew she was sliding on her face, but there wasn't time to change positions. Finally, he stood over her, daring her to get up. Karen was afraid to move. The dog was still hiding in the truck; Hal carried it to the house and threw it against the concrete of the patio until he apparently thought he'd killed it. Then he made Karen go inside.

Several days later, a friend helped Karen get to the emergency room of a local hospital. Karen had been in so much pain she could hardly breathe, and walking was difficult. They found that several ribs were broken, and there seemed to be damage to her spleen. The doctor was sympathetic and tried to get her to report it, but she told him, "That is how I got hurt so badly in the first place . . . trying to report it." She finally agreed to go to a local shelter and to receive outpatient care, but when they called to make arrangements they learned that the shelter wouldn't take dogs. Karen went home. The animal had survived, but it was badly hurt, and Karen felt responsible. She wanted to be there to take care of it; she knew Hal would kill it in retaliation if she left. After this, Karen was afraid to seek any more help. Instead, she began thinking about dying. She had always feared it, but now she thought it might not be so bad; like passing out, only you never got beaten again.

———————

It is important to remember that, had these women been able to leave their abusers, this still would not have guaranteed their safety from further assault. The case of Sharon and Roy Bikson provides an example of repeated attempts at self-protection, and the continuation of harassment and assault after separation and divorce.

Sharon had been separated from Roy for over two years and was divorcing him, yet he continued to harass her. He broke into her home, destroyed her furniture, poured acid in the motor of her car, and slit the seats with a knife. He cut power and phone lines to the house, set small fires, and bragged to others about how he was going to kill her. He attacked and severely injured her at work, and she finally took a leave of absence from her job. She had unlisted phone numbers, but he always got them. She repeatedly called the police for protection, but they came only after Roy had already broken in.

Sharon left home and moved to different apartments to try to escape Roy, and sent her two small children to live with a baby-sitter. Roy found the children, threatened to kill the babysitter, and kidnapped her infant son. When Sharon appealed for help to the judge involved in the divorce proceedings, she was advised that she couldn't leave the area with the children until the divorce action was complete and the court had ruled on custody. She obtained a restraining order and several warrants, but they were never enforced. Most of her requests were simply not processed at all.

After Roy's death, the district attorney's office admitted that "her complaints were not taken seriously down here." The head deputy said that he didn't send some of the warrants on for evaluation because he "only sent those" he thought were "really important." And the hearing officer, who approves warrants for delivery, said he hadn't approved some of Sharon's because he "wasn't a marriage counselor"; they "sort of felt sorry for the guy, he seemed so upset"; and "some of these things just work themselves out, anyway." Sharon's desperate requests for help were being winnowed out at every step of the process.

―――――――

Women are often blamed, or at least severely questioned, if they don't leave an abusive man, and they are too often ignored if they do. Occasionally—as demonstrated by the reaction of the hearing officer in Sharon's case—the situation gets completely turned around, and a woman's *leaving* is blamed for the subsequent violence of her partner.

In June 1983, the Denver *Rocky Mountain News* carried an article entitled, "Work term given in wife-killing: Judge says woman's departure provoked murder." It described the killing of Patricia Burns, an elementary school teacher, who attempted to escape her husband of 15 years after an abusive incident in August 1982. There was a documented history of prior abuse; she sought legal assistance immediately after leaving; she was reportedly terrified. An excerpt from the news article read as follows:

A woman who was murdered by her estranged husband "provoked" her death by secretly leaving him without warning, according to a Denver judge who sentenced the man Wednesday to two years of work-release in the Denver County Jail.

Partly because of the "highly provoking acts" of Patricia Burns, Denver District Judge Alvin Lichtenstein ruled out a stiffer prison sentence for Clarance Burns, who shot his wife five times in the face at close range last Aug. 15.

Lichtenstein said that Mrs. Burns had deceived her husband by being "extremely loving and caring" up to the morning that she left the family home to proceed with a divorce.

Such incidents lend credence to the fears of abused women that leaving their abusers could cost them their lives, and demonstrate a blatant lack of understanding for their plight. The prosecutor in the Burns case commented, "I hope battered women hear about this. They're damned if they do, and damned if they don't."

## BATTERED WOMEN AND OTHER VICTIMS

Even given the practical problems in leaving and the risks that may accompany separation from a violent man, battered women's apparent passivity in the face of danger is still a troubling factor in their reactions to the abuse they experience. Leaving the abuser in *spite* of the difficulties and risks seems the best option. The apparent helplessness of abused women who stay for years in a situation in which they are repeatedly brutalized—especially those who never attempt to escape—leads us to search for explanations for their apparent lack of ability to cope.[9] Why didn't they just walk out one day when their abuser was away? Why don't they get in the car and drive in one direction, and figure it out when they get there? Anything seems better than living with repeated brutalization and threat.

Yet it is interesting to note that the reactions of abused women to the violence they experience correspond quite closely with the reactions of other types of victims to catastrophe or threat.[10] In contrast to theories that would interpret their behavior as indicative of a personality disorder, their response to the violence is what we would expect from any individual confronted with a life-threatening situation. This consistency in victim reaction applies whether the victims are male or female and whether they are the victims of crime, war, natural disaster, or some other trauma.[11] (For purposes of comparing the literature on victims, the term "trauma" is used here to denote an event that inflicts pain or injury, whether this event is caused by accident or by deliberate action. The term "victim" applies to one who is threatened by, or suffers from, such an event.)

For instance, research on both disaster and war victims indicates that, during the "impact phase," when the threat of danger becomes a reality, an individual's primary focus is on self-protection and survival. Like battered women, the victims experience reactions of shock, denial, disbelief, and fear, as well as withdrawal and confusion.[12] They often deny the threat, which leads to a delay in defining the situation accurately, and respond with dazed or apathetic behavior.[13] After the initial impact, disaster victims may be extremely suggestible or dependent and, during the period that follows, may minimize the damage or personal loss. This is often followed by a "euphoric" stage, marked by unrealistic expectations about recovery.[14] The victims convince themselves that they can "rebuild"; that somehow everything will be alright; that they will wake up and find it was all a horrible dream. For individuals in war situations, initial reactions also include responses of shock, disbelief, and apparent passivity. As the level of danger becomes overwhelming, individuals often respond by withdrawing and fail to employ appropriate escape behaviors, even when those are possible.[15]

In a closer parallel to the victimization of battered women, emotional reactions of victims of assault include fear, anger, guilt, shame; a feeling of powerlessness or helplessness such as is experienced in early childhood; a sense of failure, and a sense of being contaminated or unworthy.[16] Experiences of personal attack and intrusion, such as rape, often lead to acute perceptions of vulnerability, loss of control, and self-blame.[17] During a personal assault, the victim may offer little or no resistance, in an attempt to minimize the threat of injury or death. Again, the emphasis is on survival.

Long-term reactions of trauma victims are also quite similar to the responses of battered women. Victims report reactions of fear and confusion, and acute sensations of powerlessness and helplessness. They may become dependent and suggestible, and find themselves unable to make decisions or to function alone. Some victims remain relatively withdrawn and passive, and exhibit long-term symptoms of depression and listlessness.[18] Bard and Sangrey, writing about the responses of crime victims, note that even "normal" recoveries can take months, and are characterized by lapses into helplessness and fear.[19] (Remember that the majority of these reactions were based on a single occurrence of a traumatic event, whereas most abused women are reacting to continuing threat and assault.) Chronic fatigue and tension, intense startle reactions, disturbances of sleeping and eating patterns, and nightmares are often noted in assault victims.[20] With all types of trauma, whether related to a natural disaster, war, or a more personal offense, the fear is of a force that has been out of control. Victims become aware of their inability to manage their environment or to assure their own safety, and either attempt to adapt to a powerful aggressor or reassure themselves that the traumatic event will never occur again.

## Captives and Captors

Probably the type of victimization that most closely approximates the experiences of battered women is abuse in captivity, such as that experienced by prisoners of war. In these situations, the assailant or captor has a major influence on how the victim evaluates the situation and the alternatives available to him or her. Studies show that victims select coping strategies in light of their evaluation of the alternatives and their appraisal of whether a particular method of coping will further endanger them, and to what degree.[21] A crucial factor in this decision is the perceived balance of power between the captor and the victim: The coping strategy selected is weighed against the aggressor's perceived ability to control or to harm.

For example, in situations of extreme helplessness, such as in concentration camps, surprisingly little anger is shown toward the captors; this may be a measure of the captors' power to retaliate. "Fight or flight" responses are inhibited by a perception of the aggressor's power to inflict damage or death, and depression often results, based on the perceived hopelessness of the situation. The victims' perceptions of their alternatives become increasingly limited the longer they remain in the situation, and those alternatives that do exist often seem to pose too great a threat to survival.[22]

Because of the perceived power differential, victims in hostage situations may even come to view the captor as their protector, and become ingratiating and appeasing in an effort to save themselves.[23] In writing about the dynamics of captivity, Biderman discusses "antagonistic cooperation," a situation in which the dimension of conflict actually dominates the relationship, but where there is also a degree of mutual dependence. The relationship is then developed by the weaker partner in order to facilitate survival and obtain leniency. Biderman also suggests that a normal human being might be incapable of sustaining a totally hostile or antagonistic interaction over an extended period, and that periods of acquiescence might be necessary for physiological and emotional survival.[24]

Parallels also exist between the principles of brainwashing used on prisoners of war and the experiences of some women in battering relationships. Key ingredients of brainwashing include isolation of the victim from outside contacts and sources of help, and humiliation and degradation by the captor; followed by acts of kindness coupled with the threat of a return to the degraded state if some type of compliance is not obtained.[25] Over time, the victims of such treatment become apathetic, sometimes react with despair, and may finally totally submit.[26]

## SURVIVAL VERSUS ESCAPE

The responses of battered women fit in well with this model of victim reactions. The women in the present study perceived themselves as being trapped in a dangerous situation, and as having little or no control over the abusers' violent behavior. Their perception of their partners' ability to inflict harm was reinforced by each successive assaultive incident, and by threats to kill or perpetrate further violence against them. The women in these situations often attempted to appease the aggressor by compliance, and to work through the relationship to obtain leniency and safety. Their primary concern during assaultive incidents was to survive. Their main concern after abusive incidents was to avoid angering the partner again.

Like other victims, battered women's affective, cognitive, and behavioral responses are likely to become distorted by their intense focus on survival.[27] They may have developed a whole range of responses such as controlling their breathing or not crying out when in pain, in an effort to mitigate the severity of abuse during violent episodes, but not have developed any plans for escaping the abusive situation. Women in the homicide group showed a marked tendency to withdraw from outside contacts immediately after an abusive incident, rather than attempting to escape or to take action against the abuser. They experienced feelings of helplessness and fear, and found it extremely difficult to make decisions or plan ahead. They also tended to underestimate the "damage"—as shown by their tendency to under-report the severity of abusive acts and resultant injuries—and, at least early in their relationships, entertained unrealistic hopes for improvement of the abuser's behavior or of the relationship in the future.

As the violence escalated in frequency and severity, the women's perceptions of alternatives for escape became increasingly limited, and taking action on any of those alternatives seemed too dangerous to pursue. Although frequently in terror, the women felt constrained in the situation by the men's threats of harm or death if they left or attempted to leave. They were further persuaded of the dangers of this alternative if they had tried to leave and been beaten for it, or had sought outside intervention and found the intervention inadequate or that the violence only worsened after these efforts. The abusers' power to constrain and punish was supported by a lack of societal awareness of the plight of abused women, and by the difficulties in obtaining effective legal protection when your assaulter is your mate.[28]

A lack of adequate provision for safe shelter, relocation, or protection from further attack contributed to their sense of entrapment; most women in the homicide group concluded that their only alternative was to survive within the relationship. As Thibaut and Kelley noted in their theory of nonvoluntary interactions, when the probability of escape appears to be extremely low, "the least costly adjustment" for a victim may involve a "complex of adaptions," including a "drastic shortening of one's time perspective to a "moment-by-moment or day-to-day focus."[29] Trapped in an increasingly dangerous situation, women in the homicide group narrowed their focus to efforts to deal with the immediate threat of violence, and to gathering or maintaining their strength between attacks.

Still, the question remains: Why did these women *kill?* Women in the comparison group had also experienced assaults from a violent partner; they also would have had the perception of the abuser's power to inflict harm, and have experienced some victim responses to assault. Yet they did not kill their abusers, and many managed to leave them. What was different about women in the homicide group, that they were unable to escape and eventually took lethal action against their partners?

## Differences Between Women in the Homicide and Comparison Groups

As noted in Chapter Two, few differences can be found in characteristics of the women in the homicide and comparison groups; the differences exist primarily in the behaviors of the men. Men in the homicide group used alcohol and drugs more often than did those in the comparison group, and were generally more violent to others. The incidence of child abuse, for instance, was much higher among them than among men in the comparison group. They also assaulted their partners more frequently, and the women's injuries were more severe. In addition, men in the homicide group more frequently raped or otherwise sexually assaulted their partners, and many more of them had made threats to kill. Over time, physical abuse tended to become more severe in both the homicide and the nonhomicide groups, but such increases were much more common in the homicide group, while the decline in contrition was more precipitous.

In a test of which variables most clearly distinguished women who had killed their abusive mates from women who were abused but took no lethal action, seven key dynamics were identified: the frequency with which abusive incidents occurred; the severity of the women's injuries; the frequency of forced or threatened sexual acts by the man; the man's drug use; the frequency of his intoxication; the man's threats to kill; and the woman's threats to commit suicide.[30]

Thus, the women's behavior seemed to be primarily in reaction to the level of threat and violence coming in. Women in the homicide group reported that they had felt hopelessly trapped in a desperate situation, in which staying meant the possibility of being killed, but attempting to leave also carried with it the threat of reprisal or death. Their sense of helplessness and desperation escalated along with the assaultive behavior of their partners. In her book on marital rape, Dianna Russell suggests that: "The statistics on the murder of husbands, along with the statistics on the murder of wives, are both indicators of the desperate plight of some women, not a sign that in this one area, males and females are equally violent."[31]

## THE TURNING POINT

Given the extreme level of abuse and injury to which they were subjected, how did women in the homicide group go from a seemingly passive response of helplessness and adaption to the highly active one of homicide? Although individuals have the legal right to defend themselves against the threat of imminent serious bodily harm or death, the process by which a woman makes the transition to this mode of reacting is still largely unknown.

One way to understand the shift from victim to perpetrator is suggested by the principles of social judgment theory.[32] For example, Sherif and Hovland's model of social judgment involves the concept of a continuum on which incoming stimuli—or experiences—are ordered. The "latitude of acceptance" is that range of possibilities an individual is willing to agree with or adapt to; stimuli that fall outside that range are either in the latitude of rejection or the latitude of noncommitment (neither acceptable or unacceptable).[33] These latitudes are defined by endpoints, or anchors, that determine the extremes of the scale. Internal anchors are those originating within the individual, while external anchors are provided by outside factors or social consensus. Past learning experiences also affect how acceptable or unacceptable a person will find a particular stimulus. In the absence of outside factors, a person's internal anchors play a major role in how he or she evaluates a situation. According to social judgment theory, if an event falls at the end of the continuum, or even slightly above the endpoint, it will produce a shift of the range toward that anchor—or *assimilation*. However, if the stimulus is too far beyond the others, a *contrast* effect will ensue, and the stimulus will be perceived as being even more extreme than it really is.

If one views the escalation of violent acts by the abuser as ordered along a continuum, then the latitude of acceptance for a battered woman would be that range of activities to which she can adapt. This latitude would be affected by the degree to which she had been socialized to adjust to or accept a partner's behavior, by prior experiences with similar stimuli—such as violence in her childhood home—and by the degree to which she perceives herself as trapped within the violent situation and as having to incorporate the abuse of her partner. Because society's standards on violence against wives are ambiguous, and because abused women rarely discuss their victimization with others, most battered women are quite dependent on such "internal" anchors to determine the latitude of behaviors they will accept.

As abusive acts continue to fall near the endpoints of the range, a battered woman's latitude of acceptance shifts in order to incorporate them. As demonstrated by the findings on victims of various kinds of trauma, human beings in extreme environments are able to alter their behavior quite dramatically if it seems necessary to survive. Thus, when the behaviors of the abuser are extreme, a woman may adapt far beyond normal limits, in order to coexist peacefully with him. A certain level of abuse and tension becomes the status quo: Women progress from being horrified by each successive incident to being thankful they survived the last one. Survival becomes the criterion. The latitude of acceptance is what these women think they can live through. By the end of their relationships, women in the homicide group were experiencing attacks they would not have thought endurable at an earlier stage. They were involved in a constant process of assimilation and readjustment.

According to the principles of social judgment theory, a contrast phenomenon should come into effect when an act occurs that the woman perceives as significantly outside the "normal" range of violent behavior. In recounting the events that immediately preceded the lethal incident, women frequently said, "He had never done *that* before." Often there was a sudden change in the pattern of violence, which indicated to them that their death was imminent. One attack would be so much more brutal or degrading than all the rest that, even with their highly developed survival skills, the women believed it would be impossible to survive the next one. Or an act would suddenly be beyond the range of what the women were willing to assimilate. Frequently, this involved the physical abuse of a child or the discovery that the man had forced sexual activity on a teenage daughter. The women would say, "He had never threatened the baby before," or "It was one thing when he was beating me, but then he hurt my daughter.''

Contrast theory would predict that, once the woman had defined an act as significantly outside the latitude of what she could accept, she would then perceive that act as being more extreme than it actually was. However, given the amount of minimalization and assimilation engaged in by all types of victims, and the tendency of abused women to understate the levels of violence in their relationships, it is more probable that women in the homicide group were at last simply making a realistic appraisal of the danger. Their final hope had been removed. They did not believe they could escape the abusive situation and survive, and now they could no longer survive within it either.

The current study focused on the perceptions of women victims, and their reactions to abuse by their partners. These perceptions are crucial, both from a legal and a psychological standpoint, if we are to understand the dynamics that lead an abused woman to take lethal action against her mate. Lack of effective response by the legal system to assaults in which the victim is a wife, along with a lack of adequate and established alternatives to assure the woman's protection from further aggression, allows the violence in abusive relationships to escalate, leaving a battered woman in a potentially deadly situation from which she sees no practical avenue of escape. As is typical of victims, women who are being attacked by their partners react with responses of fear and adaption, weighing their alternatives in accordance with their perceptions of the threat and attempting to choose options which will mitigate the danger and facilitate their survival.

Yet, in some cases, the violence escalates beyond the level a victim can assimilate. By the end of their relationships, women in the homicide group were subjected to frequent and injurious attacks from partners who were likely to be drinking heavily, using drugs, sexually assaulting them, and threatening murder. Most of these women had no history of violent behavior; yet, in these relationships, the women's attempts to adapt to an increasingly violent and unpredictable mate eventually resulted in an act of violence on their part as well.

# 8

# Even
# unto Death

## WHEN HOPE IS GONE

In 1983, Jim Johnson got drunk three or four times a week. The next year, he drank heavily nearly every day. By summer, he was rarely sober. He wasn't working anymore, except for a few odd jobs, and his violence outside the home was escalating. But some things were better: Jim was letting Molly work again—she had started a seamstress business at home, and was saving money secretly. She had even gotten a phone. And Jim was there much less now. He came by to check on her periodically during the day, and sometimes worked on his cars in the shed, but he spent most of his evenings and nights at his girlfriend's and was much less abusive to Molly. Molly suspected it was the girlfriend who was being beaten; still, she welcomed the relief. From May through September, Molly worked and saved and gained strength. She began to plan for her and Kevin's departure, wondering where they should go to live, estimating how much money they would need to get started. Molly had hopes that, soon, Jim would completely lose interest in them and she and Kevin would be free.

But then the girlfriend started running away because of the threats and beatings, and Jim would come home to Molly in a rage. He beat her so badly in October that her whole arm turned purple—she had used it to shield herself from his kicks—and took weeks to heal. The girlfriend only went as far as her parents, and each time Jim found her and brought her back, but he was always angry and his renewed abuse of Molly continued. No one cared about him. Everyone was out to make a fool out of him. He began threatening to kill them all.

In November, the girlfriend started talking about leaving again, because of the beatings and because Jim was threatening her with a gun. She told Molly it sounded like Jim was planning to shoot her and then kill himself. She was very young and very frightened. She begged Molly to tell her what to do.

Molly's spirits sagged. It seemed to her that they were all in danger. She began checking bus fares to any city she thought far enough away, and counted her money to see if she and Kevin would have enough to live on when they got there. She needed to stay with her business long enough to finish the orders she had for the Christmas season. She would skip the rent for December and save everything. She tried to continue with her work and avoid angering Jim. But the renewed threats and beatings, and the fear, were pretty hard to take. Nothing had really changed, after all—it had only gotten worse.

### Friday, December 14, 1984

Jim's girlfriend took everything out of her house while he was away, leaving a note saying she couldn't stand any more beatings. He checked at her parents, but she wasn't there, and no one would tell him where she had gone. Jim came over to show the note to Molly. At first, he seemed more sad than angry. Molly fixed him supper and tried to sound sympathetic, hoping that would keep him calm. Then he started drinking, and began to hit Molly in the head with his fists. Once unleashed, his violence was totally uncontrollable. He pounded her head against the kitchen cabinets, flung her to the floor, kicked her in the ribs and stomach, and shouted at her that it was her fault his girlfriend had left. He seemed to suspect that she had come to Molly for advice, and kept demanding to know what she told her. Molly tried to dial 911 for help, but Jim grabbed that hand and dislocated the fingers. He told Molly he would break them all if she touched the door.

Jim decided that Molly knew where the other woman was, and that he was going to make her tell. He shoved her down on the sofa, grabbing her hair on both sides of her head and pulling it out by the handful, gouging at her eyes, punching her in the stomach, putting his thumb in her mouth and trying to dislocate her jaw, and breaking off the arm of the sofa by the force with which he slammed her against it. He battered Molly for several hours, dragging her around the house, hurling her across rooms, pounding her with his fists. Finally, he left her bleeding on the living room floor and fell asleep on the couch beside her. Molly was still there when Jim woke up the next morning. He made sure she could hear him and then told her, "You find her. It's up to you: You know where she is. If you don't find her today, I'll kill you, you know. She means too much to me to lose. I'll shoot you, you son-of-a-bitch. I'll kill you dead." Molly remembers him saying, "Dead, D-E-A-D, dead" over and over before he left.

## Tables Turn

It took Molly half a day to drag herself up and take care of Kevin. And then she remembered what Jim had said. She knew she was hurt and in danger, and that she should do *something*—get some kind of help—but she couldn't seem to think. She became more and more frightened as it got later in the afternoon; she wandered around the house, sobbing; but even then, nothing seemed real. Jim burst in the door about 10:30 that night, stumbling drunk. He didn't even question her; just threw open the door and said, "You ready?" He grabbed her by the throat and slammed her back against the door jamb, choking her hard. Just when she started to faint, he stopped and shook her until she was breathing again, and then started hitting her methodically with his fists, waiting until she caught her breath before striking again. At some point, she realized he was laughing. Molly had seen him beat a dog like that once, slowly, until it died. She remembered that he had laughed then, too.

Jim staggered backward, and Molly escaped through the door. She ran to the pickup to get Jim's guns so she could hide them. She found the automatic he kept in the glove compartment and was frantically searching for his other pistol when Jim rushed out of the house. Molly crouched in the corner of the shed and prayed he wouldn't see her. Jim wasn't laughing now. He was angry, shouting profanities and warnings, yelling, "You don't understand. I don't care anymore. I just don't *care*."

He went back into the house and came out waving the rifle, but Molly had removed the bolt from it so it wouldn't fire. Jim was enraged. He shouted, "I'll get you. I'll find a rubber band and *make* it work. I'll get you."

Molly was afraid to go too far from the house because Kevin was still inside. She knew the neighbors were home and ran there to get help, but no one came to the door. She circled around the house and was looking in Kevin's window to make sure he was alright when, suddenly, Jim came around the corner and lunged at her. Molly fled back toward the neighbors', screaming for help. She remembers feeling like her chest was exploding; feeling caught in a cage. It seemed inevitable she would die. Jim was ransacking the pickup, looking for his guns. He finally found the pistol and, yelling at her that it was all over, aimed it at her and fired. Molly flung herself behind some oil barrels. Molly remembers thinking, "He's shooting at me. He really is shooting at me!" Jim fired again. Again the shot went wide.

Then she heard Jim yell, "Alright. I'll take the only thing that really matters to you! I'm going to kill Kevin if I have to do it with my bare hands." Molly screamed, "No, Jimmy, NO!" and jumped out into the light where he could see her. But Jim had already gone into the house. Molly didn't know if he meant it; he had never threatened the baby before. She was rushing toward the door when Jim came out, carrying Kevin. It was late at night now, and very cold. The first thing Molly noticed was that Jim had left the baby in nightclothes and barefoot, although usually he insisted that he be bundled up. Now she really believed he intended to kill him. Jim pushed Kevin into the seat of the pickup and Molly panicked. She ran around the end of the truck, trying to see if Jim was hurting him. Jim's hands were around the baby's neck. Molly screamed at him, "Get away from him, Jim! Get away!" But he just laughed at her. She told him again to get away, but he didn't move.

Molly was terrified. She knew how quickly he could kill Kevin; she had been choked by Jim, and knew his strength. There was no longer time to get help. Molly looked down at her own hands, still locked around the automatic. She raised the gun and fired. Jim fell backward, and Molly stepped over him and grabbed Kevin. She ran with him to the neighbors', and this time they let her in. They helped her call the police and an ambulance, but Jim was already dead. Molly was arrested and taken to jail, where pictures were taken of her injuries. The next day, she was charged with murder in the shooting death of her husband.

────────

## THE KILLING OF THE ABUSER

Molly's story illustrates a typical scenario in the escalation toward a lethal incident for women in the homicide group. By the end of their relationships, these women perceived their partners' behavior as totally out of control: In most cases, the men were intoxicated or using drugs nearly every day, their violence was more frequent and the severity of the violence more extreme, and their awareness of or contrition for their actions seemed almost nonexistent. Not only had their aggression toward and threats to kill their mates escalated, it frequently generalized to others as well, placing other intimates, particularly children, in danger. Women who had observed the patterns of these men's violence for years now judged the abusers as beyond the point where they would be able to stop short of murder. It seemed only a matter of time before someone would be seriously hurt or killed. Considering their history as the men's primary target, women in the homicide group expected that they were the ones most likely to die.

Most of the women in the homicide group reached a point at which they lost all hope of improvement or relief. For some women, like Karen Simon or Irene Miller, this was when they were forced to return to the man after the last failed escape attempt. For others, like Molly Johnson, hope was lost with the onset of renewed violence after a period of surcease that suggested the possibility of freedom.

Another component of the buildup toward a lethal incident was the focus on dying. For women like Molly, it was an absolute conviction that death was inevitable within a certain timeframe; usually, this conviction was based on specific threats by the men. Others, like Karen Simon, began to look toward death as the only solution to the escalation of violence and their inability to escape the abuser, and either considered taking their own lives or assumed that their partner would soon do it for them. In every case, women in the homicide group believed that they (or a child) would be the victim if someone were to die. Recalling the man's dominance and their perception of his power as an aggressor, none of the women thought the abuser would be the final victim.

Typically, the killing of the abuser was unplanned and occurred in the midst of an attack against the woman, during the warning phase when it became apparent that an attack was about to begin, or during an escape attempt by the woman. In some cases, the woman waited until the man was sleeping or otherwise inattentive after an assault, sure that the attack would resume in a relatively short while. These delayed homicides were often related to an explicit threat by the abuser to "get" the woman or a child within a specific time; women killed the abuser to avert the threatened outcome.


## *Protection of a Child*

Molly's case is an example of a woman killing to protect the life of a child. Although Molly was carrying a gun during much of the final incident, she didn't shoot at Jim—even when he was firing at her—until after she saw his hands around Kevin's neck and had warned him twice to move away. Similarly, Bella Harris endured severe abuse from her husband Isaac for 20 years, and killed him only when he told her he was going to shoot their oldest daughter when she came home. Bella remembered the time she had gone to the movies and Isaac threatened the same thing; he would have killed Bella that night, if someone hadn't intervened. When Isaac fell asleep, Bella and her younger daughter shot him and then set the house on fire. (This was the only completed homicide in which arson was involved, although, in this case, arson was not the cause of death.)

Wanda Bowles was also attempting to protect a child. After a particularly severe beating of her daughter Christie, Wanda could not shake the image of Randy's fist going toward Christie's face, the way his features were contorted with rage, his intention to do harm. Wanda's concentration narrowed to one thing: He must not ever hurt Christie again. Finally, she called her brother and asked, "How much does it cost to put a contract out on someone?" She felt she had tried everything else: She had talked to Randy about his drinking, but it did no good; talked to him about getting help, but he only laughed at her; tried to get away from him, but he always found them and threatened to kill them both. By the next day, Wanda had abandoned her idea and was getting information on safe houses, but that night her brother killed Randy, with the help of another man. (Wanda was unusual in even considering this plan of action. Only three women in the homicide group were charged with conspiracy to commit murder.)

## *Homicides during an Assaultive Incident*

More typically, the abuser was killed during an assaultive incident in which the woman was the victim.

Maggie and Duke Ortega had just returned home from a party
at which Duke had been drinking heavily. Maggie knew Duke
was in a bad mood, but they hadn't been arguing. She went into
the bedroom to change clothes and when she came out, Duke
was there. Without warning, he hit her in the head with his fist.
Her neck snapped back against the door jamb and her glasses
flew off (she has very poor vision). Maggie tried to run to the
kitchen door, but Duke knocked her into a chair by the stove
and began hitting her. He had that look on his face again; "like
another person, not like Duke; not like anyone who recognized
me." Maggie kept thinking that if she could just get outside it
would be alright. It was a weekend and people were home in
the apartments around them. Someone would protect her.

Duke was towering over Maggie, choking her, digging in his
thumbs. She reached over and pulled out a drawer by the sink
to swing at him, hoping to divert his attention so she could run.
But the drawer was heavy, full of utensils, and it fell to the
floor, scattering the contents across the room and under the
chair where Maggie was sitting. Duke was on top of her now,
pounding and screaming. Maggie reached down and picked up
the first thing she touched and struck him with it. Duke backed
off and Maggie stood up. Then she saw the knife handle in his
neck and realized what she'd done. She pulled the knife out,
and tried to stop the bleeding. She helped him sit down on the
floor, propped up against the cabinets, and ran next door to call
the ambulance and the police. Then she ran back and got some
ice to put on his neck, telling him everything was going to be
alright. Duke started leaning toward the floor and she laid him
down, holding him in her arms until the police arrived.

Later, Maggie said, "It happened so fast. I didn't know why I
was getting hit. I didn't know what I hit him with. When the
police came, they took me away: They wouldn't even let me
stay with him, and he was still alive." The detectives questioned her and had her strip to the waist so that pictures could
be taken of her injuries. A couple of hours later, they told her
that Duke was dead. Maggie doesn't remember much after that.

Often, homicides occurring during battering incidents were committed with the abuser's weapon. Sometimes, the men dared the women to kill them; it is difficult to know whether this was out of their own suicidal tendencies, or whether they simply believed the women would never carry out such an act. In the case of Karen and Hal Simon, Hal's final behaviors almost appeared as though he wanted to die.

Hal was angry with Karen again, and told her to go get the gun. She brought it to him; she knew if she disobeyed, the assault would be worse. He was yelling at her about nagging him, saying, "I've heard this shit and heard this shit, and I've had it. I'm going to fix you up right now." He shoved her down into a chair by the couch, pushing the gun up under her chin, then took the butt of the gun and began hitting her in the abdomen. Karen could smell food burning in the kitchen and told him she needed to go and turn off the stove, hoping he would change moods while she was away. But Hal said, "You're not going anywhere." He began pressing the gun against her head, clicking the hammer, talking about killing her. Suddenly, Karen was just tired of being threatened this way and never knowing if she was going to live or die. So she said to Hal, "Are we going to continue doing this? Every time I turn around, you're threatening to kill me, making me get the gun, saying you're going to blow me away. Why don't we get it over with? Why don't you just go ahead now and shoot me?"

Hal stared at her and then retorted, "You have so goddam much guts. . . . You kill me." He threw the shotgun at her, and laid down in a curled position on the floor in front of the couch with his back toward her. Karen thinks she intended to go and put the gun away, and turn off the stove. The next thing she remembers, she was standing in the kitchen and realized that Hal was shot. She went back to check on him, and then ran next door to call for help. The neighbors returned to the house and stayed with her until the police arrived. The police description of Karen at the scene notes that she was terrified and disoriented, and that they found it "very unusual to see somebody who wants to go back and just hold the deceased."

## *When Assault Was Imminent*

Other homicides occurred during the warning phase, when it appeared that an assault was imminent. Sharon Bikson's killing of her husband Roy is one such case.

Although Sharon tried to hide from him, Roy found her latest apartment and broke in several times. Sharon would come home at night and find the lock just hanging out of the door and be too afraid to go in. Roy attacked and severely injured her at work, and kidnapped and threatened her infant son. He spent much of his time threatening Sharon, and she never got over the fear that he would jump out at her from somewhere and finally kill her. She was just trying to get through their custody hearing, so that she and the children could go away. On one occasion, Roy came by her apartment and kicked in the door, but he left when Sharon ran toward the phone. The gun she purchased was stolen; Sharon wondered if Roy took it, since he was the one breaking in. She bought another handgun and hid it behind a cupboard. The fear and the tension were constant.

One afternoon, Roy called Sharon just to let her know he'd found her new phone number. He was verbally abusive, threatening and calling her names until Sharon finally hung up. When the phone rang again, she didn't answer. She considered calling the police, but knew they wouldn't come out just for a phone call. They usually didn't come at all until after something had happened. Sharon tried to brace the door, just in case. It wouldn't lock properly, since the last time Roy had broken in, but she placed a chair under the door handle and wedged another chair between that and the wall. A few minutes later, she heard Roy outside, cursing and shouting. Sharon's children were with her, playing in the bedroom, and she thought he could probably hear their voices. She was afraid of what he would do to her for hanging up, and worried that he might take one of the children.

Roy started to force the door open. Sharon was attempting to drag a dresser in from the other room when the doorknob came off and the chair fell over. Roy pushed his way into the room, shouting, "Get the gun, you bitch, 'cause I'm going to kill you and the bastard." (She thinks he meant the baby.)

Sharon was so scared she couldn't think. She ran to the kitchen and got the handgun, struggling with the zipper on the case, afraid if Roy got to her and got his hands on the gun, he would kill her for sure. Roy was coming through the living room and Sharon met him there, pleading, "Don't come up on me, Roy. Don't come up on me now." He saw the gun in her hand, but still came toward her—arms out, yelling, "Shoot me. Shoot me, bitch!" Sharon fired once. Roy still moved toward her. She shot again. He gasped, and Sharon could see the stain on his chest. She warned him, "Please, don't come up on me," and he replied, "I won't. I won't."

Roy walked out of the apartment and told a neighbor he'd been shot and to call an ambulance. Then he came back in and sat down in the chair Sharon had used to brace the door. Sharon put the gun up then, and called an ambulance too. Roy was groaning, struggling to get a breath. Sharon stayed at a distance, watching him. She wanted to believe he was going to be alright, but she saw his last breath and knew. Then she heard the police loudspeaker, telling her to come out with her hands up, and was terrified again, thinking they would shoot her as she walked out the door. She raised her arms up over her head and stepped past Roy's body into the hall.

## Weapons of Homicide

Guns were used in 81 percent of the homicide or attempted murder cases; knives were used in 7 percent; autos were involved in 7 percent (or 3) cases, and other methods were used in the remaining 5 percent of cases. In many of the homicides involving firearms, the men were killed with the same guns they had used earlier against the women: Even when several guns were available, the weapons they had been threatened with were the ones the women reached for in their moment of panic.

During a last desperate escape attempt, Irene Miller attempted to hold off Mark until help could arrive by threatening him with a .22. This was the gun that Mark had threatened to kill *her* with when he thought she was having an affair. All Irene knew about this gun was that Mark said it was old and not very powerful.

Janet VanHorn shot Rick with the .357 Magnum he had formerly made her hold to his head; she had hidden all the guns together, convinced he was planning to shoot her, and when she heard him coming up the stairs after her, this was the gun she picked up. Similarly, Bella Harris shot Isaac with the rifle he kept by the bed and had threatened to use on her—the one she sometimes woke up to find him pointing at her in the morning.

## *Women's Reactions to the Deaths of Their Mates*

For some women in the homicide group, their fear of their partners—and their perceptions of the abusers as much stronger than
they were and able to retaliate against them—dominated their
immediate reactions after the killing. A few women were unable
to realize that they were safe, even after their abusers were dead,
and took further protective measures against the retaliation they
expected to follow an aggressive attack. One woman locked her
husband's body in the closet after she shot him: As long as she
could see him, she was afraid he was going to reach out and grab
her. Another hid outside in the shrubbery until the police arrived,
and kept warning them as they entered the house to be careful;
her husband was angry and might attack them. Even after Wanda
Bowles was told by her brother that Randy was dead, she stayed
up all night, watching for his return; expecting that he would be
beaten up and angry, and that she and her daughter would be in
danger. It was only the next afternoon, when the police came and
showed her pictures of Randy's body lying in a field, that Wanda
finally realized Randy was gone and broke down completely.

Most women reacted to the wounding or killing of their mates
with sorrow and horror. Almost all of them called an ambulance
and the police for assistance, and some attempted to give medical
aid until other help arrived. Reports by officers at the scene frequently noted the women's attempts to reassure and comfort the
men, and their requests to be allowed to remain with them, or to
go back and spend time with their bodies, before they were transported to jail.

At the time of the homicide evaluations, their grief was still
intense. In talking about the death of Hal Simon, Karen Simon
began to cry, exclaiming, "I didn't want him dead! I thought it
would be me. I didn't want him to have to die!" Janet VanHorn,
disoriented and hospitalized, spent the first week after Rick's
death asking for him and begging someone to bring him to her.
Her attorney's first task was to try and convince Janet that Rick was
dead. Susan Jefferson, although she had left Don several times and
was separating from him at the time of the incident, still seemed
bewildered by the loss six months later, saying, "Now I'm in this
strange world where it's so still and I'm all alone. Now it will
never be okay." Even Sharon Bikson, after all of Roy's harrassment
and violence and her struggles to escape him, later said, "You
know, I never stopped loving him. I was willing to go through

hell to get away from him, but I never stopped loving him." The anguish of many of the women over the deaths of their abusers was captured in a statement by one of them, who told me, "He had gotten so wild, and so reckless. I was afraid he was going to die somehow. But why by my hand? Why did it have to be by *my* hand?"

Bella Harris gave one of the most complete descriptions of the aftermath of a homicide, in recounting the sensations and behaviors that followed the killing of her husband Isaac.

After Bella and her daughter set fire to the house, they walked down the hill to the community hospital and told them that Bella was ill; she was so cold and thirsty, and she felt like she couldn't breathe. Bella remembers a nurse saying, "Mrs. Harris, I just heard on the radio that your house is on fire." Bella thinks she said, "How could that happen?" She wondered how the fire could have started. It was like she was in a daze; she didn't really think she did it. Then someone told her that Isaac had been in the house, and that he was dead. She thinks she cried then, but all she really remembers is how strange she felt: All these people talking to her, the police there; she could see them all talking, but she couldn't hear anything. She doesn't think she answered at all. She says, "It was like I was a long way from home, and trying to find my way back."

Bella remembers that she could not get herself together. She spent too much money on the funeral, and although people tried to talk to her about it, it just didn't seem to matter. She was charged with first degree murder and two counts of arson, and she and her daughter were jailed pending trial, but that hardly seemed real either. She kept trying to understand who had set the fire, who had killed Isaac, why Isaac was dead. Finally, one night, it all came back to her. Bella says, "I could just *see* it, then—see the fire, see shooting him, see myself walking away." It was like a huge weight came down on her head. Bella sat down and tried to understand it, but the pressure on her head was too great. So she wrapped her sweater up into a ball and laid down on it, pressing her head against its firmness until she went to sleep. In jail, Bella says, that's what you do when things hurt.

There is much we do not know about these incidents. In a phenomenon as unknown—and as complex—as the occurrence of homicide between partners, the context of the situation, as well as the myriad personal and relational dynamics leading up to the incident itself, are vital in understanding the event; yet these nuances cannot be captured by relying solely on a questionnaire or structured interview format. In the current study, women were asked to describe the homicide and the factors leading up to it in their own words, and therefore much of the data on the homicides is qualitative in nature. Yet patterns or similarities can be derived from these accounts. Such factors as a final loss of hope, or the men's seeming to dare the women to kill them during the final incidents, were frequently reported. A darkening of their surroundings, or an effect of tunnel vision, was also reported by several of the women as occurring just prior to the lethal incident. For example, Wanda Bowles told of feeling as though she had "blinders" on, after Randy's final battering of Christie. Although it was only afternoon, she went around the house turning on all the lights, in an effort to dispel the darkness around her. Observations such as this are not easily reducible to categories or lists, yet such findings suggest new dimensions for future study.

## COMPARISON OF THE WOMEN'S REPORTS WITH OTHER STUDIES OF HOMICIDE

Although in the current study we have only the women's reports of the abusers' behavior and the circumstances preceding the homicide event, these findings are supported by other, more localized, studies on homicide. For example, in a study of men and women in Florida who were charged with killing a spouse, Barnard, Vera, Vera, and Newman note that men who had killed their wives tended to be less educated than the female defendants, and were more likely to have a previous arrest record as well as a history of alcohol abuse. Women defendants were more likely to have a history of suicide attempts.[1]

Like women in the homicide group, women in the Barnard et al. study reported the primary problem in their relationships as verbal and physical violence by their mates, as well as substance abuse by their spouses: 73 percent reported having been battered by their partners; 73 percent also reported alcohol abuse by their husbands. Forty-six percent of the women reported a history of separation from the spouse victims, although only 9 percent of the women were living separately from their partners at the time the homicide occurred.

In contrast, of men who had killed their partners, 61 percent reported a major problem in their relationships as their suspicion of infidelities on the part of their wives, and 52 percent reported "desertion" by their wives. Fifty-seven percent of the men were in fact living separately from their wives at the time they killed them; further evidence that separation from a partner does not necessarily end the risk of violence, and may increase the risk of lethal violence in some cases. Fifty-seven percent of the men also reported that they had a problem with alcohol abuse.

### Factors Precipitating Spousal Homicide

The Barnard study, in looking at both male and female perpetrators of homicide, found different factors to be operational in the killing of wives by husbands and husbands by wives. For men, the precipitating event was usually some form of perceived rejection by the partner. The most frequent type of male homicide was what Barnard et al. call "sex-role threat homicide." They note that "a walkout, a demand, a threat of separation were taken by the men to represent intolerable desertion, rejection, and abandonment."[2] In killing the women, men in this group believed they were reacting to a previous offense against them (e.g., leaving) by their wives. Barnard et al. note that "the theme most often expressed by [the men] as the precipitating event for the homicide was their inability to accept what they perceived to be a rejection of them or of their role of dominance over their eventual victims." Barnard and his colleagues see the men's "unspoken sense of dependency" on their wives as the key to this type of homicide; as well as the sex role stereotypes that encourage men to believe they have the right to control their wives' whereabouts and activities, and that lead them to express the pain of separation or rejection in aggressive, rather than more sensitive, ways.

In contrast, for females, the triggering event to the killing of their mates was usually a verbal or physical attack or threat by the partner. Following Marvin Wolfgang's earlier work, Barnard et al.

term these "victim-precipitated homicides." They note that over 70 percent of the women charged with the deaths of their husbands had previously been beaten by them, and cite the physical abuse of wives as the major factor in the precipitation of lethal actions by wives against husbands.

As mentioned earlier, this conclusion is well-supported by more general studies of homicide. Wolfgang, in his foundational study of homicides in Philadelphia, reported that over 25 percent of the male victims of a partner's violence "provoked" their own deaths by being the first to use physical force, strike blows, or threaten with a weapon; compared to only 5 percent of the wife victims.[3] (This was based on "provocation recognized by the courts," and would not necessarily reflect the number of wives who had actually experienced physical abuse or threat from their spouse victims.) William Willbanks, in a recent study of male and female homicide offenders in Dade County, Florida, also found cases involving women perpetrators much more likely to have circumstances that made their homicides justifiable in self-defense.[4] Similarly, Peter Chimbos, in a study of spousal homicides in Canada, noted that the lethal act was usually the end point in an ongoing series of conflicts or threats.[5] Fifty-three percent of the respondents reported prior threats to kill on the part of the victim or offender, and 70 percent reported prior physical violence in the relationship. All of the women in the study had experienced beatings by their partners prior to the homicides.

Studies focusing solely on women perpetrators report similar observations. In a pretrial study of women charged with homicide in Missouri, Daniel and Harris note that 75 percent of women charged with the death of their husbands had been physically abused by them prior to the homicide. They observe that "these victims posed substantial threat to the lives of the perpetrators," and, like Barnard et al., conclude that "wife beating constitutes a major contributing factor in interspousal murder."[6] Jane Totman, studying women serving time in a California prison for the killing of their partners, found that the usual homicide situation tended to be triggered by an immediate crisis that followed a long-term problem or struggle with the victim. Of these women, 93 percent reported being physically abused by their partners, and 67 percent said that the homicide was in defense of themselves or a child. As with findings in the current study, Totman reports that a major contributing factor to these homicide events was a perceived lack of viable alternatives to an "overwhelming and entrapping life situation" on the part of the women.[7] Women tried a series of alternatives prior to the occurrence of the lethal incident. Nearly one-third had left home. Many others said they wanted to leave, but were afraid to because of their partners' threatened retaliation. One had attempted suicide as a way out. Totman observes that, as these alternatives failed, the "situation seemed to become even more limited in its possibilities for modification . . . more than ever a "trap" from which there was no escape."[8]

The importance of the perception of entrapment, based on specific studies of abused or threatened women who have killed their partners, is supported as well by a larger body of theory about the genesis of crime. For example, Seymour Halleck, writing about the perpetration of criminal behavior in general, asserted that "helplessness" or the "feeling of being oppressed and not being able to do anything about it. . . . plays an important role in the genesis of criminal action"; and further contends that "criminal behavior becomes more likely . . . when alternative adaptions are actively restricted by other people."[9]

For women in the homicide group, the escalation of violence and threats, combined with this perception of entrapment and the impact of failed alternatives, culminated in eventual lethal action against their abusers. The following case provides a summary of the dynamics found to be crucial in the progression of intimate relationships toward homicides perpetrated by physically abused women.

## REPRISE: THE CONTEXT OF A HOMICIDE—KIM AND BILLY HALL

Kim Hall was 29 when I met her, but still looked somewhat like a child—just over five feet tall and weighing 100 pounds. She had both witnessed and experienced abuse for the first 10 years of her life; almost all her early childhood memories involved some form of physical force and threat:

Kim's first memories were of her father beating her mother. She remembers seeing blood and running screaming to the neighbors. After Kim's father left, her mother had a succession of boyfriends—many of whom beat her—and Kim remembers several occasions when she saw her mother badly hurt. Some of the men were physically violent with Kim as well; when she was little she thought that was just the way men were. When Kim was about 8, her mother lived with a man who sexually abused Kim. He would take her for rides and stop the car along the road, or take her to his beach house, where he forced her into sexual acts and took pictures of her. Kim remembers that he often had other children around the beach house, too.

On one occasion, this man tried to force Kim to perform oral sex on him in the car; she refused, crying and struggling to get away. He was furious and began throwing her around, grabbing her by the arms and shaking her, banging her head against the window and dashboard, slapping her repeatedly. Kim cried all the way home, curled up on the floor in back. She told her mother what had happened, but her mother did not believe her, even though her face was bruised and swollen. And when her mother asked the man about it, he beat Kim again for telling.

Shortly afterward, Kim was severely injured in a car accident and was hospitalized for a long time. Her mother did not want to resume caring for her after that, so Kim was put up for adoption and went to live with her grandmother, with whom she was very close. A year later, Kim's adoption was final and she was sent to live with a family in another state. Her new parents were not violent, but they did not believe in "spoiling" children and there was no demonstration of affection. Kim adored her adopted mother, but never quite felt she belonged in the family. When she was 18, she left in search of her real parents.

Billy Hall, Kim's husband, is another example of someone whose earliest memories were of witnessing abuse:

Billy's father beat his mother often and severely until she left him. Billy lived with his grandparents until he was nine years old, when his mother remarried; then, he moved in with his mother and stepfather. His stepfather was a harsh man who kicked the children and made them carry cinder blocks around and around the house when they displeased him.

As an adolescent, Billy was in constant trouble at school and with law-enforcement authorities; most of his offenses involved violence. By the time he was 30, he had a long record of arrests and convictions, over a dozen of those for assault and battery.

Everyone in the county knew Billy: He was a big man—6'2" and over 250 pounds—and was known for his temper and his tendency to use his fists. Even the men he worked with were afraid of him and did whatever he said. He drank heavily, and when he was drinking, he was mean. But he could also be charming and sweet, and was well-liked in spite of his unpredictability. Kim described him as a big teddy-bear of a man.

When Kim met Billy in May 1979, she had just moved from out of state. Their attraction for each other was immediate and lasting, and they were together from then on. Billy perceived Kim as a tiny little thing who needed his protection. Kim saw him as big, strong, and loving, and she felt she needed that. She was 25 and had already been married twice. Although neither of her husbands was abusive, Kim was unable to overcome her fear in close relationships and eventually left both. In Billy, she thought she had found the safety and security she was seeking.

═══════════

## The First Incident: August 1979

Kim and Billy had been living together for about three months, and were going sightseeing to another town with his sister and brother-in-law. They were drinking some on the way, and then went to a bar after they arrived. Kim was teasing Billy about paying attention to the waitress when, suddenly, he dragged her out of the restaurant by the hair and began assaulting her in the parking lot—hitting her and knocking her down, dragging her to her feet and knocking her down again, slapping, and yelling. Billy's brother-in-law came out and tried to intervene, but Billy turned on him and threw him to the ground, tearing his shirt. Finally, his sister wrapped her arms around Kim and refused to let go. Billy did not want to hit his sister, so he stopped attacking Kim. The police arrived and suggested that Kim press charges, but she was too afraid and confused to do so. They all returned to their motel and went to bed.

The next morning, Kim woke up and burst out crying. Billy held her and comforted her, saying, "Honey, it's all right. Go ahead and cry. It will be okay. It will never happen again."

Both of Kim's eyes were black, her face was scratched, and her lips were swollen. The four went sightseeing anyway. The others acted as though nothing had happened and seemed to be having a good time. Kim remembers how unreal that day seemed, as though she were floating through a slow-motion dream; as though no one could see that she was hurt. Billy had never hit her before. She kept trying to understand why it had happened and decided it was because—as Billy said—she had been "running off at the mouth." Billy was especially loving for several weeks after this incident. The next assault occurred one month later.

## Patterns of Violence

Abuse usually started when Billy was drinking. Kim did not know when the beatings were going to happen; Billy's mood would change and they would begin to argue, but there usually was not much talking. It became physical very quickly. Billy got a certain look on his face—jaw set, mouth tight—he would turn and stare at her, and then begin hitting. He rarely said anything once the violence began. It was as though something inside of him had to run its course. Then he would stop suddenly, usually when Kim was down. During these attacks, Kim would plead with him, "Billy, please quit. Please quit. I love you, Billy. Please quit." She did not know if it had any effect, but it was the only thing she knew to try.

Billy made it clear that he would kill Kim if she ever gave him a reason; he often threatened to kill her when he felt she had not obeyed him, or when he thought she was talking back. In January 1981, some of his friends were visiting. He was showing them his .357 magnum and Kim was standing in the doorway. Suddenly, he said to her, "I ought to blow you away." He pointed the gun at her head and fired. The bullet went high and into the door jamb; Kim thinks he intended to aim high. She just stood still for a minute, then went over and took the gun from him and hid it upstairs. Nothing more was said, and the next week she got rid of that gun.

Early in the relationship, Billy seemed sorry when he hurt Kim. After an especially bad beating, he would sit and look at her with tears in his eyes. Kim remembers once, when she was badly hurt, Billy rocked her in his arms and moaned, holding her against his chest like he was mourning a dead child. Sometimes she would come to after being hit and hear Billy saying, "Be okay. Be okay, baby, I didn't mean to. Oh, God, please be okay!" Yet he would force her to go out with him after beatings, even when she was badly bruised and her face was swollen. He did not seem to care what others thought, and no one dared mention it to him. Billy would keep his arm around Kim and become aggressive if anyone came too near. Other people were afraid to talk to Kim, for fear Billy would take offense or they would put themselves in danger. Increasingly, when she was injured, Kim felt invisible. Billy attacked her in front of his relatives and in public places, as well as at home, but usually no one intervened.

Kim left Billy over and over after these incidents, but he looked for her until he found her. He would cry and tell her how much he loved her and promise to do anything in the world if she would come back; Kim would think, "Maybe if I try harder. . . . Maybe if he doesn't get mad again. . . . Maybe if we both quit drinking. . . ." She missed him, and she could not stand to be away from home. She felt out of place staying with others—like a child again; and she hated to ask for favors or money. Everywhere she went, people she stayed with were afraid Billy would come after her, and she knew they were relieved when she left. So she would stay a few days and go home. Billy would promise to be better, and sometimes it seemed like he really tried. But there was always another assault, and nearly every time, it was more severe.

One of the worst beatings occurred at the local restaurant and bar where they first met. Kim and Billy had been getting along well that evening. They were in the car getting ready to leave, when Kim said something that made Billy angry. He grabbed her and started slapping her. She jumped out of the car and ran, but Billy caught her and flung her to the ground, kicking and hitting her with his fists. Kim tried to roll away, but Billy jerked her to her feet and threw her face forward against a phone booth, cutting her mouth and breaking off a tooth. She fell, and Billy began dragging her around the parking lot on the gravel. Kim's shirt was torn, her arms scraped and bleeding. She was screaming at Billy to stop. Someone came running toward them, shouting, and Kim got to her feet and fled into the restaurant with Billy in pursuit. Billy tried to drag her back outside, but the owner and some other men pulled him off.

Kim ran to the kitchen and hid in the cupboard under the stove, curled up into a little ball, but Billy found her. She heard him growl as he reached in to drag her out and the beating started all over again. The owner eventually drove Billy off with a shotgun and called Billy's relatives to come get Kim. Her shirt was torn off, she was covered with blood, and both eyes were swollen nearly shut. She crawled back under the stove counter and hid there until they lifted her out and took her home.

Billy's family helped Kim clean up and put her to bed. But the next morning, Billy's relatives told her she would have to go on home: Billy would be looking for her, and they didn't know what Billy would do if he found her there or they helped her get away. They gave Kim a ride to a corner near her house. When she walked in, Billy just sat down at the table and cried, saying, "Jesus! Oh, Jesus. . . ." over and over. He did not remember the night before and could not believe she was so badly hurt. He was much better for weeks after that. Of these quiet times, Kim says, "Everything was so great and loving that sometimes you'd almost believe maybe that *would* be the last time." The next beating was two months later.

## Sexual Assault

Billy frequently forced Kim to have intercourse—he just picked her up and threw her on the bed. And during or after beatings, he often made her perform oral sex on him, even when her mouth was injured and bleeding, or he raped her. This sort of abuse occurred every week or more often by the end of the relationship.

One evening, Kim and Billy went to his aunt's after work to play cards. Billy had been drinking heavily; he was losing and becoming increasingly angry. Finally, he threw down the cards and told Kim, "Come on. We're going." Kim refused. She was afraid to leave with him so upset, for fear he would hurt her. Billy slammed out the door and drove off. Kim waited for a few minutes, then left to walk to a friend's house, where she could spend the night. The aunt checked outside and thought Billy was gone, but as soon as Kim reached the street, he came out of the darkness and grabbed her; throwing her down, throwing her around the yard, hitting and kicking. He hit her hard in the face with his fist and told her, "When I tell you to leave, you leave!"

Billy dragged Kim toward the pickup, parked just around the corner, and pinned her against the side, holding her off the ground with his forearm across her throat, saying, "I ought to kill you. I ought to kill you, bitch!" Kim was choking and could not breathe. The aunt heard shouting and looked out, calling to Kim. Billy released her and told her to say that she was alright, and that they were going. Kim did, and Billy literally threw her in the truck and drove off.

On the way home, Billy was driving very fast, swerving all over the highway and barely missing other cars. He started trying to throw Kim out of the truck while it was moving— pushing her toward the door, struggling to hold the door open and still steer. Kim was terrified, clinging to him, pleading, "Billy please. You're going so fast. Billy, you'll *kill* me if you do that!" Billy pulled over and slammed on the brakes. He grabbed a revolver from under the seat and pushed Kim toward the open door, saying, "Get out then. The truck's not moving now." Kim was sure he would shoot her if she did, so she sat still, trying to talk him out of it. Eventually, he slammed the door shut and took off, but he made her perform oral sex on him even though her mouth was cut and bleeding and held the gun to her head as he drove.

Halfway home, Billy pulled over and made Kim undress. He forced her to have intercourse with him in the truck, choking her and banging her head against the dashboard. Finally, he restarted the truck and drove on. When they got home, Billy passed out in a chair. Kim washed her face and dressed, and then sat up all night in another chair, watching him. She was afraid of what Billy would do to her if he woke up and she was asleep.

The next day, Kim's eyes were swollen, her lower lip was split, and the left side of her face was puffed up and black. Her cheekbone seemed to be broken too; she had difficulty opening her mouth wide enough to eat. Billy left for work in the morning without saying a word. Kim slept all day, and drank liquor and took aspirin to dull the pain and fear. When Billy returned that night, he brought a friend with him. He called Kim into the kitchen where they were drinking beer, and bragged to his friend about her—telling him what a good woman she was, how well she cooked, how much he loved this little lady; hugging and kissing her. Kim just stood there, and the friend tried not to look at her face.

The following day while Billy was at work, Kim went to stay on a friend's house boat, where she could hide. She intended to leave permanently, and got a kitten to keep her company.

After four days, though, she called Billy. She was confused and in pain from her injuries; unused to being alone; frightened Billy would find her, but unsure of what to do now and where to go. Billy was upset; his voice was cracking and he begged to know where she was. Kim kept insisting that she could not tell him—that she was afraid he would kill her, *afraid* to come back—and at first kept her hiding place a secret. But on the seventh day, she could not hold out any longer and told him where she was.

That evening Billy arrived, quiet and contrite. He told her he understood why she was scared and that he had quit drinking; he would not hurt her anymore. Finally, Kim let Billy take her home, telling herself all the while what a fool she was for going back, but thinking at the same time that there was nowhere she could go to get away from him.

### August 1982 to January 1983

During the last six months Kim and Billy were together, things were very bad. Billy was getting moodier; less loving and more threatening. He never had anything kind to say to Kim anymore, and the abuse was almost constant. Kim was on edge every evening, wondering if Billy would come home drunk and what he would do to her. She could hardly eat or sleep, and began drinking more to handle the constant anxiety. Kim tried to tell Billy that she was afraid, but he just told her she was being stupid. She could not find any trace of the love that used to be there. After some attacks, she thought about pressing charges against Billy, but he was already on probation and she was afraid to be the one to put him back in jail.

Kim made repeated attempts to leave Billy, spending several days away practically every other week, but she was so worn down—no money, no job, and she knew everyone else was tired of her situation—she could not think of what to do. She was also terrified of Billy's anger if he should come after her and, when she was away, spent all her time watching out of windows and doors so she could run if she saw him coming. After a few days and nights of this, Kim would go home. Billy never beat her for returning, only if he had to come and find her. Kim would stay at home until the next bad beating, and then leave again, numb now with exhaustion, alcohol, and fear.

Little things made Billy irrationally angry. That fall, it was her cats. Kim had two older cats, plus the kitten she had gotten on the house boat. Pets were terribly important to her; they were her only source of comfort and affection. One afternoon, Billy said he had had it with her damn cats and started screaming that he was going to kill them. Kim didn't take it too seriously. She knew he really liked the cats, but sometimes he just did things to get a rise out of her, to give himself a reason to beat her. So she said, "Well, do what you want, Billy," never thinking he'd really do it.

The kitten was sitting in the yard. Billy got his rifle, walked up to it, and shot it. Then he hunted down the other two cats and shot them. Kim was hysterical—following him around, tugging on him, jumping up and down and screaming. She begged him not to kill the cats, and after he had, she begged him not to leave them there. So he picked them up and threw them over the fence. After Billy went to sleep that night, Kim crept out, found the cats, and buried them. Then she lay down in the field and cried. She blamed herself for their deaths. She should never have brought them to live around Billy. It seemed like all that was left was for Billy to kill her. Her diary for that day reads, "I wish I were dead. I wish I had been shot, too."

### Tables Turn

One night in early February, Kim and Billy spent the evening at Billy's favorite bar. Kim was not with Billy much that evening; he was playing the pinball machines, and Kim was sitting at a table, talking to a friend. Both Kim and Billy were drinking a lot. Kim remembers them leaving the bar and driving home together. She does not think they were arguing about anything. The next thing she remembers is being in the kitchen, and the awful realization that another beating was starting. But she does not know why. Billy was wild—picking her up and actually throwing her against the walls; pounding her head on the stove and counter tops; knocking her down, dragging her up, and knocking her down again. Kim remembers holding her head down, trying to protect her face with her hands, and saying, "Please, Billy! Please, Billy. . . . Please stop! Please stop. . . . " over and over.

The next thing Kim remembers is standing in the living room facing Billy, putting a 7mm rifle to her shoulder, and firing once. She remembers a huge sound. Billy sat down. Kim just stood there and waited for him to say something; to get up, to yell at her. But he didn't move, just sighed. Kim screamed "Billy!" but he didn't seem to hear her. She put the gun down and ran to telephone Billy's brother. She said quietly, "Richard,

I just shot Billy.'' Then she called the operator for help, but was becoming disoriented and could not remember directions to their house. When the police arrived, Billy was dead and Kim was sitting at the kitchen table, crying. Her clothes were torn, she had bruises, cuts, and abrasions, and bald patches on her head. As the police were taking her out, Kim asked them, "Please, can't I just go back and say goodbye?" She couldn't believe she would never see Billy again. She was taken to a hospital for x-rays, and then to jail, where she was booked for murder.

———

Almost all the findings from the homicide study are evident in the case of Kim and Billy Hall. Child abuse was present in the backgrounds of both the woman and the man, as well as sexual abuse in the woman's childhood; and, consistent with theories on the intergenerational transmission of violence, both Kim and Billy had witnessed severe abuse of their mothers by their fathers or by another male partner. Billy had a history of violence, beginning in early adolescence, as well as a record of arrests and convictions for assaults on others. He was easily angered and known for his tendency to use his fists. His anger was extreme in relation to the events that might trigger it, and his aggression was directed toward co-workers and male friends, as well as toward female partners.

Typical of most relationships in the homicide group, Kim and Billy's became serious very quickly; they were together almost constantly from their first meeting. Kim was living with Billy by the time the first assault occurred, although, except for his relationship with her, she knew very little about him.

The first incident of violence seemed to Kim to come "out of the blue.'' She had never been hit or slapped by Billy before, and she reported responses of overwhelming shock and fear—both to the fact that the assault occurred at all and to its severity. In a typical victim reaction, she refused offers of outside intervention at the time of the first assault, and did not attempt to leave Billy after the assault; instead, she acquiesced to his wishes and his relatives' wishes to go on as if nothing had happened. Consistent with patterns in the homicide group, Billy reassured Kim that the violence would not occur again, although the "reason" for the incident was still attributed to her: It was because she had been "running off at the mouth.''

Over time, Billy's aggression escalated both in frequency and severity and, once an assault had begun, there was little Kim could do to end it. Billy also made repeated threats to kill Kim, and—as with prior accounts from the cases of Mary and Chuck Wheeler, Janet and Rick VanHorn, Bella and Isaac Harris, Karen and Hal Simon, and Molly and Jim Johnson—guns were used to threaten and intimidate. Billy was contrite after abusive incidents, particularly early in the relationship and, again like Hal Simon, Mark Miller, and others, expressed concern and remorse when he realized the extent of the damage he had done or when he was not sure that Kim would recover. However, as with the other cases, this awareness and remorse did not deter a repetition of the violence in the future. As in the reports of most women in the homicide group, by the end of the relationship it was hard to find traces of that early concern. There was also almost a complete cessation of affectionate or loving behavior between incidents in the final months before Billy's death.

As with other types of victims, Kim's reaction to Billy's repeated attacks included shock, fear, and increasing levels of anxiety. The difficulty in accurately defining the seriousness of a situation—so often noted in victims—was accentuated in Kim's case by the many ways in which others turned away from her plight: for example, as people averted their eyes from Kim's injuries or pretended they were not there, and refrained from intervention during public attacks; and as Billy's family sympathized with her after beatings, yet always returned her to his home. Kim responded to the assaults with childlike and dependent behavior; again, this typical victim reaction was intensified by Kim's prior history of victimization. The sexual abuse, especially being forced to perform oral sex and the sexual assaults that occurred in the car, were reminiscent of similar attacks Kim experienced when she was young. Her reaction of curling up and trying to hide after beatings was a response she had first developed in childhood.

Although Kim left Billy many times, she was unable to plan to carry out an effective escape, or to see other workable alternatives to her life of victimization. Because of his beatings and threats and the fear he inspired in others, as well as the extreme differences in their physical size, Kim developed a perception of Billy as so powerful that she could never completely leave him. Billy would plead with Kim to return and promise to be better; early in the relationship, Kim, like the other victims, entertained some hopes that this improvement would occur. As the violence and threats became more severe, these hopes diminished, but Kim's concerns about Billy's possible retaliation still prevented her from taking any effective action when she was away.

Typical of women in the homicide group, the final months of Kim and Billy's relationship was marked by a nearly constant level of tension and threat and by extremely frequent attacks, both non-sexual and sexual. This resulted in physical and emotional debi-litation for Kim, who reported marked changes in sleeping and eating patterns, an inability to concentrate or to reason, and a general sense of numbness and exhaustion.

The last shred of hope disappeared when Billy killed Kim's pets. Destruction of animals was reported quite frequently by women in the homicide group (e.g., in the case of Karen and Hal Simon, and in the story of Molly and Jim). As in Kim's case, these incidents often seemed to the women a representation of their own death.

Of the seven identified variables that distinguished women in the homicide group from those in the comparison group, five are found in the case of Kim and Billy Hall: frequency of assaultive incidents, severity of the woman's injuries, frequency of forced intercourse or other sexual acts by the man, frequency of the man's intoxication, and threats to kill by the man. Billy did not use drugs other than alcohol and, to my knowledge, Kim never threatened to commit suicide; however, by the end of the rela-tionship, she began to wish she were dead.

Due to alcohol intoxication, Kim does not remember much of the final incident. It is typical for pieces of these memories to be gone, even for women who were not drinking at the time, due to injuries they may have received during the incident and to the shock of the homicide itself. Yet it seemed to Kim that this beat-ing was so much more severe than the others that, in retrospect, she is still convinced that she could not have survived it had she taken no action. Like other women in the homicide group, Kim did not immediately realize how seriously Billy was injured after she shot him. She called for help immediately, and made no attempt to cover up the fact that she was the assailant. As was also typical of these cases, although Kim was obviously the victim of a physical attack—in fact her injuries seemed so serious that she was first taken to the hospital for examination—she was almost immediately jailed and booked for murder. Her claims of self-defense were not taken into account in the crime with which she was charged, and Kim's case would be the first time the application of a self-defense plea by a battered woman had been tried in her state.

# *9*

# The Legal System and Battered Women

Ironically, although many women in the homicide group had made repeated unsuccessful appeals to the police for protection and assistance (e.g., the cases of Sharon Bikson and Irene Miller), the same system that failed to protect them from their partner's violence immediately arrested and prosecuted them when they responded in their own defense. Women who had never before been in legal trouble suddenly found themselves jailed and charged with murder, while they were still experiencing the impact of their partner's final assault and the shock and horror of having killed another human being who was also their intimate and mate.

In the first few hours after their arrests, the women were fingerprinted, searched, and interrogated about the deaths of their mates. Many gave statements that would later play a crucial role in "proving" their intent and state of mind at the time of the homicide; although, in those initial hours, the women were typically severely disoriented and unable to give a clear accounting of events. In fact, most of the women remembered little of that time period except for their own terror and confusion. One woman listened in total disbelief as a tape-recorded statement she had made shortly after the incident was played back during her trial; she had no memory of even giving the statement. In some cases, police or others attempted to tell the women what "must have happened" at the scene, confusing their recall even more.

Some women also saw the male officers as threatening and powerful, and reacted to them with fear and compliance, altering their statements to agree with what they thought their interrogators were demanding to hear, out of the same survival responses they had developed in threatening interactions with their mates.

Almost all the women made every attempt to cooperate with the police and other officials, freely acknowledging that they had been the assailants and expressing disbelief and grief that they had brought harm to the abuser. Over and over, women said, "I didn't mean to kill him! I only meant to warn him, or to stop him from hurting me." For women with a history of physical assault, and especially for those who had been sexually abused by their mates, standard strip and search procedures were particularly upsetting, and sometimes seemed like another attack. Requirements that they undress and have pictures taken of their injuries, although in the best interest of the women's defense, were also threatening or terribly humiliating for some women. One woman said she was informed that her husband had died while she was stripped to the waist and standing in front of a camera. In the rapidity of events—arrest, interrogation, being jailed, being charged with murder—the fact that these women had just become widowed, albeit by their own hand, became lost in the shuffle. The killing of their partner negated any consideration they might have received for their loss; this seemed to hold true even when the woman was injured and claiming self-defense.

A few women were hysterical or in shock at the time of their arrest, and had to be hospitalized for days or weeks before they could be transferred to jail. For instance, Janet VanHorn was completely disoriented and was committed to a psychiatric setting for several weeks. And Mary Wheeler was found in a deep state of physical shock when officers arrived at the scene; she was hospitalized for medical observation and was unaware of her surroundings until late the next day. Mary remembers waking up in the hospital and not knowing why she was there. She was cold and thirsty, and—since she had been walking out of the house with the gun intending to commit suicide—thought she must have shot herself and survived. For these women, memories of the homicide itself were almost completely absent and, unlike other women in the homicide group, whose recall improved, their memories typically did not return over time.

Women were presumed guilty until proven innocent. When arrested, the women were separated from their children and, sometimes, custody was at least temporarily removed. In one case, prosecutors decided that a woman's five-year-old child—the only witness to the homicide event—was to be the star witness for the state, and attempted to deny the mother all access to her so that she would not contaminate the child's testimony.

In Molly Johnson's case, she was immediately separated from her son, Kevin, who was placed in a foster home. Molly was allowed only occasional visits with him, and her depression over the homicide incident was deepened by this separation from her child. Molly found the separation particularly upsetting, since it had been Kevin she was trying to protect.

Kevin developed severe eating problems, became unable to keep down solid foods, and lost weight rapidly. They had never been apart before, and Molly says Kevin had never been sick before. Even though the facts in her case were consistent with self-defense, Molly eventually asked to plead guilty to a lesser charge, so she could be reunited with her son.

Yet in spite of the aftermath of the homicides—the realization of the seriousness of the charges against them, and the possible ramifications of conviction—many of the women experienced an underlying sense of relief from the fact that they were no longer in physical danger. Their injuries gradually healed, although bruises and scars were still visible many months later. Some women reported that they were able to sleep through the night for the first time; others who had been nearly unable to eat during the final months of their relationships began to gain weight.

A few women became markedly suicidal, and were watched closely by family members or jail personnel. (None of the women completed a suicide during the period between arrest and coming to trial, however.) Some also reported delayed reactions of grieving their partner's death, especially after their trials had concluded and their attention was no longer so completely focused on the legal process. A typical example of this was displayed by one woman who called her attorney's office a year after the homicide. She had just been sentenced and released on probation; and now, back in her own home, was faced with her husband's clothes in the closet, personal effects in the bathroom, papers lying out on his desk in the den, just as they had been at the time of his death. Pictures of the two of them together set about on tables; his overcoat and boots still waited in the hall. The realization of his death hit her in a way she had not been able to experience in the unfamiliar surroundings of jail, and she was not sure she wanted to go on living in a world where he was gone and she had killed him.

In the homicide cases, we often noted a reactive period of acute depression just after the verdict was returned, both in those women who were convicted and sentenced, and in those who were acquitted and released. As illustrated by the example above, women attempting to return to "normal life" were especially hard hit, with the reality of their widowhood—trying to decide how to structure their futures, sorting through the deceased's belongings and personal effects, and attending to matters such as life insurance and the disposition of assets that could not be decided until the outcome of the trial was known.

Women reentering the community were also faced with the stigma of having killed their husbands, even if they had been acquitted of any wrongdoing in the death. For example, one woman, acquitted in the death of her abuser, found that she was no longer welcome in any of her friends' homes. Although several of her friends had testified on her behalf at the trial, she was no longer someone with whom they wanted to associate in their private lives. Many women reported the loss of friendships, or that acquaintances turned away in embarrassment if they met on the street. In some cases, the women's children were also shunned or ridiculed at school, or came home heartbroken because the parents of their friends would not permit them to see one another.

In addition, women were often faced with drastically altered family relationships. In some cases, the women's children had also lost their father in the homicide, and the ambivalence this could produce toward the mother who took his life caused severe strain in some relationships. Although many children were strong supporters of their mothers during the entire process, others became estranged from their mothers, adding to the women's sense of grief and loss. As would be expected, relationships with the men's families were also either terminated or very strained. In some cases, relatives of the slain husbands even threatened the women's lives, particularly if the woman was acquitted and they thought that justice had not been served. Women in the homicide group expressed a great deal of sadness over the loss of some of these relationships; again, such estrangements also affected the children of these couples, if they had been close to relatives on the fathers' side.

## *Entering a Plea*

Shortly after their arrest, women in the homicide group had to choose whether to go to trial on the charges against them or attempt to negotiate a plea and plead guilty to lesser charges. Most of these women had no prior experience with the criminal justice system, and relied heavily on their attorneys for guidance. Yet the choice was an especially difficult one.

The most common plea arrangement offered in these cases was one of voluntary manslaughter, with an agreement that the woman would be given a reduced jail sentence, or would spend several years on probation but no time in jail. Many of the women were so emotionally fragile after the homicide incidents that the thought of going through a public trial was more than they could contemplate. Even when their attorneys believed the potential for winning was strong, and advised them to seek an acquittal, some of the women preferred to negotiate a plea and end the process as quickly as possible. As in the case of Molly Johnson, these decisions were frequently made with the welfare of others in mind as well. Many women were concerned about an extended separation from their children, and accepted a plea bargain rather than take their case to trial and risk conviction. The fact that these women were charged with such a serious felony (first- or second-degree murder, rather than manslaughter) also made a plea bargain seem the safest option for many women, since the penalties if convicted would be correspondingly severe.

However, agreeing to a negotiated plea requires that the woman plead "guilty" to a criminal offense, and abandon all claim that the killing was justified under self-defense statutes provided by law. If the facts of the case were consistent with self-defense, especially if there was good corroborating evidence, the women's attorneys frequently encouraged them to go through with the trial. For some women in the homicide group, the opportunity to take their case to court offered a first step in standing up for their rights, in spite of their dread of the process and the risk of conviction. Fifty-six percent of the women eventually argued their case on the basis of self-defense, 8 percent entered a diminished capacity or insanity plea, and 33 percent pled guilty to a lesser charge in return for leniency in sentencing. (In one case, self-defense arguments were not allowed by the court, and in Sharon Bikson's case, the charges were dropped.)

When a woman decides to stand trial she enters a legal system developed over the centuries to treat men and women, husbands and wives, very differently, based on deeply rooted assumptions about appropriate male and female roles and behaviors. An understanding of these assumptions and the laws traditionally applied to marital violence is essential to an understanding of the experiences of battered women throughout their abusive relationships, as well as when standing trial for the act that ended the relationship.

## ASSAULTS AGAINST WIVES: A PART OF THE ANCIENT LAW

Assaults of wives by their husbands have long been considered a family, rather than a legal, matter. Traditionally, the courts have been reluctant to intervene between a man and his wife; to "usurp" a man's authority over the members of his household, or to invade the privacy of the home. In addition, until the late 1800s, it was *legal* for a man to physically assault his wife, even in this country.[1] The very acts discussed in the previous chapters—and that some readers find so shocking—were specifically allowed by this country's laws: Up until 1871, a man could not be punished for "beating [his wife] with a stick, pulling her hair, choking her, spitting in her face, [or] kicking her about the floor."[2]

Such physical domination of wives by husbands was firmly grounded in ancient laws and customs. The first known "law of marriage" was formalized by Romulus (who was credited with the founding of Rome in 753 B.C.) and required married women "as having no other refuge, to conform themselves entirely to the temper of their husbands and the husbands to rule their wives as necessary and inseparable possessions."[3] The attitudes contained in this directive, ancient though the formulation may be, sound hauntingly like the sentiments expressed by men in the violent relationships we have been discussing.

In the late 1400s, Friar Cherubino of Siena, in his *Rules of Marriage*, operationalized the *process* by which a husband was to rule his wife, recommending:

> When you see your wife commit an offense, don't rush at her with insults and violent blows. . . . Scold her sharply, bully

and terrify her. And if this still doesn't work . . . take up a stick and beat her soundly, for it is better to punish the body and correct the soul than to damage the soul and spare the body. . . . Then readily beat her, not in rage but out of charity and concern for her soul, so that the beating will redound to your merit and her good.[4]

In his extensive commentary on English law, Sir William Blackstone explained the powers of authority given to husbands in legal, rather than moralistic, terms. He noted:

For as [the husband] is to answer for her misbehavior, the law thought it reasonable to intrust him with this power of chastisement, in the same moderation that a man is allowed to correct his apprentices or children. . . . [5]

Blackstone went on to reassure his readers that, "this power of correction was contained within reasonable bounds. . . ."; although the notation delineates some legalized "chastisements" that sound markedly more violent than contained, as when Blackstone observes:

The civil law gave the husband the same, or a larger, authority over his wife: allowing him for some misdemeanors, to beat his wife severely with scourges and cudgels . . . for others only moderate chastisement.[6]

Even if a husband killed his wife, it was not considered a major offense. Yet for a wife to kill her husband was to kill her lord and master, and was an act comparable to treason. As Blackstone commented:

Husband and wife, in the language of the law, are styled baron and feme. . . . [I]f the baron kills his feme it is the same as if he had killed a stranger, or any other person; but if the feme kills her baron, it is regarded by the laws as a much more atrocious crime, as she not only breaks through the restraints of humanity and conjugal affection, but throws off all subjection to the authority of her husband. And therefore the law denominates her crime a species of treason, and condemns her to the same punishment as if she had killed the king. And for every species of treason . . . the sentence of woman was to be drawn and burnt alive.[7]

English common laws, as well as Blackstone's interpretation of them, greatly influenced the formation of laws in the United States. In 1824, the Mississippi Supreme Court, although specifying moderation and the application of force only in cases of "emergency," upheld the ancient principle of a man's right to physically assault his wife as judged appropriate by the man—and continued the courts' assurance that the husband could so assault her without fear of prosecution or discredit. The court directed:

> Let the husband be permitted to exercise the right of moderate chastisement, in cases of great emergency, and use salutary restraints in every case of misbehavior, without being subjected to vexatious prosecutions, resulting in the mutual discredit and shame of all parties concerned.[8]

This reassurance of impunity from prosecution was reiterated in 1864 by a North Carolina court, ruling on a case in which a man had choked his wife. Again, the justification for both the use of force and a policy of nonintervention as the supposed "right" of a husband to direct and discipline his spouse as he might a child is reminiscent of rationales offered by abusive men in the 1970s and '80s for physical attacks against their mates. The court ruled that,

> . . . the law permits [a man] to use towards his wife such a degree of force, as is necessary to control an unruly temper, and make her behave herself; and unless some permanent injury be inflicted, or there be an excess of violence, or such a degree of cruelty as shows that it is inflicted to gratify his own bad passions, the law will not invade the domestic forum, or go behind the curtain. It prefers to leave the parties to themselves, as the best mode of inducing them to make the matter up and live together as man and wife should.[9]

It is ironic that the behaviors some now suspect as pathological in abused women—their attempts to work things out with their mates and continue to live together "as man and wife should" —fit the letter and intent of the laws on which this country was founded, in addition to accurately reflecting the implied lack of societally acceptable alternatives to the violence they experience.

In 1866, the actions a husband could legally take against his wife were amended, giving a man the right to beat his wife "with a stick as large as his finger but not larger than his thumb."[10] This law was "created as an example of compassionate reform," since it modified the weapons a husband could use on his wife's person.[11] Alabama became the first state to rescind a husband's legal right to beat his wife when, in 1871, the court declared:

> The privilege, ancient though it be, to beat her with a stick, to pull her hair, choke her, spit in her face or kick her about the floor, or to inflict upon her like indignities, is not now acknowledged by our law. . . . [T]he wife is entitled to the same protection of the law that the husband can invoke for himself. . . . [12]

A North Carolina court followed suit in 1874, but qualified its ruling by limiting the cases for which the court deemed legal interventions appropriate. The court advised:

> If no permanent injury has been inflicted, nor malice, cruelty nor dangerous violence shown by the husband, it is better to draw the curtain, shut out the public gaze, and leave the parties to forget and forgive.[13]

This "curtain rule" has since been used, both officially and unofficially, to justify both the lack of responsiveness to the pleas of abused women for protection and assistance in cases of assault by husbands, and a lack of serious consideration and intervention when the women insist that their voices be heard. A woman's perception of helplessness—both against the physical strength and willingness to do harm of a violent man, and the indifference or inability of the legal system to adequately address her plight—is in some measure simply good reality testing, rather than an unfounded delusion arising out of pathology.

Today, no American jurisdiction legally permits a husband to strike his wife.[14] Physical attacks against a marital partner fall under various assault statutes, depending on the jurisdiction: assault and battery, assault and infliction of serious injury, felonious assault, assault with intent to do great bodily harm less than murder, assault with intent to commit murder, and assault with intent to maim.[15]

Many jurisdictions are now adopting new mandates about the handling of family violence cases. For example, Sherman and Berk obtained results from an experiment on police responses to domestic violence calls in Minneapolis that suggested a deterrent effect on the recurrence of violence for those men who were arrested, as opposed to those who were counseled by police or who were separated from their victims for a period of several hours.[16] Changes in police procedures based on these findings are now being implemented across the country. Other changes in procedure are a result of law suits brought against police departments or prosecutors for inaction or discrimination in cases involving battered women.[17] And individual states are now writing legislation specifically to address the problem. Connecticut recently became the seventh state to enact a domestic violence bill. This legislation requires, among other things, arrest of the individual committing the assault, whether or not the victim is willing to sign a complaint; a court hearing the day following the assault; and a mandatory program for first-time misdemeanor offenders involving a fine and compulsory attendance at a series of classes on the causes of physical violence.[18]

Yet, although there have been a variety of improvements in the past few years in the criminal justice system's response to the problem of violence by a marital partner, these policies are only now being put into effect and both the policies and their implementation are highly inconsistent across jurisdictions. The old laws are a reflection of our previous attitudes, and such deeply entrenched attitudes take a very long time to change. In 1980, Ann Jones cited a Michigan police bulletin about domestic arguments that cautions officers to "smooth things over by appealing to the woman's 'vanity'" and reminds them that "the officer should never create a police problem where there is only a *family* problem" [emphasis mine]; a county in Indiana where the sheriff recorded wife assaults "if at all, with complaints of dogs barking"; and a 1976 Chiefs of Police directive finally suggesting that "wife abuse" should not be considered "a victimless crime"![19]

Police officers still routinely classify assaults between partners as misdemeanors, rather than as criminal offenses,[20] and there is some evidence that they do not respond to the calls of a female victim as readily as calls made by a third party (or, as reported in some studies, calls made by a man).[21] When police officers do arrive at the scene of a "domestic disturbance," in most jurisdictions they rarely arrest the assailant, unless severe injury has occurred (or unless the assailant is drunk and/or assaultive or rude to the officers themselves).[22] For instance, in studying 237 female victims of a partner's violence, one study found that "arrests were made in only about half the incidents, despite the fact that . . . injuries [resulted] in 80 percent of the cases.[23] Police may also communicate to the woman their expectation that the case will not be prosecuted; and this acts to further dissuade victims from taking the risk of pressing charges.[24]

If a woman does attempt to press charges, she may find that she is again subtly discouraged from doing so. Prosecutors protest that such cases are often a waste of time because the women so frequently drop the charges, although there are no data to demonstrate that they in fact want charges dropped any more often than do other complainants who know their assailants. As long as prosecution of the man is left to the woman's discretion, rather than to the district attorney's, she will be susceptible to the abuser's loving contrition, as well as to his threats. There is also the probability that abused women are *allowed* to drop charges more often than are victims of other crimes.[25] Typically, prosecution in these cases is rarely vigorously pursued until someone is seriously hurt or killed. Effective prosecution is needed at a much earlier level, before the violence has reached life-threatening proportions.

Even when a woman comes to the court claiming that her life is in danger, her fears may not be taken seriously. On September 21, 1986, the *Boston Globe* ran a story entitled, "Judge criticized after woman's death." In March of 1986, Pamela Dunn sought police protection from her husband Paul. She reported that her husband of two months had locked her in their apartment and removed the telephone, and that he had beaten her, choked her, and threatened to kill her. Although she obtained an order restraining her husband from contacting her, district court Judge Paul Heffernan chastized her for "doing a terrible disservice to the taxpayers" by taking up the court's time when it "has a lot more serious matters to contend with." The judge's impression of the case before him was perhaps made even more clear when he told Pamela's husband, "You want to gnaw on her and she on you, fine, but let's not do it at the taxpayers' expense"—a statement that suggests the judge viewed the violence in this case as both trivial and mutual. Judge Heffernan also ridiculed Pamela's request for a police escort to accompany her to the couple's apartment so she could pack some clothes, telling her, "[Y]ou don't need the police," just to "go there and act as an adult."

On August 16, Paul Dunn accosted his estranged wife at the bus stop as she was returning to her parents' home from work. Pamela's mother was there to meet her. According to police reports, he sprayed mace in the mother's face and, when Pamela tried to escape, he shot her in the abdomen, dragged her into his car, and sped away. Pamela's battered body was found the next morning, face down in a mudpuddle at a local rubbish dump. Paul Dunn, charged with first-degree murder in the shooting, stabbing, and strangulation death of his wife, had not been found at the time of this writing.

A Massachusetts woman is murdered by her husband or boyfriend every 22 days, according to statistics compiled by the state Department of Public Health.[26] The state instituted an abuse prevention act eight years ago, specifically designed to offer protection to women whose lives were endangered by their mates. Yet, when a *Globe* reporter discussed Pamela Dunn's case with the presiding judge of the district court in which the case was heard, Judge Tampone "was candid about his contempt for the abuse prevention act" and gave his opinion that, "With all due respect . . . these are matters to be resolved within the marital relationship." Pamela Dunn's file was closed on Wednesday, September 17, the day her six-month abuse prevention order was due to run out.[27]

The handling of this case illustrates the power of those entrusted with the implementation of new laws and policies to either expedite or impede the protection those laws were meant to offer. Battered women often risk reprisal or even death, in an effort to seek out legal remedies, only to find the legal system unable or unwilling to help them. An article by Silver and Kates suggests that possibly the reason that women, who do not typically kill others, kill family members is that it is family members who are threatening their lives.[28] A lack of effective legal protection from assaults and threats by martial partners sets up the conditions whereby victims may finally believe it necessary to protect themselves.

# GOING TO TRIAL FOR MURDER[29]

Legal definitions vary somewhat by state, but designations concerning homicides have their roots in English common law and some general definitions can be given. *Murder* is legally defined as the willful killing of another person with "malice aforethought," or malicious intent. Modern definitions further divide this category into first-degree and second-degree murder. *First-degree murder* designations are given those homicides involving "deliberation or premeditation," whereas *second-degree murder* involves malicious intent without premeditation. *Manslaughter* is used to designate the unlawful killing of another person without malice. *Voluntary manslaughter* indicates an intent to kill, but implies that the act was sudden and occurred during a violent passion or with great provocation. The use of the term "passion" usually connotes extreme rage (but some courts have found the presence of other strong emotions—e.g., fright, terror, or "wild desperation"—to be sufficient).[30] *Involuntary manslaughter* is the designation used when the death of another person results by accident without the intent to kill, and this category can include assaults that end in death. *Homicide* includes both the categories of murder and manslaughter, although homicide in itself is not a crime and is *justified* if the act was committed in self-defense, or, in some cases, if it was committed in the defense of others.[31]

## *The Plea of Self-Defense*

In general, *self-defense* is defined as the justifiable use of a reasonable amount of force against an adversary, when one reasonably believes that one is in immediate danger of unlawful bodily harm and that the use of such force is necessary to avoid this harm.[32] Such imminent bodily harm need only be *reasonably* perceived by the victim. This perception may later turn out to have been erroneous. The defendant's perception of how much force is needed to prevent further attack must also be reasonable.[33] Whether the use of force against an assailant is justified on the grounds of self-defense depends in large part on the perceptions of the defender, and whether those perceptions can be shown to be reasonable in light of the circumstances of the case. Thus, the key to the use of the self-defense plea for abused women lies in the definition of what perceptions are reasonable for a female victim of a partner's violence.[34]

## Modifications of the Plea

*Imminent danger.*     The imminent danger component of the self-defense plea is predicated on the one-time violent encounter most common to male adversaries or attacks by strangers. It does not take into account the cumulative effects of repeated violence, nor does it account for the prediction of repeated violence in the future.[35] Yet women who have been repeatedly assaulted by their partners over time become sensitized to cues of impending assault. Elizabeth Bochnak, in her volume on women's self-defense, writes:

> The battered woman learns to recognize the small signs that precede periods of escalated violence. She learns to distinguish subtle changes in tone of voice, facial expression, and levels of danger. She is in a position to know, perhaps with greater certainty than someone attacked by a stranger, that the batterer's threat is real and will be acted upon.[36]

Thus, an abused woman may kill her mate during the period of threat that precedes a violent incident, right before the violence escalates to the more dangerous levels of an acute battering episode.[37] Or she may take action against him during a lull in an assaultive incident, or after it has culminated, in an effort to prevent a recurrence of the violence.[38] As traditionally applied, such cases would not be covered under the plea of self-defense.

In *People v. Garcia*,[39] case law was established that extended the interpretation of imminent danger beyond the immediate time period of the assault. Inez Garcia was physically and sexually assaulted by two men who were known to her. After the attack, the perpetrators told Garcia they would return to do her further harm. Several hours later, Inez Garcia encountered one of her assailants, who drew his knife, and she shot and killed him. Garcia's initial defense was based on a "not guilty by reason of insanity plea," but she was found to be sane and was convicted. Upon winning a retrial, Garcia asserted a self-defense explanation of her actions and was acquitted.[40] The Garcia case established an important legal precedent for self-defense, in finding that it was *reasonable* for Inez Garcia to believe that she was in imminent danger of further bodily harm or death several hours after she was attacked.

*Equal force.*   Actions taken in self-defense must also be shown to have used the least amount of force necessary to prevent imminent bodily harm or death.[41] A person may respond to an attack with an equal amount of force, but not with greater force.[42] The defender's perception of how much force is needed to prevent further attack must also be reasonable. Like the imminent danger component of the self-defense plea, this "equal force" rule rests on the assumption of two male adversaries, approximately equal in size, strength, and physical training. Because it did not take into account a disparity in physical size and strength, application of this standard to female victims of a male's violence was often problematic. As Zimring, Mukherjee, and Van Winkle observe in their study of intersexual homicide in Chicago, "The greater physical strength of most males suggests that lethal weapons are a necessary condition for women killing men."[43]

A Washington Supreme Court decision in *State v. Wanrow*[44] clarified the application of this standard of self-defense for a woman as compared to a man. The issue before the court was whether a woman could use a weapon to defend herself when threatened if her male assailant was unarmed. In her first trial, Yvonne Wanrow was convicted of murder when the trial judge instructed the jury that a reasonable person "has no right to repel a threatened assault with naked hands, by the use of a deadly weapon, in a deadly manner. . . ."[45] The Supreme Court granted Wanrow a new trial, however, and observed that "[i]n our society women suffer from a conspicuous lack of access to training in and the means of developing those skills necessary to effectively repel a male assailant without resorting to the use of deadly weapons."[46] The court directed that "care must be taken to assure that our self-defense instructions afford women the right" to have these differences taken into account.

*Accuracy of perceptions.*   The law of self-defense also allows for the defender to have been reasonable but wrong. This recognizes the effect that danger and fear have on an individual's perceptions and judgments.[47] As Justice Oliver Wendall Holmes, Jr. noted, the "law does not require detached reflection in the presence of an upraised knife.''[48] This principle may also apply when the danger, although reasonably perceived, is not borne out by events. For instance, in the case of *Wyoming v. Austin,*[49] it was found that the defendant's perception that a flash of silver light was a gun—although it later turned out to be a cigarette lighter— was reasonable, in view of her past history with her husband's assaultive and threatening behavior.

***The duty to retreat.*** In order for self-defense statutes to apply, some jurisdictions also required that the defender first exhaust all possible means of retreat before responding to force with force. An exception was usually made for attacks occurring in one's own home, where the defendant was free to stand his (or her) own ground and fight back.[50] Even in those jurisdictions in which retreat was required, the defendant need not retreat unless it could be done in complete safety. Although a majority of American jurisdictions now hold that there is no duty to retreat before using deadly force if the individual being attacked has reason to believe that the assailant will kill her or do serious bodily harm,[51] society continues to expect that a woman *should* retreat, and the response is one of unease and censure when a woman takes action in her own defense.

Traditional American attitudes encourage men to be active in defending their persons, families, and property; however, a woman is expected to have a husband, father, or son do it for her, or turn to the police for protection and help (e.g., the classic Supreme Court opinion in *Bradwell v. State of Illinois,* 16 Wall. 130, 141, 21 L. Ed. 2d 442 [1873], which asserted, "Man is, or should be, woman's protector and defender.") However, if one's *husband* is the assailant, and if the criminal justice system does not provide adequate protection against this type of assailant because of the intimate relationship, physically abused and threatened women who find themselves unable to get away are left without recourse. It is ironic that, although society is more comfortable with a *man's* claims of self-defense, it is women, at least in the case of homicides between partners, who are the most likely to actually kill in self-defense.[52] In cases in which the battered woman kills her abuser, the burden of proof usually falls on the woman to show why she could not leave the relationship, even though legally she need only demonstrate that she was in danger and was legitimately standing her ground in her own home.

## Applications of the Self-Defense Plea to Battered Women

In the case of a battered woman, it is necessary to document clearly that the use of deadly force resulted because the woman believed her life to be in imminent danger.[53] A *history* of physical abuse alone does not justify the killing of the abuser. Having been physically assaulted by the abuser in the past is pertinent to such cases only as it contributes to the defendant's state of mind at the time the killing occurred; e.g., in that it formed the basis for the woman's perception of being in imminent danger of severe bodily harm or death at the hands of her partner.[54]

Again, a knowledge of the history of the prior violence and the specific context within which the incident occurred is essential for understanding the woman's perceptions at the time of the homicide and determining whether a plea of self-defense is appropriate.[55] As Nancy Fiora-Gormally notes, the life of a battered woman is "replete with prior provocation, continuing apprehension, and the constant threat of impending danger."[56] Thus, the reasonableness of an abused woman's perception of danger and the ability to predict the imminence of an attack can be established, based on her history of past victimization.[57] The partner's reputation for violence against others is also relevant to a perception of danger when threatened or assaulted by him. The issue is not the development of a *new* standard of self-defense for women, but the adjustment of existing statutes to account for differences in the experiences of women and men—particularly women faced with a male assailant, and women who are the victims of repeated violent assaults by one assailant—so that the *same* standard can be applied to all victims.

## Impaired Mental State Defenses

*Mens rea.*   The law requires that certain elements of an act be proven, before it defines a behavior as criminal. First, it must be proven that the accused actually committed the behavior in question. For battered women who kill, this is rarely at issue. Most of these women call for assistance for the man and readily admit that they were the assailants. The second element involves the question of an individual's state of mind—or *mens rea*—when perpetrating the act. In the past, the self-defense plea was rarely applied to women who killed their spouses or other partners. An insanity or incapacity defense was routinely applied to cases of female homicide, in an attempt to "excuse" the behavior, rather than to justify it. In fact, many of the women now incarcerated—in prisons or mental institutions—for the death of an abusive mate might not be considered guilty of a criminal act if they were to be tried today.

*Insanity and diminished capacity* defenses are based on the supposition that the act in question was wrong, but that the mental state of the perpetrator was so impaired at the time of the incident that the individual should not be held accountable for those actions. Because memory loss is often associated with homicides by battered women—which might suggest a disassociated reaction at the time of the incident—and because of some abused women's disorientation and confusion just after the incident, a defense of impaired mental state is often assumed to be appropriate. As we learn more about battered women, however, those who kill do not appear to be mentally ill, but rather seem to be reacting to the level of violence perpetrated against them. An understanding of the circumstances that preceded the homicide usually leads to a conclusion of self-defense. Yet, in our society, women who commit violent acts are more typically seen as crazy or irrational than as behaving reasonably.[58] For instance, in a study of college students, the students judged female killers to be more deranged than male killers, even when their backgrounds and the details of the homicide events were held constant.[59]

Of course, the self-defense plea is not appropriate for all homicides committed by battered women against their abusers. However, application of an impaired mental state defense has several drawbacks and should not be used in those cases in which self-defense statutes would apply. Jurors are often suspicious of insanity pleas, doubting the credibility of both the defense and psychiatrically drawn conclusions. In a homicide committed by a battered woman, an impaired mental state defense also shifts the focus back toward proving pathology in the woman, and away from her *right* to be free from harm inflicted by another. In addition, in some states, an "acquittal" (e.g., a verdict of "not guilty by reason of insanity") means the individual must then undergo mandatory commitment to a mental hospital for an indeterminate length of time. Use of the insanity plea thus does a disservice to women whose actions are reasonable within the parameters of self-defense, and should be reserved only for those cases in which the commission of the act was clearly related to an abnormal mental condition.

Even when a plea of self-defense is offered, the primary focus of the defense often rests on the woman's helplessness and victimization. Much time is spent in explaining why the woman stayed with an abusive mate and the effect of repeated assaults and threats on her ability to cope effectively with her situation. Expert witness testimony on the "battered woman syndrome" (a term used both to describe patterns of violence typically experienced by battered women and the psychological impact this violence has on the women),[60] although intended to address damaging myths and misconceptions, also contributes in a subtle way to an image of maladjustment or pathology. Just the use of the term "syndrome" connotes impairment to most people, including judges and jurors.[61]

Elizabeth Schneider, in a recent article on the application of the self-defense plea to battered women, points out that an overemphasis on "the passive, victimized aspects of battered women's experience" makes it difficult to then explain the woman's *agency* in the action of self-defense, and detracts from the appropriate focus of the plea: the "circumstances which might explain the homicide as a woman's necessary choice to save her own life."[62] Schneider goes on to express concern that:

> Judicial willingness to find women's perspective acceptable may relate to the fact that the perspective courts are hearing and to which they are responding is that of *damaged* women, not of women who perceive themselves to be, and may in fact be, acting competently, assertively and rationally in light of the alternatives.[63]

Such assumptions run the risk of resurrecting the old idea of a "diminished capacity" defense for women who kill their abusive mates; again, attempting to excuse the homicide, rather than demonstrating how the actions taken by a woman in imminent fear of extreme bodily harm or death fall within the self-defense criteria provided by law.

# *10*

# Summing Up

This book has focused on patterns of violence in relationships involving physical abuse of women by their male partners, and on the unfolding of events leading up to homicide committed by the woman victim. The intent is to fill in one piece of a very complex puzzle, to shed light on the perceptions and reactions of women who kill their abusive mates and the context within which such homicides occur. Understanding these women's experiences cannot provide "all the answers" about the phenomenon. Abuse of women by male partners is embedded in, and grows out of, society's laws and practices denying women equal self-determination and protection in their relationships with men. There are many approaches to the topic of violence between partners, addressing different aspects of the problem—societal, interactional, and clinical. The emphasis here has been on the progression of violent relationships from courtship to the death of the abuser, and on some of the ways in which these interactions are extensions of our cultural expectations for romance and husband-wife relating.

Violence between partners cannot be adequately understood outside the context within which it occurs. Men's abuse of their mates is sheltered within romantic traditions that assign women the roles of response and submission and men the tasks of initiation, seduction, and control. Until recently, the actual weapons and actions of violence used by some men against their partners were permitted by laws that granted men the "privileges" of authority and the right of chastisement over their wives—privileges not equally granted to women. Although these laws have now been officially rescinded, tacit social support still exists for violence against wives in gender stereotyping that favors, or at least excuses, a man's expression of dominance and control, and in continuing societal reluctance to get involved in family matters. All relationships in this society are affected by and to some extent incorporate the romantic and role-defined prescriptions we have been discussing. Therefore, it is important to examine this continuum of relational styles, from the more normal but still primarily male-determined interactions between men and women, to extreme expressions of dominance in physical assault and brutality.

The problem of violence between partners, once considered of little importance, is now known to affect thousands upon thousands of people in our society, to account for millions of injuries, and to be implicated in a substantial proportion of the homicides occurring between women and men. Figures from nationally representative samples reveal that over 1½ million women in the United States are physically assaulted by a male partner each year. Many of the acts involved in these assaults, including punching, kicking, hitting with an object, beating up, and assaults with a knife or a gun, are quite serious, and many result in injuries to the victims. We now know that attacks by family members are actually more serious, in terms of injuries, than the attacks by strangers we have geared our system to defend against. Men are more likely to assault their female partners than women are to assault male partners, and assaults by husbands appear to involve more of the dangerous and injurious forms of violence—and more repetition of these acts—than do assaults by wives. In studies of injurious assault involving couples, 95 percent of the time it is the woman who gets hurt.

Studies of severely battered women suggest that they are not typically violent toward their mates, either in initiation or response. However, lack of effective legal intervention in cases of wife abuse, and the lack of adequate and established alternatives to protect victims from further aggression, leaves many of these women alone with a danger from which they cannot escape. Homicides that result from abusive relationships remind us of the seriousness of "domestic" violence, and highlight how the lack of adequate intervention and response by all segments of society exacerbates the danger already present in these situations. A society that allows violence against wives to continue by forcing the individual woman to stop the perpetrator's behavior runs the risk that victims may eventually take action that the society does not condone. Homicides resulting from abusive relationships must be examined within the context from which they developed, if the event is to be accurately understood—especially if that homicide is perpetrated by a previously nonviolent individual. Knowing the history of the relationship between the partners then becomes critical, both from a legal and a psychological standpoint.

In focusing on women who kill their abusers, it is important to remember that these cases are the exceptions to the general pattern: In a lethal altercation between partners, it is more typically the woman who loses her life. In 1984, two-thirds of the homicides between partners were of husbands killing wives, while one-third were of wives killing husbands. Given the finding that women are more likely than men to kill in self-defense, and that physical abuse by the man precedes many spousal homicides regardless of the perpetrator, it seems probable that a high proportion of these cases represented the culmination of a battering relationship. As Susan Jacoby points out, in many homicides between partners, the woman kills as a "desperate, final response" to physical threat and attack, whereas the man kills as a "logical extension of the . . . abuse he has been dispensing for years."[1]

Still, it is an extreme reaction for a woman, even a battered woman, to kill. In the current study, battered women charged with the death or attempted murder of their mates were compared to women from abusive relationships in which no lethal incident had occurred, to see if differences between the two groups could be identified. Women in the homicide group were somewhat older than women in the comparison group, and came from a slightly higher class background; however, their level of education and their employment patterns were not significantly different. Although nearly three-quarters of the women in the homicide group had been exposed to violence in childhood, and over half had been the victim of at least one completed or attempted sexual assault, this also did not differentiate them from abused women in the comparison group.

Significant differences appeared primarily between the men with whom the women were involved. Men in the homicide group used drugs more frequently than did men in the comparison group, and they become intoxicated much more often. They were also more frequently given to threats and assaultive behavior: Significantly more men in the homicide group threatened to kill someone other than themselves; more of them abused a child or children, as well as their women partners; and their abuse of their mates was more frequent, more injurious, and more likely to include sexual assault.

Like victims of other types of trauma, women in the homicide group responded to these assaults with reactions of depression, denial, shock, and a since of helplessness and fear. They typically withdrew after the initial assaults and did not attempt escape, or left the assaulter but were talked into returning by his contrition and assurances that the violence would not be repeated. In keeping with cultural expectations regarding women's ways of relating, most women spent a great deal of time attempting to understand why the violence occurred and making adaptations to avoid it. They continued to attach importance to maintaining their relationships with the abusers, responding with care and concern, and attempting to reason and work things out. Yet their responses had no positive effect on the aggressive behavior of their mates. In fact, for most women in the homicide group, the violence they experienced became both more frequent and more severe over the course of their relationships.

As the assaults became more brutal and the abusers seemed increasingly unconcerned about the harm they were inflicting, the women's focus shifted from attempts to understand to an emphasis on survival. Subjected to frequent attacks and living with a constant awareness of danger, their perceptions of alternatives to their violent situations narrowed, based on their knowledge of the abusers' abilities to control and to harm. Like other victims, they chose responses that seemed most likely to minimize the immediate danger, attempting to appease their mates and avoiding actions that might trigger a renewed attack. Many women attempted to leave their partners, but were found and beaten, or intimidated into returning home. Some women did succeed in leaving their abusive partners, but were still experiencing assaults and threats by them months or even years later. The abusers' power to constrain and punish was strengthened by a lack of societal awareness of the women's plight and by the legal barriers against prosecution and effective protection from attack by a mate. This lack of safe alternatives for the women, combined with the men's threats of retaliation if they left and/or prior failed escape attempts, convinced most of these women that they could not escape their partners and survive. Yet the violence within the relationships became increasingly harder to endure. Most of the women began to live with almost an expectation of death.

The women's perception of entrapment in a desperate situation led to increasingly extreme degrees of adaptation, as they shifted the range of what they could endure to incorporate the attacks they were experiencing. Yet, eventually, the violence escalated beyond the point to which the women could adapt. One attack would be so much more severe, or so far beyond the range of what she was willing to assimilate, that a formerly passive woman would suddenly take action in her own defense or in the defense of a child. Typically, the killing of the abuser was unplanned and occurred during the period of threat before an assault, in the midst of a violent episode, or during a failed escape attempt. In most cases, the homicide weapon was a gun; often, it was the same gun the man had threatened his mate with earlier.

The violence in severely abusive relationships, and the homicides that occur as a culmination of this violence, often seem inexplicable and bizarre. Yet, the phenomenon can be effectively studied and, as our findings indicate, important variables and patterns can be identified. Service providers in law enforcement and the criminal justice system, as well as in the mental health and medical professions, frequently come into contact with identified or suspected cases of domestic violence. Without specialized knowledge of the dynamics of violence between partners, it is often hard to know how to assess these cases, to determine what responses are appropriate, and to give priority to the delivery of services in individual situations. Yet findings in the homicide study suggest that it *is* possible to identify couples at particularly high risk for a lethal incident (at least one perpetrated by the female victim), based on a cluster of reported factors: frequency of assaultive incidents by the man, severity of injury, frequency of alcohol intoxication or other substance abuse by the man, forced or threatened sexual assaults of the woman partner, the man's threats to kill, and suicide ideation by the woman. (Since many of the homicides perpetrated by both women and men against their romantic partners seem to be the endpoint of a violent relationship in which the man was the aggressor, it seems likely that many of the same variables could be useful in identifying high-risk relationships in general, not just those in which the woman kills in self-defense.)

In assessing risk in violent relationships, it is important to take seriously the woman's fears and perceptions of the danger. Despite abused women's tendencies to understate the severity of their experiences and to skip the details of the more bizarre or embarrassing incidents, they are extremely knowledgeable about the patterns of violence in their relationships. Professionals confronted with these cases should make use of the woman's expertise; her ability, when encouraged, to assess the degree of risk she is facing; and her experience in predicting when another assault seems imminent. Without some knowledge of the history of violence, recommendations or interventions by outsiders may be highly inappropriate for the situation, and may actually serve to exacerbate the aggression and further endanger the lives of those involved. Information on the variables identified above—except for the sexual assault variable—is relatively easy to obtain by a asking a few simple questions; clinical expertise is not necessary to gather such information. Evaluators should also ask about changes over time in the frequency and severity of assaults and threats, to determine escalation of the violence and changes in intent, or in desperation, of both the perpetrator and the victim.

Based on the documented frequency with which battered women ask for help prior to killing their abusive mates, more active responses by the agencies and individuals to whom these women turn could undoubtedly prevent many of the homicides that are eventually committed in desperation. Given what we know of battering relationships—the tendency for abuse to escalate over time and the potential for the violence in some relationships to assume lethal proportions—the importance of informed, effective responses during early contacts with domestic violence cases cannot be overemphasized. Even "mild" abuse must be taken seriously, and assaults by partners treated with the same stringency as are attacks by strangers. Research to date suggests that the most effective method of reducing assaults by abusive husbands toward their mates involves a serious response by police officers and the criminal justice system, treating a man's assault of his wife as a criminal offense; and immediate, specialized counseling for the offender in the context of a group designed for men who physically abuse their intimates.[2] An increase in the number of abusive mates actually facing vigorous prosecution would communicate a message to society regarding the criminal nature of the offense and the seriousness with which the crime should be viewed. The necessity for a clear statement is particularly important, given our history of laws allowing and endorsing assaults against wives.

Early interventions in abusive relationships in which the level of assault is less serious than that documented here would avert at least some of the serious injuries and deaths that occur when the violence is left to run its course. Determining what interventions are actually most effective will take the cooperative efforts of both researchers and service providers. It is obvious that threatened women and their children need both legal and practical provisions to enable them to live safely and to pursue their lives away from the violent partner if they so choose. Thus, our first efforts must be directed toward protecting victims from further assault and assuring them their rights to "life, liberty, and the pursuit of happiness."

We still know relatively little about men who perpetrate violence against their partners—their motivations and perceptions, and the distinguishing features in their lives that cause them to turn to violence as a response to daily events and emotions. And this is a hindrance to effective treatment. In light of the repeated finding that characteristics of the male with whom the woman is involved, rather than characteristics of the woman herself, are the best predictors of a woman's chances of victimization, it is imperative that we make a systematic effort to understand more about the aggressors. The men's aggression seems to be more in response to internal triggers than to the realities of current relationships with others.

Men who are assaultive toward their women partners may actually be striking out in an attempt to connect with another person, to break through a sense of alienation engendered by a neglectful or violence-scarred childhood. Yet repeated perpetration of aggression against others produces alienation, and such a misguided attempt at connection can only result in a worsening cycle of abuse and despair. Descriptions of violent men indicate that there are sufficient similarities in their behaviors to suggest a violence-prone personality pattern, originating in childhood and becoming progressively more severe as the men practice aggression.[3] Yet we do not know what factors determine which individuals, exposed to violence in childhood, will later become violent, and what variables mitigate against this outcome in some children.

Psychologists and others will note the absence of psychological test reports for women in this study. Such measures are useful for assessing a battered woman's current state—i.e., the degree of her depression, fearfulness, anxiety, and her general adjustment—at the time she is evaluated. However, because there are usually no comparable measures on her *prior* to her victimization, it is difficult to determine which of her responses are a result of the trauma she has suffered, and which might have been characteristic of her psychological makeup prior to the onset of assault. Earlier theories suggesting pathology in the female victim ignored the man's initiation of violence and its effects on the woman. Though experiences of victimization have a major impact on women's choices and behaviors while they are with their abusers, behaviors specifically related to victimization tend to disappear over time when the threat of violence is no longer present. (E.g., women, when living with violence, tend to be more fearful, emotionally restricted, withdrawn from others, and guarded.)[4]

It is important to identify these women's strengths as survivors—the depth of their compassion, their willingness to try again, their endurance in the face of pain and terror—in order to encourage them to go on. Although previously applied in an increasingly hopeless situation, these are the strengths an abused woman needs to leave a violent partner and begin a new life, even in the face of threat and danger. As society clearly identifies the abuse these women experience as outside the bounds of *societal* acceptability—and demonstrates that in outrage and in sanctions—abused women will also come to share that view and refuse to accept violence in their relationships.

# Disposition of Cases Discussed in the Text

## MOLLY AND JIM JOHNSON

Although police pictures taken at the time of her arrest show facial bruises, facial and neck abrasions, and bruises on her back, arms, and legs, Molly Johnson was charged with second-degree murder in Jim's death. She was separated from her son and he was placed in foster care. After three months, Molly was released on bail, but was allowed to visit Kevin only occasionally, and then only with someone in attendance to supervise their interactions. Kevin had never been away from his mother before and reacted poorly: He became unable to eat solid foods and increasingly lost weight, which added to Molly's distress over their separation. Although Molly's attorney wanted to try her case and felt that they could gain an acquittal, Molly could not wait. Six months after her arrest, she pled guilty to a reduced charge of manslaughter, with the understanding that she could resume custody of Kevin. Molly was sentenced to three years in jail, with 90 days off for time served, and the remainder of the sentence was deferred to probation.

## MARY AND CHUCK WHEELER

Mary Wheeler was found at the scene of Chuck's death in a state of profound shock, by police officers who responded to a call from a neighbor. She was transported to the hospital for observation, and was later transferred to jail and charged with first-degree murder. Due to legal battles over the release of evidence necessary for Mary's defense, her trial was delayed for two years. Mary was convicted for manslaughter and sentenced to five years in jail, where she remains at the time of this writing.

## IRENE AND MARK MILLER

Irene Miller was charged with first-degree murder in the shooting death of her husband Mark. She went to trial pleading self-defense, and was acquitted. Irene was severely depressed and suicidal while awaiting trial. After her acquittal, she retreated into isolation and avoids all contacts that might remind her of the past. Recent reports indicate that her depression is improving.

## WANDA AND RANDY BOWLES

Wanda Bowles was charged with soliciting murder in the death of Randy Bowles. She was incarcerated during the 14 months it took her case to come to trial. Similar to the experience of Molly Johnson, Wanda's contacts with her daughter Christie—the child she had been trying to protect—were limited to brief visits in the prison waiting room, under the watchful eye of a warden. In an attempt to protect her brother, Wanda refused to turn state's evidence against him in return for leniency. She was finally allowed to plead guilty to conspiracy to commit murder. Although she was not present when the murder took place and had no certain knowledge that Randy was going to be killed, Wanda was sentenced to nine years in jail.

## JANET AND RICK VANHORN

Janet VanHorn was severely disoriented at the time of her arrest for the shooting death of her husband Rick, and was transferred from jail to a psychiatric facility, where she remained for several weeks. She was charged with first-degree murder, and attorneys at her trial employed a dual defense: claiming both grounds for self-defense and diminished capacity at the time of the shooting. Janet was convicted of voluntary manslaughter and given a sentence of 10 years on probation.

## MAGGIE AND DUKE ORTEGA

Maggie was charged with second-degree murder in the stabbing death of Duke Ortega. She was too frightened to go to trial, and pled guilty to a reduced charge of manslaughter. Maggie was given a 4-year suspended sentence, with the stipulation that she participate in an in-patient alcohol-treatment program.

## SHARON AND ROY BIKSON

Sharon Bikson was charged with first-degree murder in the shooting death of her husband Roy, after he broke into the apartment where she was staying. She was allowed to remain free on bond, but was suspended from her job without pay, pending the outcome of her trial. Sharon was unwilling to accept the offer of a plea bargain, insisting that the shooting was in self-defense and citing her numerous requests to the police and to prosecutors for assistance and protection. After 13 months, the district attorney's office finally dropped the murder charges, agreeing that the slaying was justifiable. Sharon was able to resume her job and began picking up the pieces of her life. However, she had borrowed money to support her family while she was out of work, and had incurred enormous bills for funeral expenses and attorneys' fees while awaiting trial. For the next two years, Sharon worked two jobs and attempted to pay off her debts bit by bit. At the end of the second year, her creditors forced her into bankruptcy.

## KAREN AND HAL SIMON

Karen Simon was charged with first-degree murder in the shooting death of Hal Simon. Her mother was ill at the time and needing her care, so Karen attempted to negotiate a plea in the hope that this would result in a shorter jail term. Ironically, in view of the fact that the homicide incident revolved around Hal's use of a gun, Karen was allowed to plead guilty to a charge of manslaughter without a weapon, and was sentenced to three years in prison. Karen is now out on parole.

## BELLA AND ISAAC HARRIS

Bella Harris was charged with first-degree murder in the shooting death of her husband Isaac, and was jailed for a year before her case came to trial. Her case was also tried with a dual defense of self-defense and insanity. However, Bella was convicted of first-degree murder and sentenced to life in prison. (Bella's daughter is incarcerated in the same prison.) Bella is in her late forties, but suffers from injuries sustained during the beatings by Isaac that left her permanently disabled and in very poor health. Judging from her physical condition, it seems unlikely that Bella will live to be paroled.

## SUSAN AND DON JEFFERSON

Susan Jefferson was charged with first-degree murder in the shooting death of Don Jefferson. Her baby was one-week-old at the time of the shooting, and Susan was afraid to take the risk of going to trial. In light of the evidence for Don's assaults and threats against her, Susan was allowed to plead guilty to criminally negligent manslaughter and was sentenced to one year in jail.

## KIM AND BILLY HALL

Although Kim's head and facial injuries were severe enough that she was taken to a hospital for x-rays at the time of her arrest, she was later transported to jail and charged with first-degree murder in the shooting death of Billy Hall. Kim went to trial on a plea of self-defense, but was convicted of manslaughter and sentenced to 2½ years in prison.

# Case Study Index

# The Interview Schedule

A semi-structured interview was used to gather data on both the homicide and the comparison groups. A tightly structured format would have been inadequate to obtain the breadth of responses desirable for exploratory research or to establish a detailed picture of the context in which the actions occurred. Conversely, an unstructured format—perhaps more appropriate for therapeutic work—would not have permitted careful comparison of results and would have been difficult to analyze quantitatively. The semi-structured interview schedule allowed for the systematic collection of information, while at the same time giving the women an opportunity to fill in details and background that we otherwise might not have known to ask.[1]

The inclusion of open-ended questions in the interview schedule has several advantages. Such questions have been found to produce better and more complete responses, and the opportunity to talk freely about the violence seems to foster a climate of trust between the subject and the interviewer.[2] When an unstructured response is followed by a structured question covering the same material, the interviewee's response is clarified and the data can be accurately compared with answers given by other subjects to the same question.

Structured questions were most effective when attempting to get an accurate picture of the abuse that occurred. Abused women can remember details on an abusive incident if they are asked specific questions, although they often minimize the violence and their resulting distress. This may be because they are accustomed to other people not really wanting to hear what has happened. Another possibility is that women who have been abused over a period of time have engaged in so much denial to be able to endure the abuse that it is difficult for them to acknowledge the severity of the violence, even in retrospect. As with the foundational work on battered women done by Washburn and Frieze (1980), the interview schedule included questions on violent actions and their outcomes in terms of injuries and reactions. Questions concerning sexual abuse also combined unstructured responses with forced-choice or list answers, and this method was found quite effective for gaining sensitive and detailed information.

The overall format of the questionnaire is crucial in conducting interviews on such an emotionally charged topic. The interview schedule was structured so that questions about violent incidents came during the middle of the interview, with less upsetting topics discussed at the beginning and the end. This gave subjects an opportunity to relax and adjust to their surroundings and the interviewing process before the most difficult questions were asked. It was equally important to provide closure for subjects at the end of the interview; this was accomplished by asking the woman questions about her current state and future expectations. Obviously, this "cool down" was not as effective in the homicide interviews, when women were facing trial for murder and felt that their whole future was in jeopardy. However, the opportunity to tell the whole story and place the events in context seemed to be therapeutic for most women.

The use of a semi-structured interview schedule has several practical limitations: It is much more time-consuming than a tightly structured interview format and takes more time to code and analyze. It can also be quite taxing to administer, especially in sensitive topic areas, and requires a highly trained interviewer who is skilled at obtaining information and handling the intensity of the interaction. The questionnaire took eight to ten hours to administer, and when a subject was incarcerated, it sometimes required two days to complete. This meant it was not possible to study as large a sample as could have been obtained using a more tightly structured schedule; but for exploratory research, a more thorough and in-depth technique seemed preferable to a survey method. Especially in homicide cases, in which a prior history of abuse is at issue, it is necessary to have detailed knowledge of the factors surrounding the homicide event in order to bring testimony on the case or evaluate the reasonableness of a self-defense or insanity plea.

In conducting an intensive, day-long interview, it is crucial to maintain a balance between gathering information and pacing the overall process. Interviewers must be skilled at perceiving when the woman needs support in order to continue and yet be able to stay within the structure of the questionnaire format so that consistent information can be obtained.

The interview schedule began with a section on the woman's family of origin, her health in childhood, and circumstances of her childhood. The women were asked questions about any previous physical or sexual assault as a child and whether there had been any abuse between family members in her childhood home. General questions were also asked about the background of the abusers, and about typical interactions between the woman and her mate.

In addition, women were asked to give a narrative account of four specific assaultive incidents in their relationships with the abusers: the first occurrence of violence in the relationship, a "typical" violent incident, a subsequent incident that was one of the "worst" or most frightening by the woman's definition, and the last violent incident prior to the interview. (These incidents occurred in chronological order, although the time lag between incidents, and the number of other abusive episodes that may have occurred in that interval, varied by case.) The woman's account of each abusive incident was followed immediately by a matching set of detailed questions about the occurrence. The criterion for participation in the study was to have experienced at least two instances of physical abuse from the same man, but almost every woman in both the homicide and the comparison group had experienced four or more. By asking about these four incidents, it was possible to assess more accurately the severity and escalation of the violence, and to look for patterns in the abusive relationships over time.

The interview also included an overall summary section on the abusive relationship and the woman's perceptions of patterns and threats, as well as questions about whether the children had witnessed the violence or were themselves abused. It closed with questions about the woman's current health and emotional condition, and her expectations for the future.

# Source Notes

## Introduction

1. The Battered Woman Syndrome Study, National Institute of Mental Health grant #RO1MH30147, L.E. Walker, Principal Investigator.
2. This work was performed as part of a consulting team at Walker & Associates in Denver, Colorado.
3. Chimbos, 1978; Totman, 1978.

## Chapter 1

1. Stark & McEvoy, 1970. See particularly pp. 53 and 54.
2. Early research on child abuse included the work of Kempe, Silverman, Steele, Droegemueller, & Silver, 1962; Gil, 1970; Steele & Pollack, 1968; and others.
3. Kleckner, 1978; Shainess, 1977; Schultz, 1960; and Snell, Rosenwald & Robey, 1964 were among those who espoused the psychopathological point of view, while O'Brien, 1971 and Steinmetz & Straus, 1974 adopted a more structural perspective.
4. E.g., Gelles, 1974, 1975; O'Brien, 1971; Straus, 1971, 1973.
5. See for example Gelles, 1980; Humphrey & Palmer, 1982; Kalmus & Seltzer, 1984; Parke & Collmer, 1975; and Straus et al., 1980 on stress theory; Ball-Rokeach, 1980 and Goode, 1971 on resource deprivation; Berkowitz, 1983, and Sebastian, 1983 on a conflict perspective; Davis, 1971; Dobash & Dobash, 1978, 1979; Pagelow, 1981; and Straus, 1978 on structural inequality; and Barnett et al., 1980; Dobash & Dobash, 1979; Martin, 1976; Stark, Flitcraft & Frazier, 1979; and Stark & Flitcraft, 1981 on discrimination against women—an overlapping perspective.
6. Bourdouris, 1971; Chimbos, 1978; Lindsey, 1978; Totman, 1978; Wolfgang, 1958.
7. See Straus and Gelles, 1986, for results of the follow-up survey, and Schulman, 1979, for findings from the study by Louis Harris and Associates.
8. Russell, 1982.
9. Frieze, Knoble, Zomnir & Washburn, 1980.
10. Straus et al., 1980, 1986.
11. See also Straus & Gelles, 1986; Greenblat, 1983; Maccoby & Jacklin, 1974; Russell, 1982; and Tavris, 1977.
12. Browning & Dutton, 1984; Deshner, 1984; Ewing, Lindsey, & Pomerantz, 1984; Ganley & Harris, 1978; Sonkin & Durphy, 1982, 1985. See also Szinovack, 1983, for a discussion of the use of couple data.
13. E.g., Dobash & Dobash, 1978; Frieze, 1980; Pagelow, 1981; Russell, 1982; Sonkin, 1985.

14. Frieze et al., 1981.
15. See for example Russell, 1982; Sonkin & Durphy, 1985.
16. Berk, Berk, Loseke, & Rauma, 1983.
17. E.g., Berk et al., 1981; Bureau of Justice Statistics, 1980.
18. Stark, Flitcraft, Zuckerman, Grey, Robison, & Frazier, 1981.
19. Stark et al., 1981.
20. Schulman, 1979.
21. E.g., Field & Field, 1973; U.S. Commission on Civil Rights, 1982.
22. Crime in the United States, 1984; Straus, 1985.
23. Uniform Crime Reports, 1983.
24. *Crimes of Violence,* 1969. See also Bourdouris, 1971; Fields & Kirchner, 1978; Stephens, 1977.
25. Chimbos, 1978.
26. Lindsey, 1978.
27. Police Foundation, 1976; Sherman & Berk, 1984.
28. Lindsey, 1978.
29. Fiora-Gormally, 1978; Fromson, 1977; Lewin, 1979; Martin, 1976; Wolfe, 1979.
30. Schneider & Jordan, 1981.
31. Jones, 1980, p. 308.
32. This work was performed as part of a consulting team at Walker & Associates in Denver, Colorado.
33. A subsample of 403 battered women interviewed during a National Institute of Mental Health-supported study, NIMH grant #RO1MH30147, L.E. Walker, Principal Investigator.
34. Volunteer subjects for research often differ from non-volunteers. For example, in an investigation of types of battered women, Washburn & Frieze (1980) found that abused women who responded to posted notices differed from those referred by shelters on several measures: They were more likely to work full time, had more education and somewhat higher income, and had experienced somewhat less violence than women in the shelter group. (Even then, nearly 50 percent had sustained severe or permanent injuries.) In the present study, 18 percent of women in the comparison group were referred by a battered women's shelter to the research project, whereas the rest were predominantly self-referred. With 38 of 205 women being referred from a shelter, the present sample may somewhat underrepresent levels of violence experienced by women who utilize shelter facilities. Extremely low levels of violence may also be missing from this sample; volunteers do not typically include women experiencing very minor assaults in their relationships who do not think of themselves as battered. However, although a random-sample procedure is desirable for generalizability, survey methods would have been inadequate to obtain a comprehensive history of the *context* surrounding violent episodes and the unfolding of patterns of violence over time, due to time and cost constraints implicit in survey methodology. Intensive interviewing of identified populations—the basis of this study—is the first step in approaching a detailed description of little-known events and in generating relevant hypothesis for future research.

35. See also Frieze, 1979; Pagelow, 1984; Straus, 1980; and Walker, 1979.
36. See Appendix for a more complete description of the interview schedule and procedure.
37. Dobash & Dobash, 1984; Frieze et al., 1980; Pagelow, 1985; Straus & Gelles, 1986; Walker, 1979.
38. E.g., Chimbos, 1978; Totman, 1978.

## Chapter 2

1. [$x^2(35) = 7.98$, p$<$.05]. Significance level based on Kruskal–Wallis one-way analysis of variance, which tests whether $K$ dependent samples are from the same population. The statistic $H$, based on this analysis, is distributed approximately as Chi-square, and is estimated to be 95 percent as powerful as the equivalent parametric test, $t$. (See Klugh, 1974, pp. 307–308 for a description of this test.)
2. [$t(40) = 2.80$, p$<$.008].
3. Women in the homicide group were significantly older than women in the comparison group [$t(245) = 3.42$, p$<$.001]. Although women in the homicide group had slightly larger families—2.3 children vs. 1.97 for women in the comparison group—this difference was not statistically significant.
4. [$x^2(210) = 11.90$, p.$<$.001], as based on Kruskal–Wallis one-way analysis of variance.
5. Women in the comparison group were significantly more educated than their mates [$t(203) = 4.36$, p$<$.001]. However, fewer women than men in the comparison group were fully employed [$x^2(189) = 5.99$, p$<$.05].
6. [$t(243) = 3.10$, p$<$.002].
7. As the first of its kind, this study was exploratory and results should not be treated as representative of all spousal homicides in which a woman kills her mate. For one thing, statistical procedures needed to assure generalizability—such as random-sampling procedures in which subjects are drawn at random from a population and then divided into groups to study a particular topic—are not feasible when studying battered women who have killed their abusers, since the general incidence in the population is so low. This affects the generalizability of the findings, and statistical significance must be interpreted cautiously. However, significant findings do indicate a relatively large difference or relationship in the data. Thus, these results provide a first look at relationships in which women kill a man who had been victimizing them over a period of time.
8. Bandura, 1973; Bandura & Walters, 1963; Herzberger, 1983; Pagelow, 1980.
9. E.g., Alfaro, 1978; Farrington, 1978; McCord, 1979; Sorrells, 1977; Strasburg, 1978.
10. Coleman et al., 1980; Dvoskin, 1981; Hofeller, 1980; Kalmuss, 1984; Peterson, 1980; Schulman, 1979; Washburn & Frieze, 1980; and Walker, 1984 did find a positive relationship between childhood exposure to violence and later victimization, whereas Bowker, 1983; Dobash & Dobash, 1979; Rosenbaum & O'Leary, 1981; and Star, 1978, did not.
11. Roy, 1977.

12. See also Frieze, 1979.
13. Carroll, 1977; Coleman et al., 1980; Fagan et al., 1983; Ganley & Harris, 1978; Gelles, 1974; Hofeller, 1980; Johnston, 1984; Kalmuss, 1984; Lopez, 1981, Rosenbaum & O'Leary, 1981; Rouse, 1984a, 1984b; Sonkin & Durphy, 1985; Star, 1978; Straus et al., 1980; Telch & Lindquist, 1984; Washburn & Frieze, 1980.
14. E.g., Chimbos, 1978: Totman, 1978.
15. Hotaling & Sugarman, 1986.
16. Coleman, Weinman & Hsi, 1980; Fagan et al., 1983; Kalmuss, 1984; Rosenbaum & O'Leary, 1981; Rouse, 1984a, 1984b.
17. Bandura, 1973.
18. See also Pagelow, 1984, pp. 117–124.
19. Bandura, 1977.
20. Sonkin & Durphy, 1985, p. 3.
21. Pagelow, 1984; Walker & Browne, 1985.
22. Serum, 1982.
23. E.g., Bandura & Walters, 1970.
24. E.g., Herzberger, 1983.
25. C.f. Conger, 1980; Elliott, Ageton & Canter, 1979; Fagan & Jones, 1984; Hawkins & Weis, 1980.
26. E.g., Straus et al., 1980.
27. Halleck, 1967.

## Chapter 3

1. Bernard & Bernard, 1983, 30 percent; Cate, Henton, Kaval, Christopher, & Lloyd, 1982, 22 percent; Laner & Thompson, 1982, 25–30 percent; Makepeace, 1981, 21 percent. Since these estimates are based on college student samples only, they are not necessarily representative of a non-student population.
2. E.g., Cate et al., 1982; Henton et al., 1983; Laner & Thompson, 1982; Makepeace, 1981; Legg et al., 1984; Murphy, 1984; Sigelman et al., 1984.
3. Cate et al., 1982; Henton et al., 1983 (on a high school, rather than a college student sample); Legg et al., 1984; Makepeace, 1981; Matthews, 1984.
4. Murphy, 1984.
5. Legg et al., 1984; see also Pagelow, 1984.
6. Fagan et al., 1983; Hanneke & Shields, 1981.
7. Bowker, 1983a; Dobash & Dobash, 1978; Pagelow, 1981; Rosenbaum & O'Leary, 1981.
8. E.g., Dobash & Dobash, 1978; Dutton & Painter, 1981; Pagelow, 1981; Rosenbaum & O'Leary, 1981.
9. Bowker, 1983, p. 40.
10. See for example Makepeace, 1981.
11. Laner, 1982, p. 11; as cited in Pagelow, 1984, p. 294.
12. C.f., Dobash & Dobash, 1984.
13. See also Dobash & Dobash, 1984, p. 282; and Stark et al., 1981, who, in discussing the frequency with which medical service providers use "mental health" labels for the problems of battered women, note that these labels

then "signify to other practitioners . . . that future complaints may also be less serious (or real) than initial evaluation might suggest. . . . [This labeling] is a way of telling patients that, "whatever the problem, it is certainly not anything I can help you solve." From the abused woman's perspective, this encounter minimizes her problem, discourages access to social resources, and reinforces her sense of isolation (p. 27)."

## Chapter 4

1. C.f. Dobash & Dobash, 1984a.
2. Significantly more men in the homicide group than the comparison group expressed contrition after the first assaultive incident [$x^2(233) = 8.32$, p< .004, as measured by a Kruskal-Wallis one-way analysis of variance].
3. After the "worst" incident, 58 percent of men in the homicide group expressed contrition—down from 87 percent; whereas in the comparison group, the decline was less percipitous with 64 percent expressing contrition after the worst incident, down from 72 percent.
4. See Walker, 1978, 1984; Dobash & Dobash, 1984.
5. This difference was highly significant [$x^2(241) = 8.99$, p<.003].
6. It is interesting to note in this regard, investigations by Berkowitz & LePage, 1967, which suggest that the mere presence of a weapon within reach is sufficient to increase the aggressive tendencies of one person against another, in addition to increasing the risk of lethal outcome where the weapon is used.
7. E.g., Chimbos, 1978; Totman, 1978, Wolfgang, 1958.
8. E.g., Chimbos, 1978.
9. The differences in threats to commit suicide by women in the two groups were statisticaly significant [$x^2(238) = 4.32$, p<.04].
10. Stark et al., 1981.
11. The pattern of differences in the frequency of abusive incidents over time was significant at the .001 level [$x^2(241) = 10.43$, p<.001].
12. Significantly more women in the homicide group than the comparison group reported that the severity of physical assaults worsened over time [$x^2(157) = 6.06$,p<01]. (In contrast, 14 percent of the comparison group reported that the assaults became less severe over time, whereas only 3 percent of women in the homicide group made that observation.) Similarly, more women in the homicide than the comparison group reported that the psychological abuse became more severe [$x^2(158) = 4.41$, p<.05].
13. Women in the homicide group sustained significantly more injuries than women in the comparison group [$x^2(245) = 11.64$, p<.001].
14. C.f. Patterson, 1982 and Reid, Tapling & Lorber, 1981.
15. Stark et al., 1981.
16. See the report by Stark et al., 1981, for an excellent discussion of clues to identifying battered women in the context of a medical setting.
17. More men in the homicide group than in the comparison group physically and/or sexually abused children in the home [$x^2(179) = 3.98$, p<.05].
18. Walker, 1984.
19. Estimations of the frequency of alcohol or drug use by the men are based on the women's reports of their behavior. In the homicide group, the wom-

en's reports of the men's substance abuse were frequently corroborated by other witnesses as well. In many cases, further evidence of the veracity of their reports was provided by police records documenting intoxication or drug use, as well as by medical and other records.

20. Differences in the frequency with which men in the two groups became intoxicated were significant beyond the .001 level [$x^2(244) = 20.78$].

21. The use of prescription drugs was much higher for men in the homicide group [$x^2(240) = 15.32$, p<.001]. The frequency with which the men in the homicide group used street drugs was also higher [$x^2(231) = 5.46$, p<.02].

22. Seven of nine studies that investigated this question using some sort of comparison or control group found that men who abused their female partners were more likely to abuse alcohol than men who did not. These studies ranged from nationally representative samples to small, matched samples using multiple comparison groups. (Caesar, 1985; Coleman et al., 1980; Coleman & Straus, 1983; Hofeller, 1980; Lopez, 1981; and Van Hasselt et al., 1985, all found positive relationships. Rosenbaum & O'Leary, 1981, and Washburn & Frieze, 1980, did not; as cited in Hotaling & Sugarman, 1986.)

23. Only one study (Telch & Lingquist, 1984) found a significant relationship between alcohol consumption and women's victimization by a husband's violence. The five other controlled studies that looked at this question did not find such a relationship (Shields & Hanneke, 1983; Star, 1978; Stark et al., 1981; Van Hasselt et al., 1985; Washburn & Frieze, 1980).

24. Bochnak, 1981; Coleman et al., 1980; Coleman & Straus, 1983; Hofeller, 1980, Eberle, 1982, Pagelow, 1981a, Roy, 1977, Sonkin & Durphy, 1985; Telch & Lindquist, 1984; Walker, 1979, 1984; Washburn & Frieze, 1980.

25. Gelles, 1974.

26. See Bowker, 1983a; Frieze & Knoble, 1980; Pagelow, 1981a; Roy, 1977; and Russell, 1982 for a discussion of the tendency of abused women to blame the drinking, rather than the perpetrator, for abusive incidents.

27. Sonkin & Durphy, 1985.

28. E.g., Frieze & Knoble, 1980; Roy, 1977.

# Chapter 5

1. I am indebted to Jean Baker Miller, 1976, and Carol Gilligan, 1982, for their insights on the differing "psychologies" of women and men.

2. See, for example, Freud, 1905, 1925, & 1953; Piaget, 1932; Erickson, 1950; Kohlberg, 1969. Kohlberg's early model of "moral development" (1958), for instance, was based entirely on a sample of boys.

3. McClelland, 1975. See also Miller, 1976, and Gilligan, 1982, for foundational discussions on how differently these traits appear when women's development is viewed *outside* of a male model.

4. Kaplan & Surrey, 1984.

5. Chodrow, 1974.

6. Aries & Olver, 1985; Broverman, Broverman, Clarkson, Rosenkrantz, & Vogel, 1970.

7. Cf. Hoffman, 1977. There is also, of course, the potential for damage, such as when a mother views a daughter as a total extension of herself.
8. Chodrow, 1974; Gilligan, 1982; Kaplan & Surrey, 1984.
9. Gilligan, 1982, p. 8.
10. E.g., Bardwick, 1971; Gilligan, 1982; Gutmann, 1970; Miller, 1976.
11. For a discussion of differences in these fears by gender, see, for instance, the study conducted by Pollak & Gilligan, 1982, which analyzed violent imagery in stories written about pictures on the Thematic Apperception Test. In their stories, men projected danger into situations of close personal connection, whereas women saw the potential for danger in contexts of impersonal achievement. Men's fears centered around the risk of entrapment, betrayal, or humiliation in relationships; women's around the danger of isolation in success.
12. Williams, 1977.
13. See Lever, 1976, as cited by Gilligan, 1982.
14. Miller, 1976, p. 83.
15. E.g., Miller, 1976.
16. Cf., Miller's (1976) discussion on dominants and subordinates.
17. Dutton, 1986; Williams, 1977.
18. Miller, 1976, p. 31.
19. See the work of Donald Dutton & James Browning, 1985, for a discussion of "power struggles and intimacy anxieties" in abusive men.
20. See the discussion on "Gender and Victimization by Intimates," Walker & Browne, 1985; also Walker, 1979.
21. Dutton & Browning, 1985; see also Ewing, Lindsey, & Pomerantz, 1984.
22. Ewing, Lindsey, & Pomerantz, 1984; Ganley, 1981; Sonkin & Durphy, 1985; Walker, 1984.
23. See Dutton, Fehr, & McEwan, 1982; Pleck, 1981; Fasteau, 1974; and Novacok, 1976; for discussions of the tendency of men in general to find expressions of anger more compatible with male sex-role socialization than expressions of fear.
24. Dutton, Fehr, & McEwan, 1982; Pleck, 1981.
25. Dutton & Browning, 1984. See also Ganley & Harris, 1978; Martin, 1976; and Walker, 1979, for similar observations.
26. Gilligan, 1982, p. 165.
27. E.g., Walker, 1979, 1984.
28. Gilligan, 1982, p. 171.
29. Gilligan, 1982, p. 173.
30. Gilligan, 1982, p. 165.

## Chapter 6

1. See Finkelhor & Yllo, 1985; Frieze, 1983; Pagelow, 1984; and Russell, 1982, for exceptions.
2. Frieze, 1983, p. 552. See also Bowker, 1983a, 1983b; Dobash & Dobash, 1979; Hilberman & Muson, 1978; Martin, 1976; Pagelow, 1980, 1981; Prescott & Letco, 1977; Shields & Hanneke, 1981; and Walker, 1979, for others who have found sexual violence highly related to other types of physical violence in marriage.

3. Russell, 1982, p. 357.
4. The women were asked simply, "Has he ever forced you to have intercourse (sex)?" The meaning of "force" was left up to them. Statistically, the difference between groups on the rape variable was highly significant. Using a Kruskal-Wallis one-way analysis of variance: $x^2$ (243) = 12.18, p<.001.
5. Again, this difference was highly significant: $x^2$ (241) = 8.61, p<.003.
6. Because of concerns for confidentiality, accounts in this section have not been identified with specific cases.
7. Black, 1979; Queen's Bench Foundation, 1979; Landau, 1976; Russell, 1975, as cited in Pagelow, 1984. It is important to remember in this context that, although the seriousness of assault appears to *increase* with a closer relationship between perpetrator and victim, the likelihood of prosecution and conviction *decreases.*
8. Cf. Finkelhor & Yllo, 1985; Russell, 1982.
9. E.g., Finkelhor & Yllo, 1983; Russell, 1982.
10. Frieze, 1980, 1983; Russell, 1982.
11. Russell, 1982.
12. Finkelhor & Yllo, 1983.
13. Frieze, 1980.
14. Pagelow, 1980.
15. Shields & Hanneke, 1983.
16. Pagelow, 1984.
17. Finkelhor & Yllo, 1983; Gelles, 1979; Pagelow, 1984; Russell, 1982; Walker, 1984.
18. Russell (1982) also found that marital rape was the most difficult type of *sexual* assault on which to obtain information; more difficult, for instance, than obtaining reports from incest victims (p. 39).
19. E.g., Burgess & Holmstrom, 1974; Kilpatrick, Veronen, & Resick, 1979; Katz & Mazur, 1979; Medea & Thompson, 1974; Shields & Hanneke, 1983.
20. See Pagelow, 1984; Mettger, 1982; and Russell, 1982.
21. Shields & Hanneke, 1983; Russell, 1982.
22. Russell, 1982, p. 203–204.
23. Turner, Fenn, & Cole (1981), p. 31. See Stuart's (1981) chapter on Violent Behavior for an excellent review of theories on aggression.
24. Geen, Stonner, & Shope, 1975. See also Buss, 1966b; Geen, 1968; Keating & Brock, 1976; and Berkowitz, 1979.
25. Bandura, Underwood, & Fromson, 1975, p. 256.
26. Festinger, 1957; Brock & Buss, 1962, 1964; Lerner & Simmons, 1966; Aronson, 1972; Bandura, 1973; Bandura, Underwood, & Fromson, 1975; Goldstein, Davis & Herman, 1975; and Sebastian, 1983.
27. Goldstein, Davis, Kernis & Cohn, 1981.
28. At present, the majority of studies on police responses to domestic violence calls suggest that arrest of the male abuser with effective prosecution and treatment appears to afford the best protection to women victims, and the greatest potential to deter further attacks. See Bard & Zacker, 1974; Jaffe & Burris, 1984; Levens & Dutton, 1980; Loving & Farmer, 1981; and Sherman & Berk, 1983; as cited in Dutton, 1986, p. 19.
29. Goldstein, Davis & Herman, 1975.
30. Laurie Wardell, Dair Gillespie, and Ann Leffler (1983) in a biting critique

of the provocation theory of wife abuse, noted that "whenever [a husband] swings, a way can be found to claim she drove him to it. . . . Thus the operational definition of provocation becomes empirically equivalent to 'anything she does or does not do which, after hitting her, he reports disliking' (p. 74)."

31. Berkowitz, 1974, 1977; Sebastian, 1983.
32. Cf. Perry & Perry, 1974, on the effect of perceived signs of victim suffering on the perpetration of aggression by children.
33. E.g., Azrin, Holz, & Hake, 1963. This fits in well with Dutton's theory of a batterer's need for a renewed, discernible impact, whether that be through violence or remorse (Dutton & Browning, 1984; Dutton, 1986).

## Chapter 7

1. Moore, 1979.
2. See Schechter (1982) for an excellent history of the development of shelters, and the battered women's movement, in the United States.
3. See, for example, report by the National Center on Women and Family Law, July 1982; Walker & Edwall (in press).
4. See Jones' (1980) chapter, "Totaling Women," pages 298–299; see also Lindsey, 1978; Martin, 1976; Pagelow, 1980, 1981.
5. Fields, 1978; Fiora-Gormally, 1978; Lewin, 1979; Pagelow, 1980, 1981.
6. See, for example, Ewing, Lindsey & Pomerantz, 1984.
7. E.g., Barnett, Pittman, Ragan, & Salus, 1980; Ewing et al., 1984, Pagelow, 1981, 1984; Tanay, 1976.
8. See Tanay's (1976) chapter, "Until Death Do Us Part."
9. E.g., Lenore Walker's (1979, 1984) theory of learned helplessness in battered women; Donald Dutton and Susan Painter's (1981) application of theories on traumatic bonding.
10. See the works of Alexandra Symonds, 1979, and Martin Symonds, 1975 and 1978, for discussions of psychological effects and aftereffects in female victims of violence and their parallels to known responses of other victims.
11. Browne, 1980.
12. For example, see the works of Chapman, 1962; and Mileti, Drabek, & Haas, 1975.
13. E.g., Bahson, 1964; Miller, 1964; Powell, 1954.
14. Mileti, et al., 1975; Powell, 1954.
15. Grinker & Spiegel, 1945; Speigel, 1955.
16. Bard & Sangrey, 1979.
17. Burgess & Holmstrom, 1974; Notman & Nadelson, 1976.
18. E.g., Chapman, 1962.
19. Bard & Sangrey, 1979.
20. Burgess & Holmstrom, 1974; Hilberman & Munson, 1977–78; Nathan, Eitinger & Winick, 1964.
21. E.g., Arnold, 1967; Lazarus, 1967.
22. E.g., Lazarus, 1967.
23. Bettleheim, 1943; M. Symonds, 1978; Stentz, 1979.
24. Biderman, 1967.

25. E.g., A. Symonds, 1979.
26. Meerloo, 1961.
27. Walker & Browne, 1985.
28. Blair, 1979; Field & Field, 1973; U.S. Commission on Civil Rights, 1982.
29. Thibaut & Kelley, 1959, p. 180.
30. Based on a discriminant function analysis (Klecka, 1975, pp. 434–467) using all of the abuse-related variables for which between-group differences reached the .001 significance level. The analysis identified seven of these variables which, in linear combination, best discriminated between women in the homicide and comparison groups. Using these seven variables, one could correctly classify 77 percent of the homicide subjects and 83 percent of the comparison subjects (or 82 percent of all subjects).
31. Russell, 1982, p. 299.
32. This discussion is based on the (1961) model of Sherif and Hovland. Although experimental testing of their theory has produced some contradictory results (Wrightsman, 1972), their concept of a "latitude of acceptance" for stimuli may make a contribution to our understanding of the evolution in a violent relationship toward a homicide committed by the woman.
33. See Browne, 1986.

## Chapter 8

1. Bernard, Vera, Vera, & Newman, 1982. All the respondents in this study were interviewed as a part of psychiatric evaluations required by the courts, either to determine their competencey to stand trial or their legal sanity at the time of the alleged crime; obviously a very non-random sample. However, all but one male defendant were judged competent to stand trial at the time they were evaluated.
2. See also Tanay's (1976) chapter, "Until Death Do Us Part," on homicide precipitated by the threat of abandonment, and Simon's (1978) conclusion that the separation or the threat of separation is usually the trigger for this type of homicide.
3. Wolfgang, 1958, p. 252.
4. Willbanks, 1983. Willbanks studied all homicides perpetrated by females in Dade County, Florida, for the year of 1980, and compared these cases to homicide perpetrated by male offenders in that same jurisdiction. Study of these repondents began at the arrest level and followed the subjects from arrest through disposition of their cases, using data obtained from police records.
5. Chimbos, 1978. This study was conducted post-adjudication with individuals convicted of a crime in the killing of their spouses. Most respondents were serving time in a penal institution at the time of the interview, or had served time prior to the interview.
6. Daniel & Harris, 1982. Again, women in this study were those who had been referred to a State Hospital for psychiatric evaluation. Women charged with homicide were compared to a group of other female offenders admitted for evaluation in relation to other crimes. This sample would exclude women

charged with homicide but not referred for psychiatric evaluation, and women for whom homicide charges were dropped due to mitigating circumstances.

7. Totman, 1978, p. 105.
8. Totman, 1978, p. 92.
9. See Halleck's section on "Oppression and Limitation of Adaptational Alternatives," 1967, pp. 67–72.

## Chapter 9

1. For a more complete discussion of laws and customs bearing on a man's treatment of his wife, see *Violence Against Wives: A Case Against the Patriarchy,* Dobash & Dobash, 1979; and *The Marriage Contract: Spouses, Lovers, and the Law,* Weitzman, 1981; see also Davidson, 1977; Eisenberg & Seymour, 1978; Kanowitz, 1969; May, 1978; and Pleck, 1979.
2. Eisenberg & Micklow, 1974.
3. O'Faolain & Martines, 1973, as cited as Pagelow, 1984, p. 281.
4. As quoted in Terry Davidson, 1978, p. 99.
5. Blackstone, *Commentaries on the Laws of England,* 1765, p. 444.
6. W. D. Lewis, *I Commentaries on the Laws of England,* Blackstone, 442 (1897).
7. William Blackstone, *Commentaries on the Laws of England,* bk. 4 (Philadelphia: R. Welsh & Co., 1897), p. 1602.
8. *Bradley v. States,* 2 Miss. 156, 158 (1Walker 1824), as cited in *Under the Rule of Thumb,* 1982, p. 2.
9. *State v. Black,* 60 N.C. 162, 163, 86 Am. Dec., 436 (1864), as cited in Tong, 1984.
10. *State v. Rhodes,* 61 Phil. L. (N.C.) 453 (1866).
11. Davidson, 1977, p. 18.
12. *Fulgham v. State,* 46 Ala. 146–147 (1871).
13. *State v. Oliver,* 70 N.C. 60, 61–62 (1874) (Criminal Liability).
14. U.S. Commission on Civil Rights, 1982.
15. Tong, 1984.
16. Sherman & Berk, 1984.
17. See, for example, *Bruno v. Codd,* 90 Misc. 2d 1047, 396 N.Y.S.2d 974 (Sup. Ct. 1977), *Rev'd in part, appeal dismissed in part,* 407 N.Y.S.2d 165 (App. Div. 1978), *aff'd,* 47 N.Y.2d 582 (1979); and *Scott v. Hart,* No. C76-2395 (N.D. Cal., filed October 28 and November 18, 1976), both against police departments; and *Raguz v. Chandler* (No. C74-1064, N.D. Ohio, filed November 20, 1974), and *Tedesco v. Alaska,* Alaska Superior Court, Fourth Judicial District, (No. 4FA-81-593 Civil, filed May 19, 1981), for examples of cases against prosecutors— *Tedesco v. Alaska* being an attempt to collect damages after the death of the complainant at the hands of her abuser.
18. Treen & Wildeman, October 1986.
19. Jones, 1980, pp. 303–304.
20. Cf., Tong, 1984.
21. Berk & Loseke, 1981; Berk, Berk, & Newton, 1984; Ford, 1983.

22. Berk & Loseke, 1981; Berk, Berk, & Newton, 1984; Ford, 1983; Worden & Pollitz, 1984.
23. Berk, Berk, & Newton, 1984, p. 8.
24. E.g., Ford, 1983.
25. Blair, 1979.
26. As reported in the *Boston Globe,* March 1986.
27. "Judge criticized after woman's death." The *Boston Globe,* March 1986, Eileen McNamara, *Globe* Staff.
28. Silver & Kates, 1979.
29. I am indebted to Lenore Walker and Roberta Thyfault for the insights and knowledge gained in the years we worked together on the evaluation of battered women's homicide cases; and to Nancy Fiora-Gormally, Elizabeth Schneider, Susan Jordan, and Elizabeth Bochnak for their practical and theoretical work on the application of the self-defense plea to women victims of violence.
30. See *Commonwealth v. Colandra,* 231 Pa. 343, 80 A. 571 (1911), and *People v. Borchers,* 50 Ca. 2d 321, 325 P.2d 87 (1958), as cited in Fiora-Gormally (1978), p. 136; also LaFave & Scott (1972), p. 573.
31. E.g., LaFave & Scott, 1972, p. 528.
32. LaFave & Scott, 1972, p. 391.
33. LaFave & Scott, 1972.
34. See Fiora-Gormally, 1978; Schneider, 1980; Schneider & Jordan, 1981; Thyfault, 1984; and Walker, Thyfault, & Browne, 1982 for a further discussion of the self-defense plea and its applicability to cases of abused women who kill their assailants.
35. Schneider, 1980.
36. Bochnak, 1981, p. 45. See also the Supreme Court decision in *State v. Gladys Kelley,* 97 N.J. 178, 478 A.2d 364 (1984).
37. E.g., Bochnak, 1981.
38. See Fiora-Gormally, 1978, p. 156; Thyfault, 1984, p. 493, notes 84 and 85.
39. Cr. No. 4259 (Superior Court, Monterey County, Cal., 1977).
40. See Schneider & Jordan, 1981 for a more complete description of the case.
41. La Fave & Scott, 1972.
42. Schneider & Jordon, 1981.
43. Zimring, Mukherjee, & Van Winkle, 1983, p. 922.
44. 88 Wash, 2d 221, 559 P.2d 548 (1977).
45. 559 P.2d at 558–559.
46. "Wanrow," supra, at 558.
47. E.g., Fiora-Gormally, 1978; Kadish, S.H., & Paulsen, M.G., *Criminal Law and Its Processes,* 499 (3rd ed. 1975); Schneider & Jordan, 1981; Thyfault, 1984.
48. *Brown v. United States,* 156 U.S. 335, (1921):343.
49. No. 7828 Natrona Co. D.C., 1979.
50. See *Rhoades v. Superior Court,* 80 Cal. Rptr. 169; *Watkins v. State,* 197 So. 2d 312 (1969); *State v. Bonano,* 284 A.2d 345, 59 N.J. 515 (1967), as cited in Fiora-Gormally, 1978. See also *People v. McGrandy,* 156 N.W.2d 48, 9 Mich, App. 187 (1967), in which a wife, prosecuted for fatally stabbing her husband, was not obliged to retreat from the family

dwelling before using extreme resistance in self-defense (Fiora-Gormally, p. 138, note 57).
51. E.g., LaFave & Scott, 1972, p. 395, 396.
52. E.g., Barnard, Vera, Vera, & Newman, 1982; Campbell, 1981; Chimbos, 1978; Daniel & Harris, 1982; Lindsey, 1978; Totman, 1978; Wilbanks, 1983; Wolfgang, 1958.
53. See Thyfault, Browne, & Walker, in press, for a discussion of evaluation and expert witness testimony techniques in the application of the self-defense plea.
54. Bochnak, 1981; Thyfault, 1984.
55. Amicus Brief filed by the American Psychological Association in *State v. Hawthorne, No. An-35* (Fla. Dist. Ct. APP. Feb 11, 1983). See also Zimring et al., 1983, p. 929, for a discussion of the necessity of detailed knowledge in order to "make the punishment fit the crime."
56. Fiora-Gormally, 1978, p. 141.
57. Bochnak, 1981; Fiora-Gormally, 1978; see also opinion in *Hawthorne v. State,* 408 So. 2d 801 (Fla. 1st DCA 1982), rev. denied, 415 So. 2d 1361 (Fla. 1982).
58. E.g., Jones, 1980; Schneider & Jordan, 1981; Scheider, 1986; Tong, 1984; Wilbanks, 1982, 1983.
59. Blum & Fisher, 1978, as cited in Wilbanks, 1982, p. 173.
60. Walker, 1979; Walker, 1984; Thyfault, 1984.
61. See Schneider, 1986 (note 146).
62. Schneider, 1986.
63. Schneider, 1986; emphasis mine.

## Chapter 10

1. Jacoby, 1983, p. 185.
2. E.g., Dutton, 1986; Ganley, 1978, 1981; Sherman & Berk, 1984.
3. Walker & Browne, 1985; Hotaling & Sugerman, 1986.
4. Walker & Browne, 1985.

## Appendix

1. Similar interview formats were used by Washburn & Frieze, 1980, and Chimbos, 1978.
2. E.g., Bradburn & Sudman, 1979; Chimbos, 1978; Walker, 1981, 1984; Washburn & Frieze, 1980.

# References

ALFARO, J.D., *Project Director* (1978). Summary report on the relationship between child abuse and neglect and later socially deviant behavior. New York State Select Committee on Child Abuse.

ARIES, E.J. & OLVER, R.R. (1985). "Sex differences in the development of a separate sense of self during infancy: Directions for future research." *Psychology of Women Quarterly, 9* (4), 515–531.

ARNOLD, M.B. (1967). "Stress and emotion." In M.H. Appley & R. Trumbull (Eds.) *"Psychology Stress."* New York: Appleton-Century-Crofts.

ARONSON, E. (1972). *The Social Animal.* San Francisco: Freeman.

AZRIN, N.H., HOLZ, W.C., & HAKE, D.F. (1963). "Fixed ratio punishment." *Journal of Experimental Analysis of Behavior, 6,* 141–148.

BAHNSON, C.B. (1964). "Emotional reactions to internally and externally derived threats of annihilation." In G.H. Grosser, H. Wechsler, & M. Greenblatt (Eds.) *The Threat of Impending Disaster.* Cambridge, MA: MIT Press.

BALL-ROKEACH, S.J. (1980). "Normative and deviant violence from a conflict perspective." *Social Problems, 28,* 45-62.

BANDURA, A. (1973). *Aggression: A Social Learning Analysis.* Englewood Cliffs, NJ: Prentice-Hall.

BANDURA, A. & WALTERS, R.H. (1973). *Social Learning and Personality Development.* New York, NY: Holt, Rinehart and Winston.

BANDURA, A., UNDERWOOD, B., & FROMSON, M.E. (1975). "Disinhibition of aggression through diffusion of responsibility and dehumanization." *Journal of Research in Personality, 9,* 253–269.

BARD, M. & SANGREY, D. (1979). *The Crime Victim's Book.* New York: Basic Books.

BARDWICK, J. (1971). *Psychology of Women: A Study of Bio-Cultural Conflicts.* New York: Harper & Row.

BARNARD, G.W., VERA, H., VERA, M., & NEWMAN, G. (1982). "Till death do us part: A study of spouse murder." *Bulletin of the American Academy of Psychiatry and Law, 10* (4), 271–280.

BARNETT, E.R., PITTMAN, C.B., RAGAN, C.K., SALUS, M.K. (1980). "Family violence: Intervention strategies." Department of Health and Human Services, Washington, DC: Government Printing Office. Pub. No. (OHDS)80-30258.

BERK, R.A., BERK, S.F., LOSEKE, D.R., AND RAUMA, D. (1983). "Mutual combat and other family violence myths." In R.J. Gelles, G.T. Hotaling, & M.A. Straus (Eds.), *The dark side of families; Current family violence research.* Beverly Hills, CA: Sage

BERK, R.A., BERK, S.F., & NEWTON, P.J. (1984). "An empirical analysis of police responses to incidents of wife battery." Paper presented at the Second National Conference of Family Violence Researchers. University of New Hampshire, Durham, NH.

BERK, S. & LOSEKE, D. (1981). "Handling family violence: Situational determinants of police arrest in domestic disturbances." *Law and Society Review, 15*(2), 317–344.

BERKOWITZ, L. (1974). "Some determinants of impulsive aggression: Role of mediated associations with reinforcements for aggression." *Psychological Review, 82,* 165–176.

BERKOWITZ, L. (1977). "Simple views of aggression: An essay review." In J.C. Brigham & L.S. Wrightsman (Eds.), *Contemporary Issues in Social Psychology (3rd ed.).* Monterey, CA: Brooks/Cole.

BERKOWITZ, L. (1983). "The goals of aggression." In D. Finkelhor, R.J. Gelles, G.T. Hotaling, & M.A. Straus (Eds.), *The Dark Side of Families: Current Family Violence Research.* Beverly Hills, CA: Sage.

BERKOWITZ, L. & LEPAGE, A. (1967). "Weapons as aggression-eliciting stimuli." *Journal of Personality and Social Psychology, 7,* 202–207.

BERNARD, M.L. & BERNARD, J.L. (1983). "Violent intimacy: The family as a model for love relationships." *Family Relations, 32,* 283–286.

BETTLEHEIM, B. (1943). "Individual and mass behavior in extreme situations." *Journal of Abnormal and Social Psychology, 38,* 417–452.

BIDERMAN, A.D. (1967). "Captivity lore and behavior in captivity." In G.H. Grosser, H. Wechsler, & M. Greenblatt (Eds.) *The Threat of Impending Disaster.* Cambridge, MA: MIT Press.

BLACK, C. (1979). "Children of alcoholics." *Alcohol Health and Research World, 4*(1), 23–27.

BLACK, D. (1980). *The Manners and Customs of Police.* New York, NY: Academic Press.

BLACKSTONE, W. (1765). *Commentaries on the Laws of England, Book 4.* Philadelphia, PA: R. Welsh & Co., 1897.

BLAIR, S. (1979). "Making the legal system work for battered women." In D.M. Moore (Ed.) *Battered Women.* Beverly Hills: Sage.

BLUM, A. & FISHER, G. (1978). "Women who kill." In I. Kutash et al. (Eds.), *Violence: Perspectives on murder and aggression.* San Francisco, CA: Jossey Bass.

BOCHNAK, E. (1981). "Case preparation and development." In E. Bochnak (Ed.), *Women's Self-defense Cases: Theory and Practice.* Charlottsville, VA: The Michie Company Law Publishers.

BOURDOURIS, J. (1971). "Homicide in the family." *Journal of Marriage and the Family, 33,* 667–676.

BOWKER, L.H. (1983a). *Beating Wife-Beating.* Lexington, MA: Lexington Books.

BOWKER, L.H. (1983b). "Marital rape: A distrinct syndrome?" *Social Casework: The Journal of Contemporary Social Work,* (June), 347–52.

BROCK, T.C. & BUSS, A.H. (1962). "Dissonance, aggression, and evaluation of pain." *Journal of Abnormal and Social Psychology, 65,* 197–202.

BROCK, T.C. & BUSS, A.H. (1964). "Effects of justification for aggression and communication with the victim on postaggression dissonance." *Journal of Abnormal and Social Psychology, 68,* 403–412.

BROVERMAN, L.K., BROVERMAN, D.M., CLARKSON, F.E., ROSENKRANTZ, P.S., & VOGEL, S. (1970). "Sex-role stereotypes and clinical judgements of mental health." *Journal of Consulting and Clinical Psychology, 34,* 1–7.

BROWNE, A. (1980). "Comparison of victim's reactions across traumas." Paper presented at the Rocky Mountain Psychological Association annual meeting. Tucson, Arizona.

*Brown v. United States,* 156 U.S. 335, (1921):343.

BROWNE, A. (1986). "Assault and homicide at home: When battered women kill." In M.J. Saks & L. Saxe (Eds.), *Advances in Applied Social Psychology, Vol. 3.* Hillsdale, NJ: Lawrence Erlbaum Associates, Inc.

BROWNING, J.J. & DUTTON, D.G. (in press). "Using couple data to quantify the Pirandello Effect." *Journal of Marriage and the Family.*

*Bruno v. Codd,* 90 Misc. 2d 1047, 396 N.Y.S.2d 974 (Sup. Ct. 1977), *Rev'd in part, appeal dismissed in part,* 407 N.Y.S.2d 165 (App. Div. 1978), *aff'd,* 47 N.Y.2d 582 (1979).

Bureau of Justice Statistics (1980). *Intimate victims: A study of violence among friends and relatives.* (U.S. Department of Justice.) Washington, D.C.: U.S. Government Printing Office.

BURGESS, A.W. & HOLMSTROM, L.L. (1974). "Rape trauma syndrome." *American Journal of Psychiatry, 131*(9), 981–86.

BUSS, A.H. (1966). "Instrumentality of aggression, feedback, and frustration as determinants of physical aggression." *Journal of Personality and Social Psychology, 3,* 153–162.

CAMPBELL, J. (1981). "Misogyny and homicide of women." *Advances in Nursing Science, 3,* 67–85.

CARROLL, J.C. (1977). "The intergenerational transmission of family violence: Long-term effect of aggressive behavior." *Aggressive Behavior, 3,* 289–299.

CATE, R., HENTON, J., KAVAL, J., CHRISTOPHER, S., & LLOYD, S. (1982). "Premarital abuse: A social psychological perspective." *Journal of Family Issues, 3,* 79–91.

CHAPMAN, D.W. (1962). "A brief introduction to contemporary disaster research." In G.W. Baker & D.W. Chapman (Eds.) *Man and Society in Disaster.* New York: Basic Books.

CHIMBOS, P.D. (1978). *Marital Violence: A Study of Interspousal Homicide.* San Francisco: R & E Research Associates.

CHODOROW, N. (1974). "Family structure and feminine personality." In M.Z. Rosaldo & L. Lamphere (Eds.) *Women, Culture and Society.* Stanford: Standord University Press.

COLEMAN, D.H. and STRAUS, M.A. (1983). "Alcohol abuse and family violence." In E. Gottheil, A. Durley, I.E. Skolada, & H.M. Waxman (Eds.) *Alcohol, Drug Abuse and Aggression.* (pp. 104–123). Springfield, MA: C.C. Thomas.

COLEMAN, K.H., WEINMAN, M.L., & HSI, B.P. (1980). "Factors affecting conjugal violence." *Journal of Psychology, 105,* 197–202.

Colorado Association for Aid to Battered Women (CAABW) (1980). *A Monograph on Services to Battered Women.* (DAHS Publication NO. OHDS 79-05708) Washington, D.C.: U.S. Government Printing Office.

*Commonwealth v. Colandra,* 231 Pa. 343, 80 A. 571 (1911).

CONGER, R.D. (1980). "Juvenile delinquency: Behavior restraint or behavior facilitation?" In T. Hirschi & M. Gottfredson (Eds.), *Understanding Crime.* Beverly Hills, CA: Sage.

*Crimes of Violence* (1969). A staff report to the National Commission on the Causes and Prevention of Violence. Washington, DC: U.S. Government Printing Office.

DANIEL, A.E. & HARRIS, P.W. (1982). "Female homicide offenders referred for pretrial psychiatric examination: A descriptive study." *Bulletin of the American Academy of Psychiatry and Law, 10*(4), 261–269.

DAVIDSON, T. (1977). "Wifebeating: A recurring phenomenon throughout history." In M. Roy (Ed.), *Battered Women: A Psychosociological Study of Domestic Violence.* New York, NY: Van Nostrand Reinhold Co.

DAVIDSON, T. (1978). *Conjugal crime: Understanding and Changing the Wifebeating Pattern.* New York, NY: Hawthorne Books.

DAVIS, E.G. (1971). *The First Sex.* New York, NY: Penguin.

DESCHNER, J.P. (1984). *The Hitting Habit.* New York, NY: Free Press.

DOBASH, R.E. & DOBASH, R.P. (1979). *Violence Against Wives: A Case Against the Patriarchy.* New York, NY: Free Press.

DOBASH, R.E. & DOBASH, R.P. (1984). The nature and antecedents of violent events. *British Journal of Criminology, 24*(3), 269–288.

DUTTON, D. & BROWNING, J. (1984). "Power struggles and intimacy anxieties as causative factors of wife assault." In G. Russell (Ed.) *Violence in Intimate Adult Relationships.* New York: Spectrum Press.

DUTTON, D., FEHR, B., & MCEWAN, H. (1982). "Severe wife beating as deindividualized violence." *Victimology, 7*(1–4), 13–23.

DUTTON, D. & PAINTER, S.L. (1981). "Traumatic bonding: The development of emotional attachments in battered women and other relationships of intermittent abuse." *Victimology, 6,* 139–155.

DUTTON, D. (1986). Wife assault: Social Psychological Contributions to Criminal Justice Policy. *Applied Social Psychology Annual, 4.*

DVOSKIN, J.A. (1981). *Battered Women—An Epidemiological Study of Spousal Violence.* Unpublished doctoral dissertation, University of Arizona.

EBERLE, P. (1982). "Alcohol abusers and non-users: A discriminate function analysis." *Journal of Health and Social Behavior, 23.*

EISENBERG, S.E. & MICKLOW, P.L. (1974). *The Assaulted Wife: "Catch 22" Revisited.* Ann Arbor, MI: University of Michigan Law School. Unpublished manuscript.

EISENBERG, A.D. & SEYMOUR, E.J. (1978). "Self-defense plea and battered women." *Trial, 14*(7) 34–36, 41–42, 68.

ELLIOTT, D.S., AGETON, S., & CANTER, R. (1979). "An integrated theoretical perspective on delinquent behavior." *Journal of Research on Crime and Delinquency, 19*(1).

ERIKSON, E.H. (1950). *Childhood and Society*. New York, NY: W.W. Norton.

EWING, W., LINDSEY, M., & POMERANTZ, J. (1984). *Battering: An AMEND Manual for Helpers*. Denver, CO: Littleton Heights College.

FAGAN, J.A. & JONES, S.J. (1984). "Toward a theoretical model for intervention with violent juvenile offenders." In R.A. Mathias (Ed.), *Violent juvenile offenders*. San Francisco, CA: National Council on Crime and Delinquency.

FAGAN, J.A., STEWART, D.K., & HANSON, K.V. (1983). "Violent men or violent husbands?" In D. Finkelhor, R.J. Gelles, G.T. Hotaling, & M.A. Straus (Eds.), *The Dark Side of Families: Current Family Violence Research*. Beverly Hills, CA: Sage.

FARRINGTON, D.P. (1978). "The family backgrounds of aggressive youths." In L. Hersov, M. Berger, & D. Shaffer (Eds.), *Criminal Violence*. Beverly Hills, CA: Sage.

FASTEAU, M.F. (1974). *The Male Machine*. New York, NY: McGraw-Hill.

FESTINGER, L. (1957). *The Theory of Cognitive Dissonance*. Evanston, IL: Row, Peterson.

FIELD, M.H. & FIELD, H.F. (1973). "Marital violence and the criminal process: Neither justice nor peace." *Social Service Review, 47,* 221–240.

FIELDS, M.D. (1978). "Does this vow include wife-beating?" *Human Rights,* 7(20), 40–45.

FIELDS, M.D. & KIRCHNER, R.M. (1978). "Battered women are still in need: A reply to Steinmetz." *Victimology, 3*(1–2): 216–222.

FINKELHOR, D. & YLLO, K. (1985). *License to Rape: Sexual Abuse of Wives*. New York, NY: Holt, Rinehart & Winston.

FIORA-GORMALLY, N. (1978). "Battered wives who kill. Double standard out of court, single standard in?" *Law and Human Behavior, 2*(2): 133–65.

FORD, D.A. (1983). "Wife battery and criminal justice: A study of victim decision-making." *Family Relations, 32,* 463–475.

FREUD, S. (1905). *Three Essays on the Theory of Sexuality*. Vol. VII.

FREUD, S. (1925). "Some psychical consequences of the anatomical distinction between the sexes." Vol. XIX.

FREUD, S. (1961). *The Standard Edition of the Complete Psychological Works of Sigmund Freud,* trans. and ed. James Strachey. London: The Hogarth Press.

FRIEZE, I.H. (1979). "Power and influence in violent and nonviolent marriages." Paper presented at the Eastern Psychological Association meetings, Philadelphia, PA.

FRIEZE, I.H. (1980). "Causes and consequences of marital rape." Paper presented at the annual meeting of the American Psychological Association. Montreal, Canada.

FRIEZE, I.H. (1983). "Investigating the causes and consequences of marital rape." *SIGNS, 8*(3), 532–553.

FRIEZE, I.H. & KNOBLE, J. (1980). "The effects of alcohol on marital violence." Paper presented at the annual meeting of the American Psychological Association. Montreal, Canada.

FRIEZE, I.H., KNOBLE, J., ZOMNIR, G., & WASHBURN, C. (1980). "Types of battered women." Paper presented at the meeting of the Association for Women in Psychology. Santa Monica, CA.

FROMSON, T.L. (1977). "The case for legal remedies for abused women." *New York University Review of Law and Social Change, 6*(2), 135–174.

*Fulgham v. State,* 46 Ala. 146–147 (1871).

GANLEY, A. (1981). "Counseling programs for men who batter: Elements of effective programs." *Response, 4*(8), 3–4.

GANLEY, A.L. & HARRIS, L. (1978). "Domestic violence: Issues in designing and implementing programs for male batterers." Paper presented at the annual meeting of the American Psychological Association. Toronto, Canada.

GEEN, R.G. (1968). "Effects of frustration, attack, and prior training in aggressiveness upon aggressive behavior." *Journal of Personality and Social Psychology, 9,* 316–321.

GEEN, R.G., STONNER, D., & SHOPE, G.L. (1975). "The facilitation of aggression by aggression: Evidence against the catharsis hypotheses." *Journal of Personality and Social Psychology, 31,* 721–726.

GELLES, R.J. (1974). *The Violent Home: A Study of Physical Aggression Between Husbands and Wives.* Beverly Hills, CA: Sage Publications.

GELLES, R.J. (1975). "Violence and pregnancy. A note on the extent of the problem and needed services." *Family Coordinator* (January), 81–86.

GELLES, R.J. (1980). "Violence in the family: A review of research in the seventies." *Journal of Marriage and the Family, 42,* 873–885.

GIL, D.G. (1970). *Violence Against Children.* Cambridge, MA: Harvard University Press.

GILLIGAN, C. (1982). *In a Different Voice.* Cambridge, MA: Harvard University Press.

GOLDSTEIN, J.H., DAVIS, R.W., & HERMAN, D. (1975). "Escalation of aggression: Experimental studies." *Journal of Personality and Social Psychology, 31,* 162–170.

GOLDSTEIN, J.H., DAVIS, R.W., KERNIS, M., & COHN, E. (1981). "Retarding the escalation of aggression." *Social Behavior and Personality, 9*(1), 65–70.

GOODE, W.J. (1971). "Force and violence in the family." *Journal of Marriage and the Family, 33,* 624–636.

GREENBLAT, C.S. (1983), "A hit is a hit is a hit ... Or is it? Approval and tolerance of the use of physical force by spouses." In D. Finkelhor, R.J. Gelles, G.T. Hotaling, & M.A. Straus (Eds.), *The Dark Side of Families: Current Family Violence Research.* Beverly Hills, CA: Sage.

GRINKER, R.R. & SPIEGEL, J.P. (1945). *Man Under Stress.* New York, NY: Blakiston.

GUTMANN, D. (1970). "Female ego styles and generational conflict." In J. Bardwick, E. Douvan, M. Horner, & D. Gutmann, *Feminine Personality and Conflict,* pp. 76–96, Belmont, CA: Brooks/Cole.

HALL, D.J. (1975). "The role of the victim in the prosecution and disposition of a criminal case." *Vanderbilt Law Review, 28,* 931–985.

HALLECK, S.L. (1967). *Psychiatry and the Dilemmas of Crime*. New York, NY: Harper and Row.

HANNEKE, C.R. & SHIELDS, N.M. (1981). "Patterns of family and non-family violence: An approach to the study of violent husbands." Paper presented at the National Conference for Family Violence Researchers. Durham, NH.

HAWKINS, J.D. & WEIS, J.G. (1980). *The Social Development Model: An Integrated Approach to Delinquency Prevention*. Seattle: Center for Law and Justice, University of Washington.

*Hawthorne v. State,* 408 So. 2d 801 (Fla. 1st DCA 1983), *rev. denied,* 415 So. 2d 1361 (Fla. 1982).

HENTON, J., CATE, R., KAVAL, J., LLOYD, S., & CHRISTOPHER, S. (1983). "Romance and violence in dating relationships." *Journal of Family Issues, 4,* 467–482.

HERMAN, J.L. (1981). *Father-Daughter Incest*. Cambridge, MA: Harvard University Press.

HERZBERGER, S.D. (1981). "A social cognitive approach to the cross-generational transmission of abuse." Paper presented at the National Conference for Family Violence Researchers. University of New Hampshire, Durham, NH.

HERZBERGER, S.D. (1983). "Social cognition and the transmission of abuse." In D. Finkelhor, R.J. Gelles, G.T. Hotaling, & M.A. Straus (Eds.), *The Dark Side of Families: Current Family Violence Research*. Beverly Hills, CA: Sage.

HILBERMAN, E. & MUNSON, K. (1978). "Sixty battered women." *Victimology 2*(3/4), 460–471.

HOFELLER, K.H. (1980). *Social, Psychological and Situational Factors in Wife Abuse*. Unpublished doctoral dissertation, Claremont Graduate School.

HOFFMAN, M.L. (1977). "Sex differences in empathy and related behaviors." *Psychological Bulletin, 84*(4), 712–722.

HOTALING, G.T. & SUGARMAN, D.B. (1986). "An analysis of risk markers in husband to wife violence: The current state of knowledge." *Violence and Victims, 1*(2), 101–124.

JACOBY, S. (1983). *Wild Justice*. New York, NY: Harper & Row.

JOHNSTON, M.E. (1984). "Correlates of early violence experience among men who are abusive toward female mates." Paper presented at the Second National Conference for Family Violence Researchers. University of New Hampshire, Durham, NH.

JONES, A. (1980). *Women Who Kill*. New York, NY: Fawcett Columbine Books.

KADISH, S.H. & PAULSEN, M.G. (1975). *Criminal Law and Its Processes, 3rd Ed.* Boston, MA: Little Brown.

KALMUSS, D.S. (1984). "The intergenerational transmission of marital aggression." *Journal of Marriage and the Family, 46*(1), 11–19.

KALMUSS, D.S. & SELTZER, J.A. (1984). "The effect of family structure on family violence: The case of remarriage." Paper presented at the Second National Conference for Family Violence Researchers. Durham, NH.

KANOWITZ, L. (1969). *Women and the Law: The Unfinished Revolution*. Albuquerque, NM: University of New Mexico.

KAPLAN, A.G. & SURREY, J.L. (1984). "The relational self in women: Developmental theory and public policy." In L.E. Walker (Ed.) *Women and Mental Health Policy*. Beverly Hills, CA: Sage.

KATZ, S. & MAZUR, M.A. (1979). *Understanding the Rape Victim: A Synthesis of Research Findings*. New York, NY: John Wiley & Sons.

KEATING, J.P. & BROCK, T.C. (1976). "Effects of prior reward and punishment on subsequent reward and punishment: Guilt vs. consistency." *Journal of Personality and Social Psychology, 34,* 327–33.

KEMPE, C.H., SILVERMAN, F.N., STEELE, B.F., DROEGEMUELLER, W., & SILVER, H. (1962). "The battered child syndrome." *Journal of the American Medical Association, 181,* 107–112.

KILPATRICK, D.G., VERONEN, L.J., & RESICK, P.A. (1979). "The aftermath of rape: Recent empirical findings." *American Journal of Orthopsychiatry, 49*(4), 658–669.

KLECKA, W.R. (1975). "Discriminant analysis." In N.H. Nie, C.H. Hull, J.G. Jenkins, K. Steinbrenner, & D.H. Bent (Eds.), *SPSS—Statistical Package for the Social Sciences, 2nd Ed.* New York, NY: McGraw Hill.

KLECKNER, J.H. (1978). "Wife beaters and beaten wives: Co-conspirators in crimes of violence." *Psychology, 15*(1): 54–56.

KLUGH, H.E. (1974). *Statistics: The Essentials for Research*. New York, NY: John Wiley & Sons.

KOHLBERG, L. (1969). "Stage and sequence: The cognitive-development approach to socialization." In D.A. Goslin (Ed.) *Handbook of Socialization Theory and Research*. Chicago, Il: Rand McNally.

LAFAVE, W.R. & SCOTT, JR., A.W. (1972). *Handbook on Criminal Law*. St. Paul, MN: The West Publishing Company.

LANDAU, S.F. (1976). "The rape offender's perception of his victim: Some cross-cultural findings." Paper presented at the Second International Symposium on Victimology. Boston, MA.

LANER, M.R. & THOMPSON, J. (1982). "Abuse and aggression in courting couples." *Deviant Behavior, 3,* 229–44.

LAZARUS, R.S. (1967). "Cognitive and personality factors underlying threat and coping." In M.H. Appley & R. Trumbull (Eds.) *Psychological Stress*. New York, NY: Appleton-Century-Crofts.

LEGG, J., OLDAY, D.W. & WESLEY, B. (1984). "Why do females remain in violent dating relationships?" Paper presented at the Second National Conference for Family Violence Researchers. University of New Hampshire, Durham, NH.

LERMAN, L.G. (1981). "Criminal prosecution of wife beaters." *Response to Violence in the Family, 4*(3), 1–19.

LERNER, M.J. & SIMMONS, C.H. (1966). "Observer's reaction to the 'innocent victim': Compassion or rejection?" *Journal of Personality and Social Psychology, 4,* 203–210.

LEVER, J. (1976). "Sex differences in the games children play." *Social Problems, 23,* 478–487.

Levinson, D. (1978). *The Seasons of a Man's Life.* New York, NY: Alfred A. Knopf.

Lewin, T. (1979). "When victims kill." *National Law Journal, 2*(7), 2–4, 11.

Lindsey, K. (1978). "When battered women strike back: Murder or self-defense." *Viva* (September) pp. 58–59; 66–74.

Lopez S.C. (1981). *Marital Satisfaction and Wife Abuse as a Function of Sex-Role Identity, Self-Esteem and Interpersonal Style.* Unpublished doctoral dissertation, Georgia State University.

McCord, J. (1979). "Some child-rearing antecedents of criminal behavior in adult men." *Journal of Personality and Social Psychology, 37,* 1477–1486.

McClelland, D.C. (1975). *Power: The Inner Experience.* New York, NY: Irvington.

Maccoby, E. & Jacklin, C. (1974). *The Psychology of Sex Differences.* Stanford, CA: Stanford University Press.

Makepeace, J.M. (1981). "Courtship violence among college students." *Family Relations, 30,* 97–102.

Makepeace, J.M. (1983). "Life events stress and courtship violence." *Family Relations, 32,* 101–109.

Martin, D. (1976). *Battered Wives.* San Francisco, CA: Glide Publications.

Mathews, W.J. (1984). "Violence in college couples." Paper presented at the Second National Conference for Family Violence Researchers. University of New Hampshire, Durham, NH.

May, J. (1978). "Violence in the family: An historical perspective." In J.P Martin (Ed.), *Violence and the Family.* New York, NY: John Wiley and Sons.

Medea, A. & Thompson, K. (1974). *Against Rape: A Survival Manual for Women: How to Cope with Rape Phsycially and Emotionally.* New York, NY: Farrar, Straus & Giroux.

Meerloo, J. (1961). *The Rape of the Mind.* New York, NY: Grosset & Dunlop.

Mettger, Z. (1982). "A case of rape: Forced sex in marriage." *Response, 5*(2), 1–2, 13–16.

Mileti, D.S., Drabek, T.E., & Haas, J.E. (1975). *Human Systems in Extreme Environments.* Institute of Behavioral Science, University of Colorado.

Miller, J.B. (1976). *Toward a New Psychology of Women.* Boston, MA: Beacon Press.

Miller, J.G. (1964). "A theoretical review of individual and group psychological reactions to stress." In G.H. Grosser, H. Wechsler, & M. Greenblatt (Eds.) *The Threat of Impending Disaster.* Cambridge, MA: MIT Press.

Moore, D.M. (1979). *Battered Women.* Beverly Hills, CA: Sage.

Murphy, J.E. (1984). "Date abuse and forced intercourse among college students." Paper presented at the Second National Conference for Family Violence Researchers. University of New Hampshire, Durham, NH.

Nathan, T.S., Eitinger, L., & Winick, Z. (1964). "A psychiatric study of survivors of the Nazi holocaust." *Israel Annals of Psychiatry.*

National District Attorneys Association (1978). *The Victim Advocate*. Chicago, IL: The National District Attorneys Association.

NOTMAN, M. & NADELSON, C.C. (1976). "The rape victim: Psychodynamic considerations." *American Journal of Psychiatry, 133*(4), 408–412.

NOVACO, R. (1976). "The functions and regulation of the arousal of anger." *American Journal of Psychology, 133*(10), 1124–1128.

O'BRIEN, J.E. (1971). "Violence in divorce prone families." *Journal of Marriage and the Family, 33,* 692–698.

O'FAOLAIN, J. & MARTINES, L. (1973). *Not in God's Image: Women in History from the Greeks to the Victorians*. New York, NY: Harper & Row.

PAGELOW, M.D., (1980). "Does the law protect the rights of battered women? Some research notes." Paper presented at the annual meeting of the Law and Society Asociation of the ISA Research Committee on the Sociology of Law, Madison, WI.

PAGELOW, M.D. (1980). "Double victimization of battered women: Victimized by spouses and the legal system." Paper presented at the annual meeting of the American Society of Criminology, San Francisco, CA.

PAGELOW, M.D. (1981). *Women-Battering: Victims and Their Experiences*. Beverly Hills, CA: Sage.

PAGELOW, M.D. (1984). *Family Violence*. New York, NY: Praeger.

PARKE, R.D. & COLLMER, C.W. (1975). "Child abuse: An interdisciplinary analysis." In M. Hetherington (Ed.), *Review of child development research, Vol. 5*. Chicago, IL: University of Chicago Press.

PARNAS, R. (1970). "Judicial response to intra-family violence." *Minnesota Law Review, 54,* 585–644.

PATTERSON, G. (1982). *Coercive Family Processes*. Eugene, OR: Cataglia Press.

*People v. Borchers,* 50, Ca. 2d 321, 325 P.2d 87 (1958).

*People v. Garcia,* Cr. No. 4259 (Superior Court, Monterey County, Cal., 1977).

*People v. McGrandy,* (156 N.W.2d 48, 9 Mich. App. 187 (1967).

PERRY, D.G. & PERRY, L.C. (1974). "Denial of suffering in the victim as a stimulus to violence in aggressive boys." *Child Development, 45*(1), 55–62.

PETERSON, R. (1980). "Social class, social learning and wife abuse." *Social Service Review, 54,* 390–406.

PIAGET, J. (1932). *The Moral Judgement of the Child*. New York, NY: The Free Press.

PLECK, E. (1979). "Wife beating in nineteenth century America." *Victimology, 4*(1), 60–74.

PLECK, J.H. (1981). *The Myth of Masculinity*. Cambridge, MA: MIT Press.

Police Foundation (1976). *Domestic Violence and the Police: Studies in Detroit and Kansas City*. Washington, D.C.: The Police Foundation.

POLLAK, S. & GILLIGAN, C. (1982). "Images of violence in thematic apperception test stories." *Journal of Personality and Social Psychology, 42*(1), 159–167.

POWELL, J.W. (1954). *An Introduction to the Natural History of Disaster (Vol.*

*2)*. Final Contract Report, Disaster Research Project, Psychiatric Institute, University of Maryland.

PRESCOTT, S. & LETCO, C. (1977). "Battered women: A social psychological perspective." In M. Roy (Ed.) *Battered Women: A Psychosociological Study of Domestic Violence.* New York, NY: Van Nostrand Reinhold Co.

Queen's Bench Foundation (1976). *Rape: Prevention and Resistance.* San Francisco, CA: Queen's Bench Foundation.

*Raguz v. Chandler,* (No. C74-1064, N.D. Ohio, filed November 20, 1974).

REID, J.B., TAPLIN, P.S., & LORBER, R. (1981). "A social inter-actional approach to treatment of abusive families." In R.B. Stuart (Ed.), *Violent Behavior: Social Learning Approaches to Prediction, Management and Treatment.* New York, NY: Brunner/Mazel.

*Rhodes v. Superior Court,* 80 Cal. Rptr. 169.

ROSENBAUM, A. & O'LEARY, K.D. (1981). "Marital violence: Characteristics of abusive couples." *Journal of Consulting and Clinical Psychology, 49,* 63–71.

ROUSE, L.P. (1984a). "Conflict tactics used by men in marital disputes." Paper presented at the Second National Conference for Family Violence Researchers. University of New Hampshire, Durham, NH.

ROUSE, L.P. (1984b). "Models, self-esteem, and locus of control as factors contributing to spouse abuse." *Victimology, 9*(1), 130–144.

ROY, M. (1977). "Research project probing a cross-section of battered women." In M. Roy (Ed.) *Battered Women: A Psychosocial Study of Domestic Violence.* New York, NY: Van Nostrand Reinhold Co.

RUSSELL, D.E.H. (1975). *The Politics of Rape: The Victim's Perspective.* Briarcliff Manor, NY: Stein and Day.

RUSSELL, D.E.H. (1982). *Rape in Marriage.* New York, NY: MacMillan.

SCHECHTER, S. (1982). *Women and Male Violence.* Boston, MA: South End Press.

SCHNEIDER, E.M. (1980). "Equal rights to trial for women: Sex bias in the law on self-defense." *Harvard Civil Rights-Civil Liberties Law Review, 15,* 623–647.

SCHNEIDER, E.M. (in press). "Describing and changing: Women's self-defense work and the problem of expert testimony on battering." *Women's Rights Law Reporter.*

SCHNEIDER, E.M. & JORDAN, S.B. (1981). Representation of women who defend themselves in response to physical or sexual assault. In E. Bochnak (Ed.), *Women's Self Defense Cases: Theory & Practice.* Charlottesville, VA: The Michie Company Law Publishers.

SCHULMAN, M. (1979). *A Survey of Spousal Violence Against Women in Kentucky.* Study #792701 for the Kentucky Commission on Women. Washington, DC: US Department of Justice—LEAR.

SCHULTZ, L.G. (1960). "The wife assaulter." *Journal of Social Therapy, 6,* 103–12.

*Scott v. Hart,* No. C76-2395 (N.D. Cal., filed October 28 and November 18, 1976.

SEBASTIAN, R.J. (1983). "Social psychological determinants." In D. Finkelhor, R.J. Gelles, G.T. Hotaling, & M.A. Straus (Eds.), *The Dark Side of Families: Current Family Violence Research,* pp. 182–192. Beverly Hills, CA: Sage.

SERUM, C.S. (1982). "A profile of men who batter women." Paper presented at the conference of the Bozeman Area Battered Women's Network. Bozeman, Montana.

SHAINESS, N. (1977). "Psychological aspects of wife-battering." In M. Roy (Ed.), *Battered Women,* pp. 111–119. New York, NY: Van Nostrand Reinhold Co.

SHERIF, M. & HOVLAND, C. (1961). *Social Judgement.* New Haven, CT: Yale University Press.

SHERMAN, L.W. & BERK, R.A. (1984). "The Minneapolis domestic violence experiment." *Police Foundation Reports 1.* Washington, D.C.: The Police Foundation.

SHERMAN, L.W. & BERK, R.A. (1984). "The specific deterrent effects of arrest for domestic assault." *American Sociological Review, 49,* 261–272.

SHIELDS, N. & HANNEKE, C.R. (1981). "Battered women's reactions to marital rape." Paper presented at the National Conference for Family Violence Researchers. Durham, NH.

SHIELDS, N. & HANNEKE, C.R. (1983). "Battered wives' reactions to marital rape." In D. Finkelhor, R.J. Gelles, G.T. Hotaling, & M.A. Straus (Eds.) *The Dark Side of Families.,* pp. 131–48. Beverly Hills, CA: Sage.

SIGELMAN, C.K., BERRY, C.J. & WILES, K.A. (1984). "Violence in college students' dating relationships." *Journal of Applied Social Psychology, 14*(6), 530–548.

SILVER, C.R. & KATES, D.B. (1979). "Self-defense, handgun ownership, and the independence of women in a violent sexist society." In D.B. Kates (Ed.), *Restricting Handguns: The Liberal Skeptics Speak Out.* Croton-on-Hudson, NY: North River Press.

SIMON, R.I. (1978). Type A, AB, B murders: Their relationship to the victims and to the criminal justice system. *Bulletin of the American Academy of Psychiatry and Law, 5,* 344–362.

SNELL, J.E., ROSENWALD, R.J., & ROBEY, A. (1964). "The wifebeater's wife: A study of family interaction. *Archives of General Psychiatry, 11,* 107–113.

SONKIN, D. & DURPHY, M. (1982, 1985). *Learning to Live Without Violence: A Handbook for Men.* San Francisco, CA: Volcano Press.

SORRELLS, J.M. (1977). "Kids who kill." *Crime and Delinquency, 23.*

SPIEGEL, J.P. (1955). "Emotional reactions to catastrophe." In S. Liebman (Ed.) *Stress Situations.* Philadelphia, PA: J.B. Lippincott.

STAR, B. (1978). "Comparing battered and non-battered women." *Victimology,* 3(1–2), 32–44.

STARK, E. & FLITCRAFT, A. (1981). "Therapeutic intervention as a situational determinant of the battering syndrome." Paper presented at the National Conference for Family Violence Researchers. Durham, NH.

STARK, E., FLITCRAFT, A., & FRAZIER, W. (1979). "Medicine and patriarchal violence:

The social construction of a 'private' event." *International Journal of Health Services, 98*(3): 461–491.

STARK, E., FLITCRAFT, A., ZUCKERMAN, D., GREY, A., ROBINSON, J., & FRAZIER, W. (1981). *Wife Abuse in the Medical Setting: An Introduction to Health Personnel.* National Clearinghouse on Domestic Violence, Monograph Series #7.

STARK, R. & McEVOY, J. III (1970). "Middle-class violence." *Psychology Today* (November): 52–54, 110–112.

*State v. Black,* 60 N.C. 162, 163, 86 Am. Dec., 436 (1864).

*State v. Bonano,* 284 A.2d 345, 59 N.J. 515 (1967).

*State v. Gladys Kelley,* 97 N.J. 178, 478 A.2d 364 (1984).

*State v. Hawthorne, No. An-35,* (Fla. Dist. Ct. APP. Feb 11, 1983).

*State v. Oliver,* 70 N.C. 60, 61–62 (1874) (Criminal Liability).

*State v. Rhodes,* 61 Phill. L. (N.C.) 453 (1866).

*State v. Wanrow,* 88 Wash, 2d 221, 559 P.2d 548 (1977).

STEELE, B. & POLLOCK, C. (1968). "A psychiatric study of parents who abuse infants and small children." In R. Helfer & C.H. Kempe (Eds.), *The Battered Child,* pp. 103–148. Chicago, IL: University of Chicago Press.

STEINMETZS, S.K. & STRAUS, M.A. (1974). *Violence in the Family.* New York, NY: Harper & Row.

STEPHENS, D.W. (1977). "Domestic assault: The police response." In M. Roy (Ed.), *Battered Women: A Psychosocial Study of Domestic Violence.* New York, NY: Van Nostrand Reinhold Co.

STRASBURG, P.A. (1978). *Violent delinquents.* New York, NY: Monarch.

STRAUS, M.A. (1971). "Some social antecendents of physical punishment: A linkage theory interpretation." *Journal of Marriage and the Family, 33,* 658–663.

STRAUS, M.A. (1973). "A general systems theory approach to a theory of violence between family members." *Social Science Information, 12*(3), 105–25.

STRAUS, M.A. (1978). "Wife beating: How common and why?" *Victimology, 2*(3/4): 443–458.

STRAUS, M.A. (1980). "Victims and aggressors in marital violence." *American Behavioral Scientist, 23,* 681–704.

STRAUS, M.A. & GELLES, R.J. (1986). "Societal change and change in family violence from 1975 to 1985." *Journal of Marriage and the Family, 48.*

STRAUS, M.A., GELLES, R.J., & STEINMETZ, S. (1980). *Behind Closed Doors: Violence in the American Family.* New York, NY: Doubleday.

STUART, R.B. (Ed.) (1981). *Violent Behavior: Social Learning Approaches to Prediction, Management and Treatment.* New York, NY: Brunner/Mazel.

SYMONDS, A. (1979). "Violence against women: The myth of masochism." *American Journal of Psychotherapy, 33,* 161–173.

SYMONDS, M. (1978). "The psychodynamics of violence-prone marriages." *American Journal of Psychoanalysis, 38,* 213–222.

Szinovacz, M.E. (1983). "Using couple data as a methodological tool: The case of marital violence." *Journal of Marriage and the Family, 45,* 633–644.

Tanay, E. (1976). *The Murderers.* Indianapolis/New York: The Bobbs-Merrill Co., Inc.

Tavris, C. & Offier, E. (1977). *The Longest War: Sex Differences in Perspective.* New York, NY: Harcourt Brace Jovanovich. (Rev. ed., 1983).

*Tedesco v. Alaska,* Alaska Superior Court, Fourth Judicial District, (No. 4FA-81-593 Civil, filed May, 19, 1981).

Telch, C.F. & Lindquist, C.U. (1984). "Violent versus non-violent couples: A comparison of patterns." *Psychotherapy, 21*(2): 242–248.

Thibaut, J.W. & Kelley, H.H. (1959). *The Social Psychology in Groups.* New York, NY: Wiley.

Thyfault, R. (1984). "Self-defense: Battered woman syndrome on trial." *California Western Law Review, 20,* 485–510.

Thyfault, R., Browne, A., & Walker, L.E. (1987). "When battered women kill: Evaluation and expert witness testimony techniques." In D.J. Sonkin (Ed.), *Domestic Violence on Trial: Psychological and Legal Dimensions of Family Violence.* New York, NY: Springer.

Tong, R. (1984). *Women, Sex and the Law.* Totowa, NY: Rowman & Allenheld.

Totman, J. (1978). *The Murderess: A Psychosocial Study of Criminal Homicide.* San Francisco, CA: R & E Research Associates.

Treen, B. & Wildeman, J. (1986). *Out of the kitchen and into the prison: Toward sound social policy on domestic violence.* Paper presented at the meeting of the American Society of Criminology. Atlanta, GA.

Truninger, E. (1971). "Marital violence: The legal solution." *The Hastings Law Journal, 23,* 259–276.

Turner, C.W., Fenn, M.R., & Cole, A.M. (1981). "A social psychological analysis of violent behavior." In R.B. Stuart (Ed.) *Violent Behavior: Social Learning Approaches to Prediction, Management and Treatment.* New York, NY: Brunner/Mazel.

Uniform Crime Reports. (1983, September). *Crime in the United States.* Federal Bureau of Investigation. U.S. Department of Justice, Washington, DC.

United States Commission on Civil Rights. (1982). *Under the Rule of Thumb: Battered Women and the Administration of Justice.* Washington, DC: U.S. Government Printing Office.

Walker, L.E. (1978). "Battered women and learned helplessness." *Victimology, 2*(3/4), 525–34.

Walker, L.E. (1979). *The Battered Woman.* New York, NY: Harper & Row Publishers.

Walker, L.E. (1984). *The Battered Woman Syndrome.* New York, NY: Springer Publishers.

Walker, L.E. & Browne, A. (1985). "Gender and victimization by intimates." *Journal of Personality, 53*(2), 179–195.

Walker, L.E. & Edwall, G.E. (1987). Battered women and child custody and visitation determination. In D.J. Sonkin (Ed.), *Domestic Violence on Trial.* New York: Springer.

WALKER, L.E., THYFAULT, R.K. & BROWNE, A. (1982). "Beyond the juror's ken: Battered women." *Vermont Law Review,* 7(1), 1–14.

WARDELL, L., GILLESPIE, D.L., & LEFFLER, A. (1983). "Science and violence against wives." In D. Finkelhor, R.J. Gelles, G.T. Hotaling, & M.A. Straus, *The Dark Side of Families,* pp. 69–84. Beverly Hills, CA: Sage.

WASHBURN, C. & FRIEZE, I.H. (1980). "Methodological issues in studying battered women." Paper presented at the meeting of the Association for Women in Psychology. Santa Monica, CA.

WATKINS, C.R. (1982). *Victims, Aggressors and the Family Secret: An Exploration into Family Violence.* St. Paul, MN: Minnesota Department of Public Welfare.

*Watkins v. State,* 197 So. 2d 312 (1969).

WEITZMAN, L. (1981). *The Marriage Contract: Spouses, Lovers, and the Law.* New York, NY: Free Press.

WILBANKS, W. (1982). "Murdered women and women who murder." In N.H. Rafter & E.A. Stanko (Eds.), *Judge, Lawyer, Victim, Thief: Women, Gender Roles and Criminal Justice.* Boston, MA: Northeastern University Press.

WILBANKS, W. (1983). "The female homicide offender in Dade County, Florida." *Criminal Justice Review,* 8(2), 9–14.

WILLIAMS, J.H. (1983). *Psychology of women: Behavior in a biosocial context.* New York, NY: Norton.

WITHEY, S.B. (1962). "Reaction to uncertain threat." In G.W. Baker & D.W. Chapman (Eds.) *Man and Society in Disaster.* New York, NY: Basic Books.

WOLFE, N. (1979). "Victim provocation: The battered wife and legal definition of self defense." *Sociological Symposium,* 25(Winter), 98–118.

WOLFGANG, M.E. (1958). *Patterns in Criminal Homicide.* New York, NY: John Wiley & Sons.

WOLFGANG, M.E. (1967). "A sociological analysis of criminal homicide." In M.E. Wolfgang (Ed.), *Studies in Homicide.* New York, NY: Harper & Row.

WOLFGANG, M.E. (1978). "Violence in the family." In I.L. Kutash (Ed.), *Perspectives on Murder and Aggression.* San Francisco, CA: Jossey-Bass.

WORDEN, R.E. & POLLITZ, A.A. (1984). "Police arrests in domestic disturbances: A further look." *Law and Society Reveiw, 105.*

WRIGHTSMAN, L.S. (1972). *Social Psychology in the Seventies.* Belmont, CA: Wadsworth.

*Wyoming v. Austin.* No. 7828 Natrona Co. D.C., 1979.

ZIMRING, F.E., MUKHERJEE, S.K., & VAN WINKLE, B.J. (1983). "Intimate violence: A study of intersexual homicide in Chicago." *The University of Chicago Law Review,* 50(2), 910–930.

# Author Index

# Subject Index